Sextus Empiricus
Selections from the Major Writings on
SCEPTICISM, MAN, & GOD

Sextus Empiricus

SELECTIONS FROM THE MAJOR WRITINGS ON SCEPTICISM, MAN, & GOD

Edited with Introduction and Notes by
PHILIP P. HALLIE

Translated from the Original Greek by
SANFORD G. ETHERIDGE

New Foreword and Bibliography by
DONALD R. MORRISON

HACKETT PUBLISHING COMPANY

INDIANAPOLIS/CAMBRIDGE

Sextus Empiricus: circa A.D. 200

First Edition, 1968, by Wesleyan University Press
New Revised Edition, 1985

For further information, please address:

Hackett Publishing Co.
P.O. Box 44937
Indianapolis, Indiana 46244-0937

95   3 4 5 6 7 8 9 10

Library of Congress Cataloging-in-Publication Data
Sextus, Empiricus.
    Selections from the major writings on scepticism,
man, & God.
    "An Avatar book."
    Bibliography: p.
    Includes indexes.
    1. Skepticism—Addresses, essays, lectures.
2. Philosophy—Addresses, essays, lectures. I. Hallie,
Philip Paul. II. Title . III. Title: Scepticism, man &
God. IV. Title: Scepticism, man and God.
B620.E5 1985   186'.1   85-27059
ISBN 0-87220-007-8
ISBN 0-87220-006-X (pbk.)

The paper used in this publication meets the minimum requirements of
American National Standard for Information Sciences—Permanence of
Paper for Printed Library Materials, ANSI Z39.48-1984.

TO

Mr. and Mrs. William Hallie

AND

Mr. and Mrs. O. Etheridge

Contents

Foreword

SUPPOSE one day you meet a person who can argue so well that he can refute anyone. Whoever stands up and dares to assert a proposition will be knocked down again by this Universal Refuter. Suppose further that you have the courage, or the curiosity, to try some of your own opinions against the Universal Refuter. You say, "Lying is wrong." The Universal Refuter refutes you. You claim, "Needless cruelty should be avoided." The Universal Refuter gives you a persuasive argument that needless cruelty should not be avoided, but pursued. You insist, "I have a body, and I am alive." The Universal Refuter begins to argue, and as you struggle helplessly he draws from you a series of admissions which force you to conclude that you have no body, and are dead.

Suppose the Universal Refuter decides to work you over again. "Recall my earlier argument about cruelty," he says. "Does it now seem to you that needless cruelty should be pursued?" "Well," you admit, "that argument *was* persuasive." "That is what you think," he replies, and proceeds to construct an equally persuasive argument in favor of your original belief, that needless cruelty should be avoided.

Suppose the Universal Refuter keeps attacking you with arguments until he has argued equally persuasively both for and against a great range of your beliefs, and you expect that he can do so for the rest. Would you conclude, from your inability to defend your beliefs, that you don't *know* anything? That you have no better reason to believe any proposition than its opposite? Might the experience of having all your beliefs systematically overturned lead you to withhold belief from everything? Is it possible to live without beliefs? Or is this question too crude, because in some sense it is possible to live without beliefs, and in some sense not? What are the different senses of "belief" that might be involved here?

Furthermore, if you think that the experience of having all your beliefs overturned would make quite a difference to your view of yourself, and hence to your life, it is important to ask: is this change desirable or undesirable? Supposing a Universal Refuter exists, is he the sort of person one ought to go to, or run from? Should society promote and encourage such people, or suppress them?

Finally, stepping back, you may wonder about the validity of the supposition. *Could* a Universal Refuter exist? Does one exist now? Has one ever existed? (Was Socrates a Universal Refuter?) Even if there could be a Refuter who could always refute *you*, perhaps that is due to your own lack of skill. Are there arguments, or argumentative techniques, which would enable a Refuter to refute even the most philosophically sophisticated person, the person who is wise to all tricks and whose standards for judging arguments are the highest possible?

These are a few of the questions raised by ancient scepticism. The Pyrrhonian sceptic, as presented by Sextus Empiricus in the texts gathered together and translated in this book, seemed to himself to be a Universal Refuter. It seemed to him that he had learned a set of argumentative techniques strong enough to enable him to refute all opinions held by anyone—even the best philosophers. These techniques, known as "Modes," were few and simple enough to be easily teachable. This made it possible for the Pyrrhonian sceptic to have a school in which Universal Refuters were trained, much as boxers and wrestlers are.

The Modes of scepticism seemed to enable the Pyrrhonian sceptic to refute all opinions held by anyone, even his own. This ability to refute himself is of utmost importance. Without it, the Universal Refuter might reasonably think that, since he can refute everyone's opinions except his own, his are right and theirs are wrong; that he is a Wise Man and they are Fools. With self-refutation, the Universal Refuter is forced to the view that he has no better idea which opinions are right than anyone else; and this self-acknowledged ignorance is what makes him a sceptic.

The Pyrrhonian sceptic takes his ignorance seriously. Not only will he deny that he knows anything, he will deny that he even knows that. Claiming to know that nothing can be known is "dogmatic scepticism"; it is a scepticism that makes an exception for itself. One of the main enemies attacked by Philip Hallie in his Polemical Introduction to this volume was the traditional belief that ancient scepticism was a dogmatic scepticism. It must please Professor Hallie to see that in the twenty years since his Introduction was published, this battle has largely been won. Scholarly writing nowadays assumes that the ancient sceptic *was* genuinely unsure of his scepticism; that he was an inquirer, as Professor Hallie pointed out; and that he was always prepared for the possibility that he might discover the truth.

The importance of *ataraxia* or "unperturbedness" as the sceptic's goal in life was also stressed by Professor Hallie. Current scholarship agrees, and one focus of current research is the problem: what exactly was this "unperturbedness," and why did the sceptics (and other Hellenistic philosophers) think it was so important? Did the sceptics really aim at nothing more than, say, the simple satisfaction of a well-fed pig; or did they have in mind something nobler?

Professor Hallie emphasized the sceptics' Practical Criterion, according to which their behavior will be guided by nature, feelings, tradition, and instruction in the arts. Once again, the general view of scepticism has moved in the direction he pointed; but problems and questions remain. Recent scholarship has stressed the *passivity* of the Practical Criterion: since reason's influence will be gone, the sceptic's behavior will be determined by whatever external influences are present—nature, feelings, tradition, and instruction. Most writers have found the sceptic's passivity in the face of external influences disturbing and unattractive. But one may wonder whether this passivity is so unattractive after all—it certainly need not be *disturbing* to the person who has it—and one may wonder whether the non-sceptics, who place their faith in reason, are as active and self-determining as they may pride themselves on being. Tradition's influence on the sceptic has led people to claim that scepticism is inherently conservative. This claim is strengthened by the later examples of Montaigne and Hume. Whether such conservatism or traditionalism is essential to scepticism or accidental to it, how it arises, and whether or in what respects it is a good thing, are important unresolved questions in the study of scepticism.

In his Introduction Professor Hallie stresses the continuity of scepticism. Pyrrho, Sextus, Montaigne, Bayle, Hume, Wittgenstein—all were Sceptics, he says, in the crucial sense. Recent scholarship has, if anything, stressed the differences among these thinkers. Living in different periods, having different intellectual and emotional concerns, and—one must not lose sight of this—employing different arguments in favor of their scepticism, these thinkers prove by their very diversity the richness and vigor of the sceptical tradition.

In the end, the aim of all students of scepticism must be to understand both the continuities and the discontinuities in the sceptical tradition with as much penetration and exactitude as possible. We need the skills of the historian to locate, as precisely as possible, "the sceptic in his place and time" (the phrase is Myles Burnyeat's), and we need the skills of the philosopher to lift him out again and compare him with other sceptics from other times and places. And finally, we need honesty and self-awareness to put this knowledge to use in deciding whether scepticism, in any of its forms, is for us.

DONALD R. MORRISON

Cambridge, Massachusetts
September, 1985

Preface

YEARS of frustration are the cause of this book. Writings of all sorts, including poems, plays, histories of philosophy, and even encyclopaedia articles on the Greek Sceptics have been so often wrong about and unreasonably antagonistic towards Classical Scepticism that I have finally felt compelled to do this book. At least as much as Stoicism and Epicureanism, which many people know a great deal about, Scepticism has been a force in the history of philosophy, despite the fact that so few people know what it is. A long-time interest in Wittgenstein and Montaigne had led me to believe that Scepticism is a powerful, appealing position and that it has remained comparatively intact in these two important philosophers, as well as in many others. It is time to put into one volume a fresh translation and edition of the authoritative writings of Classical Scepticism. And it is also time, indeed long past time, that Greek Scepticism be treated as an important part of the history of Western thought. To achieve these goals, this volume is heavily annotated with aids towards understanding Scepticism in relation to Aristotle, Plato, the Stoics, the Epicureans, St Augustine, St Thomas, Montaigne, Descartes, Locke, Berkeley, Hume, Kant, and others. The purpose of these references, and of this book as a whole, is to help put this subtle and perennial movement into the publicly known history of philosophy where it belongs.

Despite rather full annotation, in many cases proper names as used in the text are left unexplained; and this is so because the translator and the editor believe that there are various sound reference works that explain these names better than a poor footnote could do. The scrupulous reader of this volume will find the following reference works admirably useful as companion volumes to this one:

Wilhelm Windelband, *A History of Philosophy*
E. H. Blakeney (editor), *Smith's Smaller Classical Dictionary.*

There are, of course, other, fuller reference works (and the Bibliography at the end of this volume suggests works of a more detailed and direct relevance to Greek Scepticism than these two possess), but these works are compact, comprehensive enough, reasonably priced, and readily available at the present time. Using them and the footnotes would make unnecessary any other use of reference works, at least as far as most purposes are concerned.

These reference works are not absolutely necessary for a philosophic grasp of the arguments put forth here. The book as it now stands could, for example, be used as part of a college history or philosophy course, or it could be read with profit from cover to cover without outside pedagogical or scholarly aids by any person interested in doubt.

I should like to thank Mrs. Lucinda Tarallo, whose efficiency is matchless. Also, I wish to thank President Victor L. Butterfield of Wesleyan University and Mr. Paul Horgan, Director of the Wesleyan Center for Advanced Studies, for the use of various facilities in the course of preparing this book.

PHILIP P. HALLIE

Middletown, Connecticut
June, 1964

Translator's Note

THE selections from the works of Sextus Empiricus here presented were made by the editor with the concurrence of the translator. In the translation I have followed the Teubner edition of the Greek text, edited by H. Mutschmann; for the selections in Part One I was able to use the recently revised edition of J. Mau. For these, see the Bibliography. The translation of Sextus by the Reverend R. G. Bury in the Loeb Classical Library, the only complete English translation, has been used with profit, and was, indeed, an inspiration to keep on when the going seemed rough. My chief endeavour, besides accuracy, has been to reproduce in English the dry, pragmatic style of the Greek original. Bury's translation seems to me rather too formal and archaistic.

Learned apparatus pertaining to the text had to be dispensed with in a book of this type. Those wishing to compare the translation with the Greek text are requested to note that variant readings and scholarly emendations, where adopted, are adopted tacitly.

To Professor Hallie's notes I have added some explanatory notes (including references for the quotations) which I thought necessary to an understanding of the text. These have been kept to a minimum. References for quotations are usually omitted where Sextus himself names the author and the quotation itself now exists only as a fragment—in some cases with Sextus as the only authority. Notes of the translator are marked thus: (—Tr.).

It may not be superfluous to add that for my translations of verse quotations there can be no pretension that they are literary. They are merely literal.

My best thanks are due Professor Hallie for urging my collaboration in this joint venture in the first place. I am also in the debt of Professor Francis L. Newton, of Vanderbilt University, who brought us together. To the officials of the Wesleyan University Press, and to their alert reader, I am most grateful for a measure of patience and assistance which, being undeserved, is the more greatly appreciated.   SANFORD G. ETHERIDGE

Tulane University
New Orleans, Louisiana
June, 1964

Sextus Empiricus
Selections from the Major Writings on
SCEPTICISM, MAN, & GOD

Classical Scepticism—A Polemical Introduction

DOUBT is the nerve of all fresh and durable thinking. If Aristotle was right in the first book of his *Metaphysics* when he said that philosophy began in wonder, philosophy could not have got very far if she had not doubted searchingly. In fact, Aristotle linked doubt with wonder and progress in knowledge: men, he said, "wondered originally at the obvious difficulties, then advanced little by little and stated difficulties about the greater matters." It is from a feeling of puzzlement or ignorance, a doubting attitude, that man's whole search for knowledge emerged. And every new intellectual movement has its backbone stiffened by its doubts of other movements, as well as by its doubts of itself. It survives and thrives only if it anticipates and answers the doubts of both its enemies and its friends. Indeed, a good case could be made for the claim that the more powerful one's capacity to doubt, the more powerful is one's intellectual position.

And yet, the Greek Sceptics, who were among the earliest and most thorough chemists and anatomists of this nerve, doubt, have been fallaciously criticized or simply ignored more than any other major group of thinkers in the history of Western thought. The writings of Plato, Aristotle, the Stoics, and the Epicureans have also been misread, but they are before us in many well-known translations and editions; translations of the Greek Sceptics, however, are few and hard to come by. And because of this ignorance of the texts—among other reasons we shall presently be discussing —the word "sceptic" has become a rather empty but highly charged swear-word. Moreover, many writers on various subjects have found it convenient to use "scepticism" as a whipping-boy, as a mute old stone on which to whet their terminological tools.

Now, it would be wrong to claim that the Greek Sceptics used doubt more subtly and more creatively than anybody before or after them. In the first place, we do not have enough of their writings to be able to substantiate any such claim as this; and in the second place, we find in what we do have before us much in the way of dreary, arbitrary hair-splitting. Socrates before them doubted more subtly and with more originality and power than they did,

3

and various philosophers who came after them, like Bayle in the seventeenth century and Hume in the eighteenth, used doubt to invade more important dogmas (important, at least, to us) than ever did the Greek Sceptics. Still though many *used* doubt better than they did, nobody (to go back to our physiological metaphor) *looked at the nerve itself* with more curiosity, more circumspection. The constituents of doubt (its "chemistry") and the function of doubt in human thought and action (its "anatomy") were their special contribution to Western thought. They made doubting self-conscious, and in so doing laid it bare for men to consider.

Perhaps one of the reasons for the widespread ignorance of Classical Scepticism, despite its contributions, is the fact that doubt is as dangerous as it is useful. It can be used to strengthen a position, or it can be used to destroy all positions. The positive, constructive powers of reason that Plato, Aristotle, the Stoics, and the Epicureans extolled and exemplified are not potentially so omnivorous as doubt. Perhaps an awareness of its great dangers is one of the reasons why of all the great movements of antiquity that we have been mentioning Scepticism has been the least carefully understood and the most despised. Galileo's critics refused to look into his telescope not only out of laziness, but also, perhaps, out of fear; and the critics of Freud attacked him without reading him for other reasons than merely a lack of time.

All of this is possible, but what is a more plausible reason for this neglect of Scepticism (though certainly a more superficial reason for it) is the previously mentioned fact that there are so few ways—in fact, only one—of getting a first-hand account of Scepticism as the Greeks practised it. As we have noticed, the writings of Plato lie before us in all their dramatic and logical power; the writings of Aristotle are before us in all their systematic subtlety; the writings of the Stoics and the Epicureans are available to us in many palatable maxims, essays, letters, even poems. But as for the Sceptics—all we have of theirs worth sitting down with are the rather loosely, drily articulated works of a Greek doctor named Sextus Empiricus. These works have some flashes of humour and imagination, but there is also, as we have observed, much logomachy in them, and no dramatic or even careful logical development. They are for the most part outlines.

Still, in the doctor's writings there is much that is clear—especially when the chemistry and anatomy of doubt are being laid bare, and when doubt is being used with respect to the gods and with respect to men. In fact, if you cut away much of the logomachy (and with so loose a structure as an outline this is not too difficult to do), what emerges is a readable and simple, sometimes even colourful and exciting, account of the funded wisdom of the Greek Sceptics. And so, whatever may be the other "deeper" causes of the neglect and blindly harsh criticism that Greek Scepticism has met with, we can with an edition such as this go a long way towards remedying one of those causes—difficulty of access to the writings of the Sceptics.

Though the writings of Sextus Empiricus speak well for themselves, it will be useful to prepare the reader for them with a few introductory remarks. Those writings are the result of a long evolution or accumulation, and a brief description of the various stages in that evolution or accumulation will help make them more fully meaningful to the reader who is not a specialist in the history of ideas. Moreover, it would be useful to see at least one of the misconceptions about Greek Scepticism stated plainly and then refuted by the history of Classical Scepticism itself. Attack and defence, the *agon*, has a way of helping us to see positions more sharply, at least if the conflict is responsibly conducted.

There is one misconception regarding Scepticism that will not only serve as a foil to illuminate its nature, but will also give unity and point to our brief description of the history of the movement. Moreover, it is the most widespread of all the misconceptions about Greek Scepticism, and so it is not a straw-man emptily standing there for the sole purpose of being knocked down.

i. *The Misconception*

In Molière's *Le Mariage Forcé* there is a Sceptic named Marphurius, who at one point in the play is being belaboured with a stick. When he starts to yell, the man wielding the stick (Sganarelle, who is apparently speaking for Molière) tells poor Marphurius that a Sceptic cannot be sure that he is being hit by a stick, nor can he be sure that he feels pain. Sganarelle and Molière believed that the Sceptic doubts everything, including his own everyday experience of sticks and pains, that he lives in a philosophically induced total anaesthesia or aphasia.

Three centuries later a more learned philosopher than Molière (or Sganarelle), the distinguished French essayist and teacher of philosophy Alain, put this same notion of Scepticism in a form no less picturesque than Molière's. In a little essay written in 1932 he described the Sceptic (and he was thinking of the founder of Scepticism, Pyrrho) as being somebody who "holds himself immobile and indifferent so that the sleep of death may take him alive; . . . for there is one true Sceptic, and he insists that nothing is true; and he insists upon it dogmatically." In an essay written in 1922 he had said that Scepticism is "systematic negation," "oriental indifference," and that it sees life as a "vain illusion." Again we see the notion of Scepticism as philosophically induced life-negation, and Alain was plainly talking about Classical or Greek Scepticism.

A glance at the historical context of Classical Scepticism makes this notion begin to look a bit queer. Scepticism thrived in the ancient world from the fourth century B.C. to the third century A.D., when practical-wisdom philosophies like Stoicism and Epicureanism were (though sporadically) important; in general, this was an era in the history of ideas when pure theoretical and pure mystical or otherworldly philosophies were the exception in the Greek world. What interested the Greeks primarily was insight into the proper conduct of life, practical wisdom for producing a happy life (what is sometimes called "eudaemonism" after the Greek word *eudaimonia* meaning "happiness in the conduct of life"). Usually historians talk about this era in terms of the break-down of Athenian and Alexandrian civilization (Alexander the Great had died in 323 B.C., immediately before Pyrrho went back to his native city and started teaching Scepticism), and they claim that into the "vacuum" of these break-downs various ethical philosophies offering practical guidance rushed, and enjoyed esteem.

But putting aside the causes of this eudaemonistic sort of philosophizing, what could stupidity and immobility, total indifference to human experience in its ordinary forms, have to do with ethics and action? Surely all anaesthesia could do is get one run over by carts and disqualified from living in human society.

Let us turn to the task of finding some relationship between the "oriental indifference" notion of Scepticism and the dominant philosophic moods and needs of the Greek world when Scepticism was evolving. All we need do is read the first few pages of text that follow this Introduction, and we shall immediately discover that the philosophical aphasia notion of Scepticism described by Molière and Alain has nothing at all to do with Scepticism as it actually is; Scepticism is, like Stoicism and Epicureanism, a eudae-monistic, practical-wisdom philosophy. If we take the word of our main—indeed our only—authority on the subject of what Classical Scepticism is, the *arche*, or motivating cause, of Scepticism is the hope of living normally and peacefully without metaphysical dog-matism or fanaticism; and part of the means for so living is the Practical Criterion of the Sceptics. This Criterion stated that one should follow "the guidance of nature, the compulsion of the feelings, the tradition of laws and customs, and the instruction of the arts." The *ataraxia*, or unperturbedness, that Stoicism, Epi-cureanism, and Scepticism sought was not a sort of paralytic anaesthesia; it was peaceful living according to the institutions of one's own country and the dictates of one's own feelings, experi-ence, and common sense. All three philosophies wanted tranquil-lity, not paralysis; a peaceful life, not an imitation of death.

Those first few pages reveal that doubt, rather than being an instrument for rolling back the veil of sense-experience, is a means of wiping off the excrescences that befoul man's life and lead him into endless, bitter conflicts with his fellow men. The function of doubt is to make room for a happy everyday life, not to do away with it. This is the "true" function of doubt, at least as far as our greatest authority on Scepticism, Sextus Empiricus, is concerned.

This special function of doubt is well though not pleasingly expressed by Sextus in the metaphor of the laxative. Doubt washes itself away along with the dubious unprovable claims it works on, and it does so, according to our Sceptical physician, "just as aperient drugs do not merely eliminate the humours of the body, but also expel themselves along with the humours." The ultimate purpose of Scepticism is to make doubting unnecessary, to let the customs of our country, our needs for food and drink and so forth, and our plain everyday speech take over the direction of our thought and life after the doubting is done.

Imagine three men, one a Roman Catholic, another a Calvinist, the third a Lutheran. Imagine them partaking of bread and wine together, around a table in a restaurant. Listen to them talking about their work, their impressions of the weather and of the food —here is a conversation full of quiet mutual understanding and even agreement. They are using language in a way that enhances communication, deepens the bonds of society, and keeps their minds and bodies at peace.

Now imagine three men all "well-read" (as we hopefully describe pedants) in the respective metaphysical doctrines of Roman Catholicism, Calvinism, and Lutheranism. The talk about ordinary matters runs out for such learned and ambitious minds. And since they too are partaking of bread and wine together, they are reminded of Christ's Last Supper, and the conversation swiftly turns, let us say, to whether *hoc*, or "this," in "This Is My Body" implies that the communion wafer is "transubstantiated" in the religious service, or is "consubstantial" with the spiritual substance of Christ. The conversation has moved from plain talk about plain experience, like the taste of "nice, dry wine" or of "good, light bread," to extraordinary, contentious talk about matters beyond ordinary experience, like the untastable, invisible substratum of bread and wine. What ensues are long, unconvincing (except for the speaker) arguments that even at their best recapitulate the centuries of ingenious and fruitless verbal battles that reached a climax in the sixteenth century; for where there is no universally accepted criterion for deciding who is right and who is wrong, there the offensive and defensive passions of men flare up and spread.

A situation similar to this characterized the Greek world in which Scepticism grew. But the contending parties were not, of course, Roman Catholic, and so on; they were Platonic, Aristotelian, Stoic, Epicurean. These contenders were hopelessly, endlessly bickering with each other all around the Sceptics.

Sextus would contend that in our first situation there is no need to introduce doubt: peaceful, unperturbed living and conversation need no therapy. On the contrary, doubt here *would* paralyze men, as the legends about Scepticism tell us. It would cause them to go hungry and thirsty without ever being aware of their hunger and thirst; it would make them like stumps and stones. But the Sceptic, as we have discovered, is a eudaemonist, and his doubt *serves* life, applying only in the second situation, with our worthy pedants.

Now, his doubt does not, as Alain believes, "insist that nothing is true" about the disputing positions. To insist that all the participants are speaking falsely is to join them in their conflict. Sceptical doubt is *not denial*; it is the suspension of judgement, the refusal to assert and the refusal to deny. The Sceptic says, "*Ouden mallon*," "No more likelihood that this is true than that that is true." When there is no universally satisfactory criterion that gives more likelihood to one position than to the others, the Sceptic suspends judgement upon them all. Then he turns his back upon the whole dispute, as well as upon his own suspension of judgement concerning it, and goes back to talking and acting like a civilized, commonsensical man instead of a pedantic dogmatist. This turning of the back, this elimination of the dispute from one's concern along with the elimination of one's doubt concerning that dispute, is what Sextus meant by the "aperient" or "laxative" function of doubting. But it has nothing to do with attributing *falsity* to any metaphysical position.

And so our (comparatively) swift answer to the accusation that "true Scepticism" involves paralytic aphasia is that all we know about the "true" Classical Scepticism, at least all that Sextus, our only first-hand authority on Scepticism, tells us, leads us to believe that Scepticism in its classical form neither insisted that nothing is true nor used doubt to destroy normal life. Our reading of the first few pages that follow this Introduction indicates a philosophy according to which doubt is not a monomaniacal denial but a process having a limited function and a limited subject-matter. Moreover, those first few pages indicate that the Practical Criterion, which takes over when the doubting is eliminated, is as important a part of this philosophy as the process of doubting itself. "True Scepticism" has two parts: the process of doubting, and the Practical Criterion.

II. *The History of Classical Scepticism*

GIVEN this situation, it is useful to offer, by way of a history of Classical Scepticism, a more detailed response to the legends about Scepticism as anaesthesia; not because we need further proof that the legends are false, but because such a history will help us to read the following pages with some perspective, and even throw a little light on how these legends came to be believed by such intelligent people as Molière and Alain (and also, incidentally, among many others, Bertrand Russell).

It is worth mentioning at the outset that the old Greek word *skeptikoi* had nothing to do with doubt, but meant "inquirers" or "investigators." It was only later that the word became associated with doubt. At first what we now call "Scepticism" was called "Pyrrhonism" after the founder of the movement, Pyrrho of Elis. By the time our brief history ends, the old meaning of the Greek word for "Sceptic" will become dominant: the Sceptics *were* "inquirers," while their enemies the dogmatists claimed to have found The Truth already, and no longer needed to inquire. Scepticism ended its history in antiquity by becoming the adopted philosophy of hard-working medical researchers, like Sextus Empiricus himself.

It will be useful to divide our history into three periods: the pre-Academic (which thrived after the death of Alexander the Great in 323 B.C.), the Academic (which overlapped the pre-Academic period chronologically and lasted into the second century B.C.), and finally the post-Academic (which thrived after the death of Christ, in the second and third centuries). A key figure in the post-Academic stage will be the author of our text, Sextus Empiricus. Now, this terminology might suggest to some that there was a straight-line development from the earliest Greek Sceptics to the later ones; this is by no means clearly the case. Some scholars, and with some plausibility, think that the Academic Sceptics never knew much about Pyrrho, and were continuing the tradition of Socratic doubt (after all, the Academy was Plato's school, and Socrates with his own dubitative methods had been Plato's teacher). Fortunately, in such a brief history as this we do not have to decide who read whom; all we have to do is discern the key figures and key doctrines in the history of self-conscious doubting that culminated in the writings of Sextus Empiricus. The exact relationships between these key figures and doctrines have been a subject of scholarly dispute, a subject made more difficult by the paucity of first-hand, dependable, detailed information about the philosophers and philosophies involved.

THE PRE-ACADEMICS (fourth and third centuries B.C.)

The founder of the tradition we are examining was Pyrrho, who was born and who died in the city of Elis on the Greek Peloponnesus. We have none of his writings, only a smattering of legends about him, and a few remarks about him from his most famous pupil, Timon, whom we shall presently be considering. From these fragments we learn that he did not achieve fame by perfecting a system or even a systematic method; rather, he offered to his followers an *agoge*, a way of living that was exemplary. Even as late as Sextus, five or six centuries after Pyrrho died, to be a Pyrrhonist was not to possess a given technique or vocabulary, to be a Pyrrhonist was to imitate the *agoge* of Pyrrho himself.

But with only these fragments left to us it is difficult to ascertain just what that way of life was. In general, we can see that he was not a logician or dialectician who did logical gymnastics in order to dazzle his opponents or for the sake of the gymnastics themselves. And in general, we know that he was primarily interested in living a peaceful, independent life within the customs and laws of his city. But when we get down to particulars, we find two different accounts of his way of life, and one of these accounts gave rise to the "oriental indifference" notion of Scepticism.

Diogenes Laertius in his entertaining life of Pyrrho, written about five centuries after the death of the subject, relates the legends that have given rise to this notion. He tells us that Pyrrho was completely apathetic to external objects, oblivious of danger or pleasure. He tells us that he would not look where he was going, and that only his faithful common-sensical friends kept him alive in the face of his disregard for "carts, precipices, dogs or what not." Once, Diogenes tells us, when his teacher Anaxarchus (of whom we shall presently speak) was stuck in a slough, Pyrrho walked right by him without offering the old man any help. From the time of Diogenes up to and including the time of Bertrand Russell (who in his so-called *Sceptical Essays* repeats this story, and apparently believes it to represent Greek Scepticism), this legend has served for many as the image and even a philosophical summary of Classical Scepticism. And Diogenes tells another story, somewhat less famous than this, that also reveals Pyrrho as a man whose ideal was utter indifference to everything. One day Pyrrho was attacked by a wild dog, and he recoiled (some accounts say he climbed a tree); soon afterwards he apologized to his friends and students for his terror, announcing that it is hard for a man to strip himself of his humanity. This whole tradition shows the *agoge* of Pyrrho to be a constant effort to do just that, to strip himself of his human sensibilities and achieve a heroic independence from the external world of men, animals, and things.

But there is another tradition concerning the *agoge* of Pyrrho, this one being by no means as popular as the first, but just as solidly a part of the old legends that surround his name. In fact, this second tradition was apparently believed in by Aenesidemus, himself one of the greatest of the Sceptics; and in the sixteenth century Montaigne also knew about and believed in this tradition as representing the *agoge* of Pyrrho. According to it, Pyrrho was a man of sound common sense and clear worldly judgement, who would not dream of endangering his health or life for the sake of a doctrinaire indifference to the senses or to human predicaments; he avoided carts, precipices, and dogs, helped his friends when they were stuck in sloughs or were in other kinds of trouble, and showed blank indifference only to the dogmaticism and fanaticism of philosophers. Rather than trying to strip off or numb his ordinary human feelings, he exercised moderation in the face of the massive, unyielding forces of nature (like death and illness) that all men must meet.

The story that makes this tradition picturesque is told by Posidonius and by the garrulous Diogenes. A ship on which Pyrrho was a passenger was caught in a wild storm, and the other passengers were wailing and cringing with horror. Pyrrho stood there calmly; and at the height of the storm, when the fears of his fellow passengers were at their height, he pointed out for their instruction a little pig standing there on the deck calmly munching its food, and he told them that the unperturbedness of that pig was the mark of wisdom. According to this second tradition, Pyrrho did not strip himself, or try to do so, of his sensibilities; he was solicitous of the feelings of his fellow passengers enough to give them a little demonstration, and he advocated a life imitative of a pig calmly eating rather than imitative of an ascetic trying to act

as if he had no body. This last story exemplifies the old Greek
notion of moderation, or *metriopatheia*, which is a common-sensical
notion having to do with keeping our passions under control when
confronted with natural forces that are beyond our control. It is a
very different matter from the extinction of all awareness, all
human sympathy. It is consistent with living a life in a community
of men; in fact, it is quite useful for such a life. And the more or
less "known" facts of Pyrrho's life attest to the success with which
he lived in the city of Elis.

Still, we shall not try to decide which of these two traditions
is the true one, or even try to show how one could manage to reconcile them. We thought that it would be useful to show both
traditions, and to point out that only one has achieved great popu-
larity, the one that reveals Pyrrho as trying to strip himself of his
humanity. In such a problematic situation as this, that is, with so
few hard facts, it is possible only to put down a broad sampling of
those "facts" that are available.

Now, we have more than stories about Pyrrho. We do know
something about the philosophy behind the legends. Timon, his
student, tells us that according to Pyrrho if a man would be happy
he must ask himself three questions and answer them as best he
can. The first is: What is the stuff of things? Pyrrho's answer to this
question was: Our sensations and the various metaphysical theories
proposed by reflective men contradict each other, at least when we
are talking about the hidden nature or inner constitution of things;
and so they cancel out each other, especially since a good case can
be made for any of these mutually contradictory theories about the
inner stuff of the universe. This last point, that with ingenuity one
can make a good case about any matter of which one is ignorant—
it is easy to get things to rush into a vacuum—came to be sym-
bolized by a balance-scale whose two plates are in equilibrium,
neither one containing more weighty evidence than the other. With
respect to *adela*, or "hidden things," human ingenuity can work
wonders in the way of supporting or making plausible a hundred
incompatible claims. And this fact has a great deal to do with the
next question and its answer.

That question is: In what relation do we stand to things around
us? According to Pyrrho, we must neither accept nor reject any of

the conflicting, equally plausible (or equally inplausible) theories about the inner nature of things that philosophers present to us: we must engage in *epoche,* or the witholding of assent *and* dissent with respect to such matters. There is some dispute amongst scholars as to whether Pyrrho used the word *epoche* before any of the other Sceptics, but it is generally acknowledged that he advocated the suspension of judgement, whatever particular words he used, that he acknowledged our *akatalepsia,* or lack of sure knowledge, concerning the inner nature of things, and that he advocated *aphasia,* or silence, concerning that inner nature. These key terms, whether Pyrrho used them in particular or not, summarize Pyrrho's answer to the second question about the relationship men should have to the inner nature of things.

The last question Timon mentions is: What is the result, as far as our happiness is concerned, of this metaphysical detachment? And the answer Pyrrho gave was: tranquillity of mind, *ataraxia,* the absence of fanaticism concerning matters that cannot be proved. We become content to live a peaceful life amongst our experiences without yearning to possess or know the inner natures of things themselves. And this peaceful life is a happy life.

We do not know whether Timon's account helps much to decide which of the two traditions about Pyrrho's *agoge* is the right one; as we have said, we shall in this Introduction suspend judgement on the whole matter. But there is one more group of "facts" worth mentioning about Pyrrho—the outwardly visible events of his life as more or less agreed on by historians. Let whoever would decide about his *agoge* use these for what they are worth.

Pyrrho was born about 360 B.C. on the Greek Peloponnesus, in the city of Elis. For a while he made a modest living as a painter. One year after Aristotle founded his Lyceum, in 334 B.C., Pyrrho joined Alexander the Great and travelled with his armies into India, where he is said to have encountered and learned much from the ascetic Gymnosophists and magi of the Indus Valley. In that same court, apparently senior to Pyrrho, was Anaxarchus, who was Pyrrho's teacher. Anaxarchus was a follower of the great materialist-atomist Democritus, and shared with Democritus the conviction that sense-perceptions contradict each other (an oar looks bent in water, but at the same time feels straight if you run your fingers along it). But Anaxarchus was called "The Happy Man," and was more interested in happiness and in living well than was Democritus, the rigorous logician and metaphysician. Pyrrho could have acquired this interest from Anaxarchus as readily as he acquired the notion that sense-experience is untrustworthy. (Incidentally, Anaxarchus was the man Pyrrho was supposed to have left stuck in the slough, according to the first tradition we have spoken of.)

When Alexander died in 323 B.C., Pyrrho returned to his native city and spent the rest of his life living with his sister Philistia, who was a midwife. He sometimes helped her clean house, wash pigs, and carry fowl to the market. He apparently lectured to large groups, and also was given to long talks and walks with a few students. Sometimes he would simply walk off with a passing traveller while talking with him concentratedly, and would miss a meal or even a night at home. The city of Elis made him a high priest, and in his honour exempted philosophers from paying taxes. He died at the age of ninety, about 270 B.C.

If we suspend judgement as to what was the *agoge* of Pyrrho, we must go further into the history of Scepticism in order to find an answer to the question: What is the "true Sceptical" way of life, in so far as the Classical Sceptics wrote about it and lived it? And this brings us to another figure, one about whom our image is much less ambiguous.

The only other figure we know anything about in the pre-Academic era of Scepticism is Timon, the witty, bitter, prolific student of the gentle Pyrrho. And in looking at him we begin to get a definite answer to the question: Are the "oriental indifference" legends about Scepticism fair representations of this philosophy? Timon was different from his teacher in many ways; from what we know of him (and we do have fragments of his voluminous writings) he was as restless and perturbed as his teacher was calm, and as slashing in his ways of criticizing as his teacher was reflective. Moreover, he was a wit, wrote in the form of rounded epigrams, and apparently did not seek to exemplify or teach his Scepticism in his actions. This verbal wit is well illustrated by a story that is quite possibly true. There were those who claimed that even though the senses alone deceive us and reason used abstractly deceives us, we can still find truth by having our senses cooperate with our understanding. To such people Timon often responded, "Birds of a feather flock together." He meant by this that the contradictions revealed by the senses and by the understanding when taken separately are not eliminated by using the two powers together—these illusions are only accumulated, like one flock of birds joining another flock of birds.

Like Pyrrho, he apparently had no elaborate logical or dialectical apparatus to throw into action. Like his teacher, he used various approaches, depending on the situation; but Timon loved irony, raillery, and humour. One of his most influential books was a book of *silloi*, or lampoons (he was often called "the sillograph"). These *silloi* were satirical poems in hexameter verse parodying Homer and presenting the great metaphysicians like Aristotle and Plato as arrogant, bickering blabber-mouths duping sometimes themselves, sometimes others, sometimes all parties with their unprovable, pedantic talk. He was especially fond of ridiculing the Academic Sceptic Arcesilaus, whom we shall be considering presently; but he spoke highly of Arcesilaus at his funeral. He even ridiculed himself, calling himself "Cyclops" because of his one eye.

A look at his extant sayings shows that this rather unlikely student of Pyrrho plainly recognized the needs of men for food, drink, and so forth, and that he defended the validity of customary patterns of action. They show no "indifference" to ordinary experience. For instance, in one work he wrote, "The apparent is omnipotent wherever it goes." In another he wrote, "I do not lay it down that honey is sweet, but I admit that it appears to be so." Phenomena, our ordinary experiences of things and of our needs and customs and habits, deserved our interest, according to him, not because they told us anything about the hidden, inner nature of things, but because by accepting them in our everyday actions we can achieve happiness. From what we know of his philosophy, its enemy was pretentious, contentious reasoning, not the obvious necessities or pleasures of life. In his writings we find the first plain evidence of the falsity of the "oriental indifference" or "systematic negation" notion of Classical Scepticism.

And if we consider Timon's life, we find more such evidence.

He was born in Phlius in about 320 B.C., and died in Athens about 230 B.C. Early in life he was a stage dancer, but gave up the stage in order to study under Pyrrho in Elis. There he lived with his wife and children until poverty drove him and his family to Chalcedon. Here he gained a great reputation as a Sophist, and acquired much money and property. He was a lover of solitude and gardens, of wine and money, in short, of life as men usually live it. By no stretch of the imagination could he be described as an ascetic. If we do not know exactly what Pyrrho's *agoge* and doctrine were with respect to total negation, we do know what Timon's *agoge* and doctrine were with respect to it: he was content to find happiness amongst the "phenomena," and to laugh and rail at those who dared go beyond them.

THE ACADEMICS (third and second centuries B.C.)

When we come to the two great Sceptical presidents of what was once Plato's Academy, we see Scepticism beginning to take on a more methodical form. As we have noticed, there is some controversy about whether the Academics knew much about Pyrrho; and we shall see that Sextus does not call them "Sceptics." But we shall also see that his reasons for not doing so are themselves rather dubious, especially since he himself admits that the way of one of the two great presidents "is almost identical with ours." But there is no doubt in anybody's mind that the Academics who took over Plato's Academy in the third century carried on the tradition of self-conscious doubting; and it is a masterpiece of understatement to say that they were far closer to Pyrrho and to Sextus himself than they were to the "Dogmatists," Aristotle, Plato, the Stoics, and the Epicureans. Sextus was making a distinction that is worth noticing, but the distinction, as he himself elsewhere admits, is not as deep as his refusal of the word "Sceptic" to them would imply.

In their teachings the basic distinction Timon had made between the phenomena and what was hidden in the "inner constitution" of things was sharpened and developed, and Scepticism became not only an *agoge* but a method with its own vocabulary and its own rules. In particular, the Academic Sceptics introduced two elements into Scepticism. The first is a sustained, systematic

attack upon certain dogmatic positions, like the metaphysics of
Plato, and far more importantly the philosophy of the Stoics. The
Academics pin-pointed their enemies and concentrated their fire
upon them, while the pre-Academics were more interested in the
living of a happy life and were satisfied to attack their opponents
piecemeal. The second element that the Academic Sceptics introduced was a detailed doctrine for living amongst phenomena in
ordinary life. They not only developed a dialectic for putting into
doubt the claims of Platonists, Stoics, and so on, but they developed a vocabulary and rules for thinking about Timon's "phenomena." And in giving Scepticism a way of dealing with human experience itself, the Academics once and for all refuted such claims
as Molière's and Alain's about the deathlike immobility and indifference that Scepticism advocates. The "true," that is, the actual,
Scepticism from their time on gave a very important place indeed
to the living of our everyday lives.

The first of the great Academic Sceptics was Arcesilaus, who
was born around 315 B.C. and died about 240 B.C., about ten years
before the death of Timon, his ardent critic. He took over the
headship of Plato's Academy, but immediately rejected the dogmatic Platonic metaphysics then being taught there. His main
enemies in Athens were the Stoics, and his opposite number in
the Stoic school was Cleanthes, the Stoic-poet. If we take Cicero's
word for it, Arcesilaus was the first to use the word *epoche* for the
suspension of judgement in Sceptical argumentation, and apparently
he used it in his attack upon the Stoics.

The crucial object of his attack upon Stoicism was the Stoics'
doctrine that there are certain perceptions self-evidently true, regarding which doubt is not possible; these *phantasiai kataleptikai*,
or certain representations, force the mind to assent to them, and
in so doing reveal the truth about the inner constitution of things
—they reveal the *logos*, the rational order that informs or that is
the cosmos. Upon this perception the Stoics built their complicated
though rather patchy metaphysic that had to do with the *pneuma*,
or fire-substance, which is providentially ordered for the ultimate
good of all things. The crown, or the keystone, of this metaphysic
was the notion of the Sage, the man who, having these *phantasiai*

kataleptikai, assents to them and builds a final vision or system not only of metaphysics and theology, but of morality.

To this Arcesilaus answered that when a "wise man" points to a given perception and calls it the truth, we follow him and also call it the truth; but when a fool points out a given perception and calls *it* the truth, we laugh at him, call it an illusion. But this is to beg the whole question about what is the truth: We have no criterion for deciding who is indeed the Sage and who is the fool; and lacking an ultimate, universally satisfactory standard, we cannot tell when we have indeed *phantasiai kataleptikai* before us or when we have representations that only look certain. And so we should engage in *epoche* with respect to such perceptions, should suspend judgement upon their truth.

But there was another important encounter between Arcesilaus and the Stoics, one that means more to us in this Introduction than the dispute about indubitable perceptions. The Stoics accused the Sceptics of using a medicine that had as its side-effect the paralysis of men; doubt, they claimed, could lead men away from a happy, healthy life by destroying their faith in experience and in prediction. In response to this extremely important criticism (at least, it was important in those difficult times, when, the historians tell us, men were casting about more and more frantically for a way of life amidst the crumbling customs, laws, and religions that surrounded them), Arcesilaus gave Timon's term "phenomena" a more carefully delineated form, and produced his famous doctrine of the *eulogon*. The "reasonable," or "probable," is that which, though not conclusive, and though not revelatory of the inner constitution of things, is defensible to some extent. That which is "reasonable" is that which has reasons that agree with and support each other, reasons that do this well enough for us to use them as a basis for our actions, passions, and practical judgements. The *eulogon* was not unlike what we call the "common-sensical." Arcesilaus went on to show that by suspending judgement upon metaphysical assertions we do not attack the realm of the *eulogon*; we only point out its limits. And by insisting upon some degree or sort of plausibility in our life with phenomena, we manage to live happily and in a manner that we can defend with some persuasiveness. By developing this doctrine, Arcesilaus helped keep Scepticism in the same eudaemonistic tradition as Stoicism and Epicureanism.

Arcesilaus was born in Pitane in Aeolia; in his prime he was a very striking man, with flashing eyes and oratorical skills that matched his great dialectical powers. He was independently wealthy, loved good food and drink, and was capable of self-effacing generosity, as even his philosophical enemies admitted. Unfortunately, as is the case with so many of the Sceptics, we have none of the writings of the first great Sceptical Academic.

The next famous head of the Sceptical Academy was Carneades, who was born in Cyrene in 213 B.C., and died about 128 B.C. He took over the headship almost a century after the death of Arcesilaus. Carneades was a very different sort of man from Arcesilaus; in his personal life he was not unlike Pyrrho. He had philosophical and rhetorical powers at least as great as those of Arcesilaus, but unlike him he dressed negligently, always declined invitations to dinner (so as to keep at his work); and far from being a man of the world like Arcesilaus, it is said that sometimes while eating he would get so absorbed in his thoughts that nearby friends had to move his hands for him so that he could eat and drink.

In about 156 B.C. he went on what was to become a very famous mission to Rome. His task was, with the help of other Athenian notables, to persuade Rome to exempt Athens from a fine that had been imposed upon her. In the course of this visit he illustrated the basic device of Classical Greek Scepticism by making two orations on successive days: on the first day he "proved" that justice was metaphysically founded in natural, universal law; on the second day he "proved" that justice was nothing but *ad hoc* expediency. This was the device of the balance-scale, of defending with equal persuasiveness two contradictory views, and thus bringing about a suspension of judgement concerning both—the basic dialectical weapon of the Sceptics.

Though we have none of his writings, his pupil Clitomachus was an indefatigable recorder of his thoughts, and by way of reports about Clitomachus' writings we seem to know a great deal about his ideas. In general, it seems plain that he developed far beyond Arcesilaus both the attack upon the Stoics and the logic of ordinary experience, or practicality.

Instead of attacking the *phantasiai kataleptikai* on the grounds of circularity as Arcesilaus had done, he went deeper. He was convinced that *phantasiai,* or representations, do not work on the human mind the way a seal does on wax; our minds are not purely passive recipients of the forms of external objects. He contended that subjective elements enter into all we think or experience, and if this were not the case, if our minds were not actively involved with knowledge, we would understand nothing of what is presented to us. This active interference or involvement of the mind with the *phantasiai* is abundantly clear in the various illusions that even the most careful and gifted men fall into: Heracles killing his own children by mistake, oars seen as crooked in water, and so on. Further, if you look at all the perceptions of men, the so-called "true" as well as the "illusory" ones, you will find, because of the various special subjective elements entering into each of them, no one mark that sets off the true ones from the illusory ones. There is no criterion (this last is a crucial term for the Sceptic) for distinguishing one sort from the other: they are all mixed in with our subjective actions, passions and physiological circumstances, and so we must suspend judgement upon whether a given experience "truly" reveals the reality behind the experience or phenomenon itself.

Carneades also attacked the Stoics' theology, and he attacked this important part of their philosophy (their theology was crucial to their search for *ataraxia,* or unperturbedness) in a dazzling variety of ways. For instance, they were fond of using the *consensus gentium,* or universally-believed-therefore-true, argument for God's existence; Carneades pointed out that not only are there atheists in the world, but there are nations we know nothing of. How valid can a universal consensus be when there are exceptions to it and when we have incompletely canvassed the field? His opposite number in the Stoic school, Chrysippus, had argued that if there is something man cannot build, then the one who builds it is superior to man. And he went on to say that since the world is such a thing that is beyond the powers of man to build, therefore there is a God, a being superior to man, who built it. One can imagine the glee with which Carneades undermined this muddled argument. He pointed out that the "superior" force need not be God—it could be the processes or forces of nature; and the word "build" begs the whole question in favour of an artisan God. Why not say that the world was not "built" but "formed"? And if we use this equally plausible and less question-begging term, we immediately make the forces of nature an equally plausible origin of the world as we know it.

Another attack Carneades made against the Stoics' belief in God involved pointing out the contradictions involved in the notion of God—for instance, if God perceives us or knows us, he is affected or changed by the process of perceiving; if he changes, he decays, and if he decays, he dies; and so this immortal God is mortal. Finally, he criticized the Stoics' notion of a providential, rational government of the world identical with God by pointing out the pestilences, the pain, the sure death for all, the fact that happiness has been denied to virtuous men—in fact, men like Socrates are killed, while Dionysius, the plunderer of temples, ruled for thirty-eight years—and so on. It is important to notice that in all these arguments Carneades was not, in the usual sense of the term, "refuting" the arguments of the Stoics; he was not trying to prove that they were false. He was simply proposing plausible reasons for contradictory beliefs, and thus seeking to bring about the now familiar suspension of judgement between atheism and the Stoics' builder-provider God.

All the three eudaemonistic philosophies of this era grappled with the problem of the freedom of man to do good or evil. Carneades found that the Stoics had willy-nilly excluded this freedom from their tight, providential causal chain. To counterbalance their deterministic scheme, he defended human freedom by a famous set of arguments: (1) Given that everything is caused, the will is also caused; but its cause is itself (like the Epicureans' atoms with their *clinamen*, or swerve); (2) Events follow each other, but succession is one thing, causation another (a dog can follow a cat without having been created or caused by the cat); events precede a man's choices, but they do not force him to make them the particular way he happens to make them—his own will always makes the last move; (3) To know the cause of something is to be able to predict the occurrence of that thing, but we cannot predict a given choice with certainty; and so, for all practical purposes we do not know that there are causes, only that there are more or less regular successions of events. To the present writer's mind this is one of the most powerful arguments for human freedom produced by antiquity; and yet it seems plain that it was used not to prove human freedom, but to bring about a suspension of judgement concerning that freedom. It is always important in reading the Sceptics to remember the balance-scale; this is what they were ultimately after, even though from time to time they forgot themselves and seemed to be carried away by a refutation or a proof.

Just as Cleanthes, the Stoic, had goaded Arcesilaus into developing the notion of the *eulogon* as a guide for everyday life, Chrysippus challenged Carneades into developing such a doctrine. In response he developed his doctrine of the *pithanon*, the probable. (In some histories Arcesilaus and Carneades are sometimes called "probabilists" because of this important term, and because of the similarities between the thoughts of Arcesilaus and Carneades on this matter; but this is not technically legitimate—Arcesilaus' *eulogon* is not concerned with "probability" or *degrees* of plausibility as is Carneades' *pithanon*.) According to Carneades, though we cannot know for sure which of our representations are true to the inner nature of things, we can have various degrees of certainty as far as successions of experiences or perceptions in everyday life are concerned. These degrees of plausibility have nothing to do with metaphysics or theology, and everything to do with our daily actions. The lowest degree of probability belongs to an experience that excites belief by virtue of its own vivacity or clarity, but is unsupported by other perceptions (a glance reveals something hanging from the door-lintel to be a snake; this glance, though vivacious and frightening, has the lowest degree of probability). The next higher degree of probability belongs to an experience confirmed by other experiences (a closer look reveals a brown silken cord, not a snake, and this is confirmed by our reaching out and touching it). The highest degree of probability belongs to an experience not only vivacious in itself, and not only supported

by other experiences, but also such that a detailed, careful investigation reveals many supporting experiences, each as vivacious,
clear, or plain as the first, if not more so. (We examine the cord
closely, to be sure it is not a special kind of snake with the appearance and texture of a cord; we pull it to find out that it rings a bell
or draws a curtain, and we examine closely the connexion between the cord—the wires or ropes—and the bell or curtain.) The
highest degree of probability belongs to the *carefully tested* rep-
resentation.

In a friend's home one might be able to know with the highest
probability that the cord is a bell-cord, because one would be free
to find many supporting experiences and to look closely at each in
its relationships with the first look at the cord; but in other circumstances we must be content with the second, or possibly only
the first, degree of probability. Different circumstances permit or
demand different degrees of probability. An unarmed man must
be content with only the lowest degree of probability when he
catches a glimpse of a hungry lion stalking him; he must act
swiftly or die, and is willing to risk running away from a frightened
fawn. On the other hand, a doctor diagnosing an abdominal pain
as being an upset stomach must achieve the highest degree of
probability, and usually has the time to do so; he is not, or should
not be, willing to risk the patient's life with only a careless glance
or squeeze.

The "probabilism" of Carneades was much misunderstood and
much criticized by his successors (we shall find Sextus attacking
it in the text that follows). But it is the most subtle, well-devel-
oped empirical logic devised by any of the Sceptics. And for our
purposes in this Introduction it shows how far from being in-
sensitive to Timon's "phenomena" the Sceptics were.

THE POST-ACADEMICS (second and third centuries A.D.)

We know nothing about the life of Aenesidemus, the first of the
two great figures we are placing in the post-Academic school of
Scepticism, except that he was probably born in Cnossus, Crete,
and that he certainly lived sometime between the death of Pyrrho
and the death of Sextus in 210 A.D. Though we do not even know
if he lived after the death of Christ, we are putting him in the

post-Academic school because his contributions are a crucial part
of post-Academic Scepticism as Sextus Empiricus presents it to us.

He was the greatest builder of Sceptical logic in the whole
history of the movement, not because he was the most original
of the dialectically adept Sceptics (like Arcesilaus and Carneades)
—we do not know exactly what he learned from his predecessors
and contemporaries—but because his distinctions and arguments
are foundational to the particular techniques of doubting used by
Sextus: we know that Sextus learned them from Aenesidemus, and
that is all we know about their provenance. Perhaps he is great
by virtue of our ignorance of the permanent contributions of
others, but we must speak from what we *do* know.

One of his contributions is the ten *tropoi*, or modes of balancing the scale. These modes are ten different though sometimes related ways of putting equally plausible beliefs in conflict with each
other. Sextus gives them in one sequence in the text that follows,
Diogenes Laertius (in his life of Pyrrho) gives them in another;
but to the later Sceptics they were the same ways of arguing, and
deserved careful scrutiny more than did any other modes of argumentation. Sextus places them in a crucial spot in his *Outlines of
Pyrrhonism*, and explains them in painstaking detail.

Another of his contributions is the so-called Aetiological Tropes,
ways of criticizing inferences about causes, and ways of showing
that causal power cannot be an intrinsic part of an object, but
must be found in the relations between objects (this is not as
distant from Hume's critique of causation, which involved "constant concomitance" of objects, as most commentators would have
us believe). Sextus tells us about these Tropes in the *Outlines*.

But for our purpose in this brief history, the most interesting
contribution made by Aenesidemus is his distinction between Indicative and Recollective Signs. Indicative Signs, like the *phantasiai
kataleptikai* of the Stoics, are supposed to indicate or reveal the essential, or real, natures of the objects they signify, and they are supposed to do this with certainty, by virtue of a kind of isomorphism,
or basic resemblance between the sign and the underlying object
that helped produce the sign. A man's movement, for instance, can
be said to indicate his soul to others, or a sense-impression can be
said to indicate the inner nature of the object causing that impres-

sion (in much the same way as in John Locke's philosophy and in some more modern philosophies certain impressions, like that of size and solidity, reveal the "primary qualities" of things themselves just as they are independently of our experience of them). Aenesidemus pointed out that the conflicting claims about what is 'indicated" by such signs show how little certainty we have regarding them: Aristotle made certain claims, Plato had made still other claims, and the Epicureans and Stoics had made still different claims as to what is the underlying stuff "indicated" by our experiences. Our incapacity to settle these claims shows that we have no criterion for deciding what is an Indicative Sign and what is not (notice the parallelism of this argument with the arguments of Arcesilaus and Carneades against the Stoics' version of Indicative Signs).

But, Aenesidemus goes on, there are signs that are not so problematic, and that we need not suspend judgement about. There are Recollective Signs, experiences that remind us not of inner essences or natures but of *other experiences,* just as a scar reminds us of its cause—the blow of a hammer and a bleeding bruise—or just as smoke reminds us of a fire we have seen accompanying smoke. Now, with regard to Recollective Signs, men can achieve comparatively firm belief, since an ill-remembered sequence can be checked up on swiftly in most cases. The legitimate province of philosophy, Aenesidemus goes on, is not Indicative Signs, but Recollective Signs (the "phenomena" of Timon, and the realm of the "reasonable" and the "probable "according to the Sceptical Academy). These are an indispensable part of our lives, and we must learn to live amongst them as competently as we must learn to throw into doubt arguments using Indicative Signs.

Sextus tells us that Aenesidemus lapsed into Heraclitean metaphysics, and believed, for instance, that the fusion of contraries (the metaphysical equivalent of the Sceptical device of balancing the scales and having arguments cancel each other out) gave birth to all things, and that the reason of man is not localized in each brain but is common to all men, like the universal *logos,* or reason, of Heraclitus. But whether or not all this is the case (and if it is, how do we reconcile this metaphysical dogmatism with his Scepticism?), it is plain that Aenesidemus made a permanent and massive contribution to the logic of doubt and to the semantics of practical empirical belief, even if he, like Sextus, was only codifying the discoveries of others and was a Heraclitean metaphysician at some time in his life. And we know about this contribution even though we have none of his writings; we do have a first-hand summary of his *Pyrrhonian Discourses* in the *Bibliotheca* of Photius.

SEXTUS EMPIRICUS

We come now to the author of the text we have before us, the definitive codifier of Greek Scepticism, Sextus Empiricus. He lived in the last half of the second century A.D., and into the first quarter of the third century A.D.; he was quite possibly a Greek, if his subtle handling of the language means anything, but we do not know where he was born, where he taught, or where he died. He was head of a Sceptical school in some great city—Rome, Athens, or Alexandria. We are not sure whether his Latin name "Empiricus" is a family name or whether it is an appellation classifying him as an Empirical medical doctor. It is quite certain that he was a physician, and we know that there were, generally speaking, three schools of medicine towards the beginning of the third century. There was the Logical, or Theoretical, school, which used *a priori* reasoning about the hidden causes of diseases; there was the Empirical school, which, according to Sextus himself, dogmatically denied that we can have knowledge of deep causes of disease; and there was the Methodical school, which studied diseases only in terms of the succession of phenomena, refusing to dogmatize about the impossibility or possibility of any knowledge concerning non-evident causes. His criticism of the Empiricist doctors indicates that he disagreed with them at least with respect to dogmatizing about the impossibility of a "deep" knowledge of diseases and their origins and cures; and so it is possible that the name "Empiricus" does not mean that he was an orthodox Empirical doctor. Still, there was no great difference between the Methodical and the Empirical schools as far as actual methods were concerned, and so he might have been thought of as an Empirical doctor. But whatever his affiliation, and whatever the provenance of his name, he was a central figure amongst the late Sceptical medical doctors. His teacher was Menodotus, a great physician and an ardent Sceptic, and the successor of Sextus as head of his school was Saturninus, also a doctor and, of course, also a Sceptic. These doctors terminated the history of Greek Scepticism with an emphasis upon inquiry, or research into the phenomenal facts of nature. They all helped bring the word "Sceptic" back to its older Greek signification, "inquirer," and in so doing showed how closely Scepticism was involved with the experience and problems of men, contrary to what various critics of Scepticism have contended.

We have avoided discussing his philosophy itself at any great length because it lies before you here in the methodical, clear, sometimes droll text that follows. Still, it would be fitting to conclude this history with one point about that philosophy. Sextus believed in the Practical Criterion as we quoted it in the first part of this Introduction, and as we discussed it in that part; he did not believe in the notions of "probability" or "reasonableness" produced by the Academic Sceptics; he felt that Carneades' degrees of probability were basically dogmatical, assertive, and he preferred to live without such subtle degrees of certainty; he wanted simply to consent to his natural drives and the experiences of his senses within the limits laid down by the customs and laws of his country. He needed no degrees of probability, with all the temptations to making claims about exact knowledge therein involved.

But the difference between his simple Practical Criterion and the various ways previous Sceptics dealt with phenomena, or everyday experience, is not as important to us as the fact that the Sceptics *did* deal with experience in a way consistent with loving life.

In fact, one could summarize our brief history as follows: You are a Sceptic—in the classical, Greek sense of that word—in so far as you try to avoid fanaticism and endless bickering by sharply distinguishing an arbitrary fiction that grabs you by your imagination from a plain fact that grabs you by your common sense.

In this sense of the word, some of the greatest thinkers in the West—Montaigne, Bayle, Hume, and Wittgenstein, amongst others —were Sceptics. They loved life too much to let it be ruined by arbitrary assertion.

PART ONE: *Scepticism*

from OUTLINES OF PYRRHONISM

BOOK ONE

CHAPTER I

The Basic Difference between Philosophies

IT is a fair presumption that when people search for a thing the result will be either its discovery, a confession of non-discovery and of its non-apprehensibility, or perseverance in the search. Perhaps this is the reason why in matters of philosophical research some claim to have discovered the truth, while others declare that finding it is an impossibility, and others are still seeking it. There are some who think they have found the truth, such as Aristotle, Epicurus, the Stoics,[1] and certain others. These are, in a special sense of the term, the so-called dogmatists. Clitomachus and Carneades,[2] on the other hand, and other Academics, claim it is a search for inapprehensibles. But the Sceptics go on searching. It is, therefore, a reasonable inference that basically there are three philosophies, the dogmatic, the Academic, and the Sceptic. For the present our task will be to present an outline of the Sceptic[3] discipline, leaving it to such others as it befits to treat of the former two. We declare at the outset that we do not make any positive assertion that anything we shall say is wholly as we affirm it to be. We merely report accurately on each thing as our impressions of it are at the moment.[4]

---

1. The Stoics were the main opponents of Scepticism, as was pointed out in the Introduction. What Aristotle, Epicurus, and the Stoics shared that was so odious to the Sceptics was a conviction that the stuff and structure of the universe (behind and including what appears in conscious sense-experience) are substantially and conclusively known, as revealed in a metaphysical system. See Windelband, *A History of Philosophy*, Part I, Ch. III, and Part II, Ch. 1. (Throughout this book, notes marked "—Tr." are the translator's; unascribed notes are the editor's.)

2. See Introduction, pp. 17-24.

3. Sextus will later cease to see such a deep distinction between what in our Introduction was called post-Academic Scepticism and Academic Scepticism. See pp. 96-97.

4. A typical and crucial phrase emphasizing the process of seeking truth that was so precious especially to medical Sceptics like Sextus

CHAPTER II

The Arguments of Scepticism

THE Sceptic philosophy comprises two types of argument, the general and the special. In the first we undertake an exposition of the character of Scepticism by stating its notion, the principles and methods of reasoning involved, and its criterion and end. We set forth also the various modes of suspension of judgement, the manner in which we use the Sceptic formulae, and the distinction between Scepticism and those philosophies which closely approach it. The special argument is that in which we dispute the validity of so-called philosophy in all its parts. Let us, then, first treat of the general argument and begin our sketch with the various appellations of the Sceptic discipline.

CHAPTER III

The Names of Scepticism

Now, the Sceptic discipline is called the "zetetic" (searching) from its activity of searching and examining. It is also called the "ephectic" (suspending) from the experience which the inquirer feels after the search. "Aporetic" (doubting) is another name for it, either from the fact that their doubting and searching extends to everything (the opinion of some), or from their inability to give final assent or denial. It is also called "Pyrrhonean," because Pyrrho appears to us[5] to have applied himself to Scepticism more thoroughly and with more distinction than his predecessors.

CHAPTER IV

The Meaning of Scepticism

SCEPTICISM is an ability to place in antithesis, in any manner whatever, appearances and judgements, and thus—because of the

---

himself: the seeker keeps finding things *relative* to his mood and condition at a given time. This relativity is analysed in detail in the following pages, especially pp. 44-72.

5. Notice the acknowledged relativity even of Sextus' knowledge concerning the founder of Scepticism. See Introduction, pp. 11-15.

equality of force in the objects and arguments opposed—to come first of all to a suspension of judgement and then to mental tranquillity. Now, we call it an "ability" not in any peculiar sense of the word,[6] but simply as it denotes a "being able." "Appearances" we take as meaning the objects of sense-perception;[7] hence we set over against them the objects of thought. The phrase "in any manner whatever" may attach itself to "ability," so that we may understand that word (as we have said) in its simple sense, or it may be understood as modifying the phrase "to place in antithesis appearances and judgements." For since the antitheses we make take various forms, appearances opposed to appearances, judgements to judgements, or appearances to judgements, we say "in any manner whatever" in order to include all the antitheses. Or, we may understand it as "any manner of appearances and judgements whatever," in order to relieve ourselves of the inquiry into how appearances appear or how judgements are formed, and thus take them at their face value.[8] When we speak of arguments which are "opposed," we do not at all mean denial and affirmation, but use this word in the

---

6. Not in the full, complicated sense in which Aristotle used the term "potency," or *dynamis*, because potency in his system was a metaphysical notion involving powers not directly experienced by us, the way the smooth redness of an apple is experienced. Sextus is trying to stay close to what we might now call a "phenomenological" description of the mind, a plain description of what we experience.

7. Sextus is concerned not with the objects that help cause sense-perception, the hidden potencies of things, but with objects, like the yellow smoothness of the apple that we experience facing us, which are the "objects of sense-perception." These are the Recollective Signs spoken of in the Introduction, the "simple ideas" of Locke, the "ideas of sense" of Berkeley, the "impressions" of Hume, and the "sense-data" of Bertrand Russell and H. H. Price. These are the "objects" with which we are directly "acquainted" in sense-experience, and which do not require a metaphysical system for their description. Of course, there are differences amongst all these terms, but the similarities are important enough to warrant our putting them all in the same group: directly experienced objects.

8. Another key phrase of Scepticism, related to the notion of sense-objects discussed in the preceding footnote. The Sceptic is not undertaking psychology (the depth study of the soul or mind), nor is he expounding the metaphysics of mind; he is not studying the hidden or inferred causes or structures of judgements or appearances. All he wants is to study the experienced relations, observable in experience, that hold amongst judgements and appearances.

sense of "conflicting."[9] By "equality of force" we mean equality in respect of credibility and incredibility, since we do not admit that any of the conflicting arguments can take precedence over another on grounds of its being more credible.[1] "Suspension of judgement" is a cessation of the thought processes in consequence of which we neither deny nor affirm anything. "Mental tranquillity" is an undisturbed and calm state of soul.[2] The question how mental tranquillity enters into the soul along with suspension of judgement we shall bring up in the chapter "On the End."

---

9. To deny something is to assert its falsity, just as to affirm it is to assert its truth; the Sceptic is not making such assertions, is not letting himself assert the falsity or the truth of a metaphysical claim. He is *suspending* judgement on such claims *via* pointing out the conflicts or oppositions between them. To involve himself in denial or affirmation would be to make the Sceptic a rival metaphysician with all the others. And so he witholds assent or denial, and observes how that rogue reason can make any metaphysical claim as plausible (or implausible) as it likes. The device of the Sceptic is the balance-scale: he suspends arguments against each other, and does not come down hard for or against any of them. Doubt then is the withholding of assent *and* of denial, the mere recognition of the conflicts or oppositions between equally plausible (or equally implausible) claims. Many who talk about Scepticism do not see this all-important point. Bishop Berkeley in his *Three Dialogues* defines the Sceptic as one who "denies the reality of sensible things" (Dialogue I), and in so doing makes about all the mistakes decried in this volume thus far, especially since the "reality" of sensible things for Berkeley lies in their relativity to a perceiving being, and it is just such a relativity that the Sceptics are *not at all* denying.

1. This equality of force is not determined by the Sceptics by means of some measuring or weighing machine which tells us exactly how much truth and how much falsity there is in a given argument. The device of the balance-scale is therefore a misleading one as far as the Sceptics' position is concerned: they have no way of determining the precise amount of truth or falsity in a claim in any precise way. If they did, they would be dogmatists, stopping their investigations when they come to the weightiest claim. As it is, they are observers of the complex set of mutually conflicting claims that make up the history of metaphysical philosophy, observers who notice that with ingenuity and luck as strong a defence can be made for any one claim as for any other. And this notion of "strength" is broad and qualitative, not as precise and quantitative as the balance-scale would suggest. This "equality" simply means that reason is a rogue, that having no decisive grounds for proving matters beyond everyday experience and custom it can make anything as plausible (or implausible) as anything else.

2. Bertrand Russell in his *Sceptical Essays* makes an interesting ob-

CHAPTER V

The Sceptic

THE definition of the Pyrrhonean philosopher is also virtually included in the concept of the Sceptic discipline. It is, of course, he who shares in the "ability" we have spoken of.

CHAPTER VI

The Principles of Scepticism

SCEPTICISM has its inception and cause, we say, in the hope of attaining mental tranquillity.[3] Men of noble nature had been disturbed at the irregularity in things, and puzzled as to where they should place their belief. Thus they were led on to investigate both truth and falsehood in things, in order that, when truth and falsehood were determined, they might attain tranquillity of mind. Now, the principle fundamental to the existence of Scepticism is the proposition, "To every argument an equal argument is opposed," for we believe that it is in consequence of this principle that we are brought to a point where we cease to dogmatize.

---

servation regarding the connexion between having a decisive "criterion" for judging the truth or falsity of a claim and having mental tranquillity. On p. 10 he says: "When there are rational grounds for an opinion, people are content to set them forth and wait for them to operate. In such cases, people do not hold their opinions with passion; they hold them calmly, and set forth their reasons quietly. The opinions that are held with passion are always those for which no good ground exists; indeed, the passion is the measure of the holder's lack of rational conviction." The Classical Sceptic might be a little wary of Russell's notion of "rational conviction," but on the whole he agrees: an empty barrel makes the most noise, an argument empty of a universally acceptable decisive criterion causes the most passion in its proponents and in its opponents, and thus destroys our tranquillity. It is with arguments having no such criteria that the Sceptic is dealing when he puts arguments in "opposition" to each other.

3. This point was emphasized in the Introduction. Scepticism is a *practical-wisdom philosophy*, one that seeks (as did post-Christian Stoicism and Epicureanism) *eudaimonia*, "happiness," by way of peace of mind, or *ataraxia*. The truth is not its ultimate goal. Moreover, the proof of the *falsity* of particular dogmatic claims is not its motivation or goal either. The *arche* of Scepticism is peaceful happiness by way of a suspension of judgement.

CHAPTER VII

Does the Sceptic Dogmatize?

WE say that the Sceptic does not dogmatize. But in saying
this we do not understand the word "dogma" as some do, in the
more general sense of "approval of a thing." The Sceptic, of course,
assents to feelings which derive necessarily from sense-impressions;
he would not, for example, when feeling warm (or cold), say, "I
believe I am not warm (or cold)." But some say that "dogma" is
"the assent given to one of the non-evident things which form the
object of scientific research." It is this meaning of "dogma" that we
have in view when we say that the Sceptic does not dogmatize, for
concerning non-evident things the Pyrrhonean philosopher holds no
opinion. In fact, he does not even dogmatize when he is uttering
the Sceptic formulae in regard to non-evident things (these formulae, the "No more," the "I determine nothing," and the others,
we shall speak of later). No—for the dogmatizer affirms the real
existence of that thing about which he is said to be dogmatizing,
whereas the Sceptic does not take the real existence of these formulae wholly for granted. As he understands them, the formula "All
things are false," for example, asserts its own falsity together with
that of all other things, and the formula "Nothing is true" likewise.[4]
Thus also the formula "No more" asserts not only of other things
but of itself also that it is "no more" existent than anything else,
and hence cancels itself together with the other things.[5] We say the
same about the other Sceptic formulae also. However, if the dogmatizer affirms the real existence of the thing about which he is
dogmatizing, while the Sceptic, uttering his own formulae, does so
in such a way that they virtually cancel themselves, he can hardly
be said to be dogmatizing when he pronounces them. The greatest

---

4. Most modern commentators on Scepticism have failed to see this
delicate, all-important point, one that has been stated in various ways in
this volume thus far. The Greek Sceptic is not denying the possibility
of knowledge; he is suspending judgement on a set of mutually contrary
or conflicting claims, claims which have no decisive rational grounds
cogent for all men at all times.

5. What this "cancellation" or "purgation" means is that life is
restored to its ordinary course when the doubting is done. See Introduction, pp. 7-9.

indication of this is that in the enunciation of these formulae he is saying what appears to him and is reporting his own feeling, without indulging in opinion or making positive statements about the reality of things outside himself.

CHAPTER VIII

Does the Sceptic Have a System?

OUR attitude is the same when we are asked whether the Sceptic has a system. For if one defines "system" as "an adherence to a set of numerous dogmas which are consistent both with one another and with appearances," and if "dogma" is defined as "assent to a non-evident thing," then we shall say that we have no system. But if one means by "system" a "discipline which, in accordance with appearance, follows a certain line of reasoning, that line of reasoning indicating how it is possible to seem to live rightly ('rightly' understood not only with reference to virtue, but more simply),[6] and extending also to the ability to suspend judgement," then we say that we do have a system. For we follow a certain line of reasoning which indicates to us, in a manner consistent with appearances, how to live in accordance with the customs, the laws, and the institutions of our country, and with our own natural feelings.

CHAPTER IX

Is the Sceptic Concerned with the Study of Physics?

To the inquiry whether the Sceptic should theorize about physics our reply is similar. We do not theorize about physics in order to give firm and confident opinions on any of the things in physical theory about which firm doctrines are held. On the other hand, we do touch on physics in order to have for every argument an equal argument to oppose to it, and for the sake of mental tranquillity. Our approach to the logical and ethical divisions of so-called philosophy is similar.

---

6. Notice the emphasis upon "simple," or everyday, obvious uses of words like "rightly." What the Sceptic is doing in general is to try to get back to plain talk.

CHAPTER X

Do the Sceptics Deny Appearances?

THOSE who say that the Sceptics deny appearances seem to me to be ignorant of what we say. As we said above, we do not deny those things which, in accordance with the passivity of our sense-impressions,[7] lead us involuntarily to give our assent to them; and these are the appearances. And when we inquire whether an object is such as it appears, we grant the fact of its appearance. Our inquiry is thus not directed at the appearance itself. Rather, it is a question of what is predicated of it, and this is a different thing from investigating the fact of the appearance itself. For example, honey appears to us to have a sweetening quality. This much we concede, because it affects us with a sensation of sweetness. The question, however, is whether it is sweet in an absolute[8] sense. Hence not the appearance is questioned, but that which is predicated of the appearance. Whenever we do expound arguments directly against appearances, we do so not with the intention of denying them, but in order to point out the hasty judgement of the dogmatists. For if reason is such a rogue as to all but snatch even the appearances from under our very eyes, should we not by all means be wary of it, at least not be hasty to follow it, in the case of things non-evident?[9]

---

7. There are at least two important meanings to this notion of "passivity," or "involuntariness" of our sense-experience: (1) When a knife cuts through one's skin, one is not free to eliminate the pain; the pain follows the knife-cut regardless of our volition or voluntary activity —we are passive to the affective consequences of our sense-experience; (2) When we see an apple as red, we believe it to be red, without any act of choosing or volition having to come between the perception and the belief. Seeing *is* believing. But the dogmatist believes in a hidden reality with special traits, while the Sceptic, and the ordinary man, simply believes what he sees as he sees it.

8. As we shall presently be seeing by way of the modes, we can speak of appearances only in a sense that keeps us mindful of the relativity of our perceptions to ourselves and to our conditions.

9. Again, the Sceptics want to keep "reason" (in the form of a dogmatic analysis of the causes "behind" experience) from turning our attention away from plain experience and towards matters that produce endless squabbling and groundless zeal. Appearances themselves are not subject to question as appearances. Notice again how close this is to Berkeley's position in particular (see the first of his *Three Dialogues*),

CHAPTER XI

The Criterion of Scepticism

THAT we pay attention to appearances is clear from what we say about the criterion of the Sceptic discipline. Now, the word "criterion" is used in two senses. First, it is the standard one takes for belief in reality or non-reality. This we shall discuss in our refu-

---

and to the Empiricists' position in general. They all want us to talk about what we actually experience.

It is important here to mention some of the similarities between the philosophy of Ludwig Wittgenstein (1889–1951) and Greek Scepticism. Both philosophies contend that when men twist or ignore their ordinary ways of talking and thinking they get into hopeless puzzles or *Sackgassen*, blind alleys. Both are suspicious of attempts to look behind our living experience of words, things, or minds; they contend that language when it is most fruitfully employed is a functional part of action or everyday life. They try to restore man's wandering attention to the particular, everyday contexts in which he learned as a child to use language. Wittgenstein brings these straying terms back to their "home" in everyday talk by thinking of many examples or situations in which these terms are used correctly, according to the customs of our way of life. The motto of both philosophies is (as Wittgenstein puts it in Section 66 of the *Investigations*) "Don't think, but look!" (*Denk nicht, sondern schau!*) Don't dream up queer entities, castles in the air—look at the way your key words are normally used, and *then* generalize cautiously. For both, the job of philosophy is to remind us of what we already have before our eyes, our way of talking and living.

The second major similarity between the two philosophies lies in their shared emphasis upon a *criterion* (*Kriterium* in Wittgenstein) for deciding whether a given claim is true. Both say, in effect, that the claims of metaphysics float in mid air away from the facts, offer no way of deciding whether or not they are true. And so these claims are squabbled over endlessly, and produce insoluble puzzles for their creators. ("How does a mode relate to a substance?" asked Spinoza. "How does a mind connect with a body?" asked Descartes.) Each great metaphysic is summarized by the insoluble puzzle it left to us by departing from plain talk and the ordinary criteria we use for deciding, say, whether this is sugar or salt.

A third basic similarity between their philosophies is that both wish to do away with philosophy itself. Both wish to make philosophy unnecessary by helping us to restore that rogue reason and the language he uses to their home in everyday life. The aperient or laxative notion of doubt which we shall presently be considering (*infra*, p. 86, fn. 7) is matched in Wittgenstein's philosophy by the conviction that analysis is a cure for a disease—the disease of arbitrariness, of building castles in the air and believing in them. Wittgenstein believes that this disease can be cured by going back to our remarkably efficient usual language about evident

tation. Second, it is the standard of action the observance of which regulates our actions in life.[1] It is this latter about which we now speak. Now, we say that the criterion of the Sceptic discipline is the appearance, and it is virtually the sense-presentation to which we give this name, for this is dependent on feeling and involuntary affection and hence is not subject to question. Therefore no one, probably, will dispute that an object has this or that appearance; the question is whether it is in reality as it appears to be. Now, we cannot be entirely inactive when it comes to the observances of everyday life. Therefore, while living undogmatically, we pay due regard to appearances. This observance of the requirements of daily life seems to be fourfold, with the following particular heads: the guidance of nature, the compulsion of the feelings, the tradition of laws and customs, and the instruction of the arts. It is by the guidance of nature that we are naturally capable of sensation and thought. It is by the compulsion of the feelings that hunger leads us to food and thirst leads us to drink. It is by virtue of the tradition of laws and customs that in everyday life we accept piety as good and impiety as evil. And it is by virtue of the instruction of the arts that we are not inactive in those arts which we employ. All these statements, however, we make without prejudice.[2]

---

or decidable matters. Once we are reminded that freedom involves freedom from jail, freedom from censorship, something being free of charge, a girl being free for a date, etc., we drop our nonsensical puzzles and learn to think about freedom fruitfully and clearly. And when we do this well and habitually, philosophy of all sorts, metaphysical as well as Wittgensteinian or Sceptical, becomes unnecessary. In both philosophies, philosophy washes itself away with the nonsense it works upon. And so with respect to staying in the world of appearance, avoiding criterionless talk, and dispensing with philosophy when it has cured us of our tendency to ignore appearance and criteria, Wittgenstein and Sextus are in the same great tradition of Western thought that includes Michel de Montaigne and David Hume.

1. Appearances can and do regulate our actions in everyday life, Molière's comments on Scepticism notwithstanding. (See Introduction, pp. 5-28.) It is very important to see that the word "appearance" does not mean "illusion"—it means "that which turns up or appears" (the way a person suddenly "appears" in a room) *without any claims being made* about the "reality" or "illusoriness" of the experience as far as hidden, "non-evident" structures of reality are concerned.

2. That is, without prejudging any tradition, custom, or art to be absolutely better than any other.

CHAPTER XII

The End of Scepticism

THE next point to go through would be the end of Scepticism. An end is "that at which all actions or thoughts are directed, and which is itself directed at nothing, in other words, the ultimate of desirable things." Our assertion up to now is that the Sceptic's end, where matters of opinion are concerned, is mental tranquillity; in the realm of things unavoidable, moderation of feeling is the end. His initial purpose in philosophizing was to pronounce judgement on appearances. He wished to find out which are true and which false, so as to attain mental tranquillity. In doing so, he met with contradicting alternatives of equal force. Since he could not decide between them, he withheld judgement. Upon his suspension of judgement there followed, by chance, mental tranquillity in matters of opinion. For the person who entertains the opinion that anything is by nature good or bad is continually disturbed. When he lacks those things which seem to him to be good, he believes he is being pursued, as if by the Furies, by those things which are by nature bad, and pursues what he believes to be the good things. But when he has acquired them, he encounters further perturbations. This is because his elation at the acquisition is unreasonable and immoderate, and also because in his fear of a reversal all his exertions go to prevent the loss of the things which to him seem good. On the other side there is the man who leaves undetermined the question what things are good and bad by nature. He does not exert himself to avoid anything or to seek after anything, and hence he is in a tranquil state.

The Sceptic, in fact, had the same experience as that related in the story about Apelles the artist.[3] They say that when Apelles was painting a horse, he wished to represent the horse's foam in the painting. His attempt was so unsuccessful that he gave it up and at

---

3. Apelles was a contemporary of Alexander the Great and also of Pyrrho, the Sceptic, in the fourth century B.C. He was famous not only for his portrait of Alexander holding a thunderbolt and another picture of Venus rising from the sea, but also for his unceasing efforts at self-improvement in his art. The proverb *Nulla dies sine linea* is not only ascribed to him but could be broadly applied to the researches of the Sceptics from Pyrrho to Sextus' medical Sceptics.

the same time flung at the picture his sponge, with which he had wiped the paints off his brush. As it struck the picture, the sponge produced an image of horse's foam. So it was with the Sceptics. They were in hopes of attaining mental tranquillity, thinking that they could do this by arriving at some rational judgement which would dispel the inconsistencies involved in both appearances and thoughts. When they found this impossible, they withheld judgement. While they were in this state, they made a chance discovery. They found that they were attended by mental tranquillity as surely as a body by its shadow.

Nevertheless, we do not suppose the Sceptic to be altogether free from disturbance;[4] rather, we say that when he is disturbed, it is by things which are unavoidable. Certainly we concede that he is sometimes cold and thirsty, and that he suffers in other such ways. But even here there is a difference. Two circumstances combine to the detriment of the ordinary man: he is hindered both by the feelings themselves and not less by the fact that he believes these conditions to be evil by nature. The Sceptic, on the other hand, rejects this additional notion that each of these things is evil by nature, and thus he gets off more easily. These, then, are our reasons for saying that the Sceptic's end is mental tranquillity where matters of opinion are concerned, and moderate feeling in the realm of things unavoidable.[5] Some notable Sceptics[6] have, however, added to these a third: suspension of judgement in investigations.

CHAPTER XIII

General Introduction to the Modes of Suspension of Judgment

WE were saying that mental tranquillity follows on suspension of judgement in regard to all things. Next, it would be proper

---

4. Scepticism is a *necessary*, though not a *sufficient*, condition for our having peace of mind. The full force of this paragraph requires that one weigh equally the necessity as well as the insufficiency of Scepticism for attaining *ataraxia*.

5. This doctrine of *metriopatheia* was shared by the Stoics and Epicureans.

6. It is possible that Sextus was thinking here of the great medical researchers who were Pyrrhonists (see Introduction, pp. 27-28), as well as others.

for us to state how we attain suspension of judgement. As a general rule, this suspension of judgement is effected by our setting things in opposition. We oppose appearances to appearances, or thoughts to thoughts, or appearances to thoughts. For example, when we say, "The same tower appears round from a distance, but square from close by,"[7] we are opposing appearances to appearances. When a person is trying to prove the existence of providence from the order of the celestial bodies, and we counter him with the observation that the good often fare ill while the evil prosper and then conclude from this that there is no providence, we are opposing thoughts to thoughts. And then appearances may be opposed to thoughts. Anaxagoras,[8] for instance, could oppose to the fact that snow is white his reasoning that "Snow is frozen water, and water is black, snow therefore is black also." And sometimes, from the point of view of a different concept, we oppose present things to present things, as in the foregoing, and sometimes present things to past or future things. An example of this is the following. Whenever someone propounds an argument that we are not able to dispose of, we make this reply: "Before the birth of the founder of the school to which you belong, this argument of your school was not yet seen to be a sound argument. From the point of view of nature, however, it existed all the while as such. In like manner it is possible, as far as nature is concerned, that an argument antithetical to the one now set forth by you is in existence, though as yet unknown to us. This being so, the fact that an argument seems valid to us now is not yet a sufficient reason why we must assent to it."

---

7. Bishop Berkeley, the great British Empiricist (1685–1753), used this example as part of his efforts to refute what he called "execrable Scepticism." And yet the Greek Sceptics did not differ from him as much as he thought they did: they and he were attacking the notion that we can have "absolute" knowledge of an object, knowledge not involved with our distance from it, or our visual capacities to perceive it, etc. They and he were insisting that all our knowledge is relative to the observer and to his relationship with the object. Of course, there were great differences between Berkeley's anti-materialist metaphysics and the Sceptics' non-metaphysical philosophy, but the similarities are far more striking and important than Berkeley ever suspected.

8. Anaxagoras of Clazomenae lived around 450 B.C. and was a friend of Euripides and Pericles. He taught that a supreme intelligence (*nus*) ruled all things by composing and decomposing numberless "seeds of all things," or basic, elemental, indivisible building blocks of the universe.

But for a better understanding of these antitheses, I shall now present also the modes by which suspension of judgement is induced. I cannot, however, vouch for their number or validity, since it is possible that they are unsound, and that there are more of them than the ones to be discussed.

CHAPTER XIV

The Ten Modes

WITH the older Sceptics the usual teaching is that the modes by which suspension of judgement seems to be brought about are ten in number, which they also term synonymously "arguments" and "forms." These are as follows. First is that in which suspension is caused by the variation in animals. In the second it is caused by the differences in human beings. Third, by the differences in the construction of the organs of sense. Fourth, by the circumstances. Fifth, by the positions, distances, and places involved. Sixth, by the admixtures present. Seventh, by the quantities and compoundings of the underlying objects. Eighth, by the relativity of things. Ninth, by the frequency or rarity of occurrence. Tenth, by the institutions, customs, laws, mythical beliefs, and dogmatic notions. This order, however, is merely arbitrary.

Transcending these are three modes: the argument from the subject judging, the argument from the object judged, and that from both. The first four modes above are subordinate to the argument from the subject judging (for that which judges is either an animal or a human being or a sense, and is in some circumstance or other). The seventh and the tenth are referred to the argument from the object judged. The fifth, sixth, eighth, and ninth are referred to the argument from both combined. These three modes are in turn referred to the mode of relativity, so that the mode of relativity is the *summum genus*,[9] while the three are its species, and the ten are subordinate. This is the most plausible statement we can

---

9. This general point must be kept in mind, because it shows how similar all philosophers are who argue for the relativity of human knowledge, from the *Theaetetus* of Plato through the British Empiricists to H. H. Price in our own day.

make concerning their number. In regard to their meaning, we have the following to say.[1]

The First Mode

As we were saying, the first argument is the argument from differences in animals. According to this mode, the same objects do not produce the same impression in different animals. This we conclude both from the fact that they have different origins and from the variety exhibited in the structure of their bodies. Now to consider origin. Some animals are produced without sexual union, others by coition. Of those which are produced without sexual union, some are generated out of fire, such as the little animals that appear in furnaces, others out of stagnant water, such as mosquitoes, and others from soured wine, such as ants. From the earth come earthworms, from mud come frogs, from dung, maggots. From asses come beetles, and from vegetables caterpillars. Other animals come from fruits, as the gall-insects from wild figs; and still others from rotting animals, as bees from bulls and wasps from horses. Of the animals produced by sexual union, some (most of them, in fact) are the offspring of parents of like kind, some of parents of different kinds, as are mules. Speaking of animals in general again, some are born alive, as are human beings, some are born as eggs, as are birds, and some are born as unformed flesh, as bears. It is reasonable,[2] then, to suppose that the dissimilarities and differences in their respective origins are a cause of greatly contrary affections in animals, and that the discordant, incongruous, and conflicting character of their affections is derived from their different origins.

Moreover, a very great conflict between sense-impressions can be produced even by differences in the most important parts of the

---

1. What follows are the modes of argument, the ways of putting arguments in opposition, supposedly set up by Aenesidemus (see Introduction, pp. 24-25). The single philosopher who drew most heavily from them was Michel de Montaigne (1533–1592) in his "Apology for Raymond Sebond."

2. One could ask here: Is it reasonable to "suppose" all that follows? What sort of notion of "reason" or the "reasonable" can a Sceptic use in such speculative matters if he is out to show what a "rogue" reason is when she deals with such matters?

body, especially the organs whose natural function is judging and
perceiving. For instance, people suffering from jaundice[3] say that
what appears to us as white is yellow, and those who have a bloodshot condition of the eyes say it is blood-red. Now, since some animals have yellow eyes, others bloodshot eyes, while others have eyes
which are white, and others have eyes of still other colours, it is
reasonable to suppose, I think, that their perception of colour is
different. Moreover, if we fix our gaze on the sun for a long time
and then look down into a book, the letters appear to be gold-
coloured and going in circles. Also, some animals have a sort of
natural brilliance in their eyes, and send off from them a fine light
which travels easily, so that they even see at night. In view of this
fact, we might well be right in supposing that the impressions they
get of external objects are different from ours.[4] And jugglers, too,
by smearing their lamp-wick with copper rust or with the ink of
the cuttle-fish, make their onlookers appear to have a copper or
black colour, as the case may be. This they effect by the application
of only a small quantity of their preparation. It is surely much more
reasonable to suppose that if the eyes of animals contain different
mixtures of fluids, the impressions they receive of external objects
will be different. Also, when we press one side of the eyeball, the

---

3. This example, too, was to become famous in modern philosophy
as an indication of the relativity of sense-perception to one's physiological
condition.

4. But if "we might well be right in supposing" this, is this supposition enough to bring about a suspension of judgement on this matter?
Later Descartes, in his *Discourse on Method* and his *Meditations*, would
(as he put it in Part IV of the *Discourse*) simply "suppose" that all of
his perceptions are illusory, without giving any really sound evidence for
their being illusory, and this would suit his over-all project of doubting
"anything of which I *could* have the *least* doubt." But with the Greeks,
suppositions are not enough: doubts must be based on evidence as
weighty as the belief we are putting in doubt; the balance-scale was the
symbol of the Sceptics, not of Descartes. How could a *supposition* have
"equality of force" with a given, firmly entrenched belief in the blackness and whiteness of books, for example? The Sceptic might respond
to all this by pointing out that we use all ten modes in order to cast a
given belief into doubt, and the total weight of these modes could be
said to counterbalance the beliefs we are putting into doubt. Still, it is
the duty of the critical, sceptical reader to ask: What solid evidence do
the Sceptics put forward in order to induce doubt, and just how solid
is it?

objects viewed appear longish and narrow in form, figure, and size. It is probable, therefore, that those animals which have a slanting and elongated pupil, such as goats, cats, and the like, receive impressions of objects which are different from and unlike the impressions had of the same objects by animals with round pupils. And then mirrors: owing to differences in their construction, they sometimes show the external objects as being very small (concave mirror), sometimes as longish and narrow (convex mirror). Some show the mirrored person's head at the bottom and his feet at the top. Now, there are similar differences in the organs of sight of animals. Some of these, owing to their convexity, protrude quite out of the sockets, while others are more concave, and others lie in a flat plane. It is natural[5] to suppose that these conditions also may cause differences in the sense-impressions. If this is so, when dogs and fishes and lions and humans and locusts look at the same objects, they would in each case see objects that are neither equal in size nor similar in shape. Rather, what each perceives would be the impression created by the particular sight that receives the object.

The same argument applies to the other senses. Take the sense of touch. One could hardly postulate a similarity of sensibility between hard-shelled animals, fleshy animals, thorny animals, and feathered or scaly ones. And as for perceptions conveyed through the sense of hearing, one could hardly say that they are the same in those animals which have a very narrow auditory passage as they are in those which have a very wide one, or the same in animals with hairy ears as in those with smooth ears. We can even see the truth of this assertion in ourselves, as far as the sense of hearing is concerned, for when we plug up our ears, our perception through this sense is different from our normal hearing. The sense of smell also would exhibit differences by virtue of the variety in animals. We ourselves, when we have a cold and the phlegm in us is excessive, are affected in one way; but when an excessive amount of blood is collected in the parts about the head, we are affected in another way, and turn away from things which to others seem fragrant, believing ourselves overpowered, as it were, by their smell.

---

5. Again, in the light of the last note, how can a Sceptic use "natural" reason on such suppositious matters?

Some animals, too, are flaccid by nature and abound in phlegm, while others are very rich in blood; and in others yellow or black bile, present in an excessive amount, is the predominant element. Hence it would be reasonable to assume that this is another reason why objects of smell appear different to each severally. It is the same with objects of taste. In the first place, the tongues of animals are different, some being rough and without moisture, some very moist. In fever our tongues too become very dry, so that we think the food set before us has an earthy, ill-flavoured, and bitter taste; and this experience of ours is caused by the varying predominance of the juices we are said to have in us. Now, since the organs of taste of animals differ from each other, and have different juices in excess, it would follow that they also receive different ideas of the taste of things.

An analogous process is the distribution of food throughout the body. In one place it becomes a vein, in another an artery, a bone, a sinew, and so on. The difference in the power it displays corresponds with the differences between the parts which receive it. Water also, which is one and uniform when it is absorbed by trees, becomes in different places bark, branch, or fruit, and further, fig, pomegranate, or whatever it may be. The breath of the musician, also one and the same when it enters the flute, becomes in turn a high-pitched tone or a low one. Similarly, the same pressure of his hand upon the lyre sometimes produces a low tone, sometimes a high one. In the same manner it is a fair supposition that external objects appear different to the animals receiving the sense-impressions of the objects, and that this is due to differences of constitution in the different animals. But this can be seen more clearly from the preferences and aversions of animals. For example, perfume seems very agreeable to men, but intolerable to beetles and bees. Olive-oil is beneficial to men, but it kills wasps and bees if sprinkled on them. Sea-water is unpleasant for men to drink, even poisonous, but for fish most pleasant—and drinkable. Pigs would much rather wash in the most stinking mire than in clear and pure water. And then some animals subsist on herbs, others on shrubs, and others live in the woods; others live on seeds, flesh, or milk. Some enjoy putrefied food, while others like it prepared by cooking; and in general, what is pleasant to some is unpleasant to others, and may be undesirable, even fatal. Hemlock, for example, fattens quails, and henbane fattens sows. The latter even like to eat salamanders, just as deer eat venomous animals and swallows eat blister-beetles. Ants and wood-lice, if swallowed by humans, produce nausea and colic, while the bear, if he falls sick, licks them up and thus regains his strength. One touch of an oak-twig is sufficient to stun a viper. The leaf of a plane-tree has the same effect on bats. An elephant will run from a ram, a lion from a cock. Sea-monsters will flee from the crackling noise produced by the pounding of beans,[6] and a tiger will run from the mere sound of a drum. We could multiply these examples, but it would mean dwelling unduly long on the subject. In short, if the same things are unpleasant to some animals but pleasant to others, and pleasure and displeasure depend on sense-impression, then the sense-impressions that animals get from the objects are different.

But if the difference in animals is a cause of things appearing different, then we shall, it is true, be able to say what—in our view—a thing is; but on the question what it really is by nature, we shall suspend judgement. And as for acting ourselves as judges between our own sense-impressions and those of the other animals, that is out of the question, because we ourselves are a party to the disagreement. For this reason, in fact, we shall be more in need of a judge than capable ourselves of judging.[7] Moreover, we are unable, either without proof or with proof, to give the preference to our own sense-impressions over those of the irrational animals. For besides the possibility (which we shall mention) that proof is non-existent, the so-called proof itself will be either apparent to us or non-apparent. If it is non-apparent, we cannot even bring it forward with confidence. But suppose it is apparent to us. Then,

---

6. This, it is quite possible, is a bit of humour on the part of Sextus, the hard-headed physician.

7. Here is a turning-point in the argument: where, Sextus is asking, is the standard, the universally persuasive, universally cogent *criterion* for deciding whose sense-impressions are "true to nature"? All of our standards are *our* standards, relative to us, to our prejudices, our condition, etc. To set them up as judicial criteria is to beg the whole question of which impressions are right. Or to put it slightly differently, it is to perpetuate the dispute by putting forward mutually warring or opposing "criteria," that is to say, standards that are not decisive *criteria* at all, since a criterion is a universally acceptable standard.

since what is apparent to animals is the question at issue and we to whom the proof is apparent are animals, we still shall have to investigate whether the proof itself is in the same degree true as it is apparent. It is absurd to attempt to establish the question at issue by means of the question at issue, since that would involve believing and disbelieving the same thing at once—which is impossible. We should have to believe it in so far as it professes to furnish the proof, and disbelieve it in so far as it itself is the thing to be proved. We shall have, then, no proof which will enable us to give the preference to our own sense-impressions over those of the so-called irrational animals. If, therefore, the sense-impressions of animals differ as a consequence of the differences which exist between animals, and we cannot possibly sit in judgement over them, we must of necessity suspend judgement in regard to external objects.

We also allow ourselves the luxury of comparing the so-called irrational animals with man in respect of sense-impressions. For after our practical arguments have done their work, we feel not unqualified to make sport of those demented braggarts the dogmatists.[8] Now, the men of our school are wont to compare the generality of the irrational animals with man. But since the dogmatists sophistically assert that the comparison is unfair, we shall base our argument on one animal only—for instance, the dog, if you please, which seems to be the most worthless—and still continue our jesting at great advantage. Even so, we shall find that as far as the trustworthiness of appearances goes, the animals we speak of are not inferior to ourselves. Now, the dogmatists concede that this animal excels us in sense-perception. His perception by the sense of smell is superior to ours, and he also has a keen sense of hearing.

Let us now turn to the faculty of reason. One kind of reason is internal reason, and the other kind is uttered reason.[9] Let us look first at internal reason. According to those dogmatists whose doc-

---

8. Here Sextus is referring especially to the favourite enemies of the Sceptics, the Stoics, whose belief in the cognitive powers of Sage (see below, p. 57, fn. 8) in particular is as strong as their belief in the great power of human reason in general, "sovereign reason."

9. I.e., thought and speech. (—Tr.)

trines are the most opposed to us, namely, the Stoics, it seems that internal reason is activated in the following cases: in the choice of congenial and the avoidance of alien things; in the knowledge of the arts that contribute to this; in the apprehension and alleviation of one's own sufferings; and in the acquisition of the virtues consistent with one's own nature. Now, the dog—the example we decided to take for the sake of the argument—makes a choice of the congenial when he seeks after food, and he avoids the harmful when he retires before a raised whip. What is more, he possesses an art by which he procures what is congenial to him, the art of hunting. He is not without virtue, either. Certainly, at any rate, if justice means to render each his due, the dog would not be without justice, for he exercises it by guarding and wagging his tail at those who are familiar to him and who treat him well, and by keeping strangers and those who harm him at a distance. But if he possesses this virtue, then, since the virtues are reciprocally implied, he possesses the other virtues also, which according to the claim of the wise men the majority of men do not possess. We see that he is brave from the way he defends us, and intelligent too, as Homer also testified when he represented Odysseus as going unrecognized by all the members of his household and as being recognized only by his dog Argus, who was not deceived by the changes that had come over the body of the man. Neither had his impression of the man lost its immediacy; in fact, it appeared that he had retained this immediacy of impression better than the humans did. But according to Chrysippus, who is hostile, if anybody is, to irrational animals, the dog even shares in the famous science of dialectic. At any rate, the aforesaid man is responsible for the statement that the dog knows intuitively the fifth complex indemonstrable syllogism.[1] He shows this knowledge

---

1. Stoic logic is at least as important in the history of logic as Aristotle's logic, especially as far as developing certain notions important to "symbolic" or "mathematical" logic is concerned. For a smattering of it see the life of Zeno in the *Lives* of Diogenes Laertius. For a fuller study, see *Stoic Logic*, by Benson Mates. They used five forms of inference as "primitives," unprovable "anapodeictic" forms of argument; they used these forms in the proving of other, provable forms of argument. The fifth of these five argument-forms was: "Either X or Y or Z is the case; neither X nor Y is the case; therefore Z is the case."

whenever he is tracking an animal and comes to a meeting of
three roads. After he has tried two of the roads and found that
the animal has not passed that way, he rushes off immediately on
the third without even stopping to pick up the scent. The old
philosopher says that the dog virtually reasons this out, as follows:
"The animal passed either this way, or this way, or this way; but
it did not take this road, nor that; therefore it must have gone by
the third road." Moreover, he is capable of apprehending his own
sufferings and of relieving them. Thus, if there is a thorn stuck
in his foot, he sets about removing it by rubbing his foot against
the ground, or by means of his teeth. And if he has a sore anywhere, because dirty sores are slow to heal and clean ones heal
easily, he gently wipes off the discharge that gathers. Why, he
even observes the teaching of Hippocrates, and very well at that;
for if he should receive an injury to his foot, he applies the general
rule (that rest will cure it) and elevates the injured foot and keeps
it as undisturbed as possible. And when he is troubled by unwholesome humours, he eats grass, which enables him to vomit up the
unwholesome matter and get well.

Now, we based our observations on the dog as an example for
the sake of the argument. If, then, it appears that he chooses what
is good for him and avoids what is troublesome, if he possesses an
art which enables him to procure the good things, if he is capable
of apprehending and relieving his own sufferings, if he is not
without virtue—these being the conditions on which the perfection
of internal reason depends—then the dog will be, in this respect,
perfect. This may be the reason why some philosophers have
exalted themselves with the name of this animal.[2]

An inquiry concerning uttered reason is for the present unnecessary, since even some of the dogmatists have rejected it on the
grounds that it is prejudicial to the acquisition of virtue. For the
same reason they also used to practise silence during the time

---

2. An ironic reference to the Cynics, a sect founded by Antisthenes,
who used to meet in the *kynosarges*, a gymnasium outside of Athens
dedicated to the use of those who were not of pure Athenian blood.
It seems just as likely that their name is derived from their place of
meeting as that it is from the Greek word for "dog" (*kyon*). See Windelband, *A History of Philosophy.*

they were learners.[3] And besides, just supposing a man were dumb, no one is going to say that he is irrational. But leaving this consideration aside also, as our subject is animals, we certainly see some animals, jays among others, that can even utter human sounds. But leaving this point aside also, we note simply that even though we do not understand the sounds made by the so-called irrational animals, it is not altogether improbable that they do converse—without our understanding them. But then when we hear the speech of foreigners we do not understand that either; we think it monotonous. Also, the sounds we hear dogs utter are different: when they are keeping people off it is one sound, when they are howling it is another; and when they receive a beating, the sound is different from the sound they utter when they are fawning. And in general, if a person were to look into this matter carefully, he would find that the utterances of both this and the other animals vary greatly under different circumstances. On this account the so-called irrational animals might fairly be said to share in uttered reason also. But if these animals are inferior to humans neither in the accuracy of their perceptions, nor in internal reason, nor—needless to say—in uttered reason, then their sense-impressions will be no more untrustworthy than ours. It is perhaps even possible to prove this by basing our argument on each class of the irrational animals separately. Who, for example, would not admit that birds excel in quickness of wit and that they possess the use of uttered reason? Their understanding is not confined to the present but extends to future things as well, and to those who are able to understand them they show the future beforehand, both by their prophetic cry and by the other signs they give.

The comparison I have here drawn is given into the bargain as a bonus. This I have indicated before. I had previously shown sufficiently, I think, that we cannot give the preference to our own sense-impressions over those of the irrational animals. But then if the irrational animals, as judges of the sense-impressions, are not less reliable than we, and if the discrepancy in sense-impressions

---

3. This is a reference to the Pythagoreans, whose rule of silence was famous. The most powerful dogmatical opponents of the Sceptics, the Stoics, apparently influenced a first-century B.C. form of Pythagoreanism. See the *Lives* of Diogenes Laertius, Bk. VIII, Ch. 10.

is due to the difference between animals, it is true that I shall be able to say what each object appears to me to be, but no more. As to what its real nature is, I shall be forced, for the reasons given above, to suspend judgement.

The Second Mode

Such, then, is the first mode of suspension. The second, as we said, is the argument from the difference between men. Let us make a concession for the sake of the argument and say that human beings are more to be believed than the irrational animals. Even so, inasmuch as we differ from one another, we shall find suspension of judgement being brought in. It is said that man is made up of two elements, soul and body. Well, in both of these we differ from one another.

As for the body, we have different figures and constitutional peculiarities. Now, the Scythian's figure is different from that of an Indian, and the difference is due, it is said, to the varying predominance of the humours. And according as different humours predominate in men, their sense-impressions also are different, as we showed in the first argument. That is why there is also much difference between them in their choice and avoidance of external things. Thus the Indian standard of taste is different from that in our country, and the fact that we enjoy different things is indicative of a difference in the sense-impressions that we get from the external objects. We differ also in our constitutional peculiarities: for some people, beef is easier to digest than rock-fish, and some suffer diarrhoea from inferior Lesbian wine. There used to be an old woman of Attica, they say, who could take thirty drams of hemlock with impunity, and Lysis used to take four drams of opium without harm. And Demophon, Alexander's butler, used to shiver when he was in the sun or in a hot bath, but when he was in the shade he felt warm. Athenagoras of Argos was not affected by the sting of scorpions and poisonous spiders; the tribe called the Psyllaeans are not injured by the bite of snakes and asps; and the Tentyritae, an Egyptian people, suffer no harm from the crocodiles. Also, the Ethiopians who live along the Astapous River on the other side of Lake Meroë eat scorpions and snakes and such-like animals without ill effect. Rufinus of Chalcis would drink hellebore without vomiting and without any evacuation at all; he could simply take it and digest it like any of the usual beverages. Chrysermus, of the school of Herophilus, ran the risk of a heart attack whenever he took pepper, and Soterichus the surgeon used to suffer from diarrhoea whenever he caught the odour of fried sheat-fish. Andron of Argos was so unaffected by thirst that he even journeyed across the waterless part of Libya without requiring a drink. Tiberius Caesar could see in the dark, and Aristotle tells us of a certain Thracian who had the hallucination that a man was continually leading the way in front of him.

Now, we shall content ourselves with the recitation of these few examples from the many found in the writings of the dogmatists. Even so, it is clear that the bodily differences between men are great, and it is thus natural to assume that these differences extend also to the very soul of man, for the body is in a sense the stamped image of the soul, as the art of physiognomy shows us. But the greatest indication of the wide, indeed infinite, variety to be found in human intelligence is the discrepancy in the statements which the dogmatists make on every subject, particularly on the question what things it is proper to choose or avoid. The poets, too, have expressed themselves on this. Pindar says:

> The honours and wreaths won by wind-swift
> horses are the delight of one man,
> Others delight in a life in gilded chambers;
> Another man, too, finds joy in traversing
> the salty main with a fast ship.[4]

And the Poet says:

> Different men take delight in different deeds.[5]

Tragedy also is full of these sentiments. For example:

> If fair and wise meant both the same to all,
> Dispute and strife would be no more.[6]

And again:

> Strange, to say the least, that what gives joy to some,
> Is an object of hate to others.[7]

---

4. Pindar, fragment 221 (242). (—Tr.)
5. Homer, *Odyssey* XIV 228. (—Tr.)
6. Euripides, *Phoenissae* 499 f. (—Tr.)
7. Author unknown. (—Tr.)

Now, since choice and avoidance depend on pleasure and displeasure, and pleasure and displeasure in turn depend on sensation and sense-impression, it is logical for us to conclude that whenever the same things are chosen by some and avoided by others they are not even affected in the same manner by the same objects, since otherwise they would agree in their choices and avoidances. But if it is because of the differences between men that the same objects affect us differently, then this would be another good reason for bringing in suspension of judgement. We are, perhaps, able to say what each external object appears to be from our several different points of view, but we are unable to give an account of its true essence. For we shall have to believe either all men or some of them; to believe all would be an impossible undertaking, as we should have to accept contradictory accounts, while if we are to believe some, let them tell us who it is we are supposed to agree with. The Platonist will say Plato, the Epicurean, Epicurus, and so on with the others. They cannot decide as between their own factions, and this only serves to bring us round to suspension again. Furthermore, to say that we should agree with the majority would be puerile, since it is in no one's power to make a survey of all mankind and determine statistically the majority opinion. It is quite possible that there are peoples unknown to us, to whom things rare with us are common occurrences and with whom the conditions obtaining with us are comparatively rare. It might turn out, for example, that those who feel no pain at the bite of spiders are in the majority, and that some feel pain only rarely; and this might be similarly the case with the other constitutional peculiarities mentioned above. The differences in men, therefore, are another compelling reason for invoking suspension of judgement.

The Third Mode

Now, the dogmatists are a rather conceited class of people, and they say that they must give themselves the preference over other men in the matter of judging things; but we know that their claim is absurd because they themselves form a party to the disagreement. Furthermore, if they are thus prejudiced in favour of themselves whenever they judge appearances, then they are begging the question before they even begin their judgement, because they are turning the decision over to themselves. Nevertheless, we can arrive at suspension of judgement even when basing the argument on a single man, for instance on the "wise man"[8] who is the product of their dreams. In order to do this we bring into play the mode which is third in order. This is the one we called the argument from the differences in the senses. And it is clear at the outset that the senses differ from one another. Take paintings, for example. To the eye they seem to have hollows and prominences, but certainly not to the sense of touch. And to some, honey appears to be pleasant to the tongue, but to the eyes it appears unpleasant; thus it is impossible to say whether it is in itself pleasant or unpleasant. With perfume the case is similar; it delights the sense of smell but is disgusting to the taste. Then there is the juice of the spurge. Since it is painful to the eyes but causes pain to no other part of the body, it will not be for us to say whether, as far as its own nature is concerned, it is in itself painful or painless to bodies. And rain-water is beneficial to the eyes, but irritates the windpipe and lungs just as olive-oil does, which to the skin is soothing. The electric ray produces stiffness if applied to the extremities, while application to the rest of the body is without ill effect. Therefore we are not in a position to say what each thing is by nature, although it is possible to say what it appears to be on each occasion.

We could easily cite more examples,[9] but to avoid waste of time, on account of the plan of the treatise, we need say just this. Each appearance that we perceive through the senses seems to present itself under many forms; an apple, for instance, seems smooth, fragrant, sweet, and yellow.[1] It is uncertain, however,

---

8. The much discussed Sage of the Stoics (who was never found) often was the subject of Sceptical assault and humorous irony. He was to be the arbiter, the judge whose experiences and judgements were to give men the final truth about the universe, and about man's role in it. Supposedly, of course, he would confirm, when he finally did arrive, what the Stoics had said about these matters.

9. The richness of the examples Sextus gives us on these physiological matters reminds us that he was a physician.

1. This smooth, sweet apple turns up again in Montaigne's "Apology for Raymond Sebond," and in the same context, though after thirteen centuries it ripened and was red for Montaigne.

whether these are really the only qualities it possesses, or whether it is of one quality only but appears in different forms because the various sense-organs are of different construction. It may also be that it has more qualities than are apparent, and that some of them are not perceived by us. Now, that the apple is of a single quality we can conclude, on the one hand, from our previous statements about the distribution of food throughout the body, of water throughout trees, and about the breathing of wind into flutes, pipes, and similar instruments. For the apple, like these, may well be of a uniform quality, yet still appear to possess several qualities by reason of the differences between the sense-organs through which its perception takes place. On the other hand, we can conclude that the apple possesses more qualities than those which are apparent to us, as follows. Let us imagine a man whose senses of touch, smell, and taste are intact, but who is congenitally deaf and blind. This man will have no idea at all that a thing is visible or audible, but will believe that only those three classes of qualities exist which he is capable of apprehending.[2] With us too it is possible that our apprehension of qualities in the apple is determined by the number of senses we possess—five only. And it is possible that there exist other qualities that fall within the province of other organs of sense. Our not possessing any such other organs of sense would be reason enough why we do not apprehend the type of sense-objects proper to them.

"But," one will say, "nature made the senses commensurate with their objects." In view of the great disagreement amongst the dogmatists on the unsettled question of the existence of nature, we can only reply, "Which nature?" On this question of the existence of nature the layman's judgement will carry no authority with the dogmatists. But a philosopher's judgement is no better, for he is not a judge, but a party to the disagreement, himself subject to judgement. However, given these possible alternatives, that there may subsist in the apple only those qualities which we seem to

---

2. Montaigne and the British Empiricists (especially Locke and Berkeley) were to discuss the differences between the senses at great length, and to try to show how, despite them (or rather using them), knowledge by way of the senses was still possible. See Bk. II, Ch. 9, of Locke's *Essay Concerning Human Understanding*.

apprehend, likewise that there may subsist more than just these; or again that even the ones we perceive may not subsist at all; it follows that it will be non-evident to us what kind of thing the apple is. And the same argument holds for the other objects of sense. But then if the senses do not apprehend external objects, the intellect cannot apprehend them either, seeing that it is led astray by its guides, which is all the more reason why suspension of judgement in regard to the external underlying objects will be indicated.

The Fourth Mode

But we can also reach suspension by basing our argument on each sense separately, or even by disregarding the senses. To this end we employ the fourth mode of suspension, which we call the mode based on the circumstances. We understand by "circumstances" the states in which we are. This mode, we say, is seen in cases of natural or unnatural states, in states of waking or sleeping, in cases where age, motion or rest, hating or loving are involved; or where the determining factor is a state of want or satiety, drunkenness or soberness; in cases of predispositions, or when it is a question of confidence or fear, or grief or joy. For example, things appear dissimilar according to whether we are in a natural or unnatural state; delirious people, and those who are possessed by a god, think that they hear divine voices, while we do not. Often they claim that they perceive, among a number of other things, the odour of storax or frankincense, or something of that sort, where we perceive nothing. And the same water that seems hot to a person when poured on inflamed parts seems lukewarm to us. The coat which appears yellowish-orange to men with bloodshot eyes does not appear so to me, yet it is the same coat. And the same honey that appears sweet to me appears bitter to those suffering from jaundice.

Now, one might object that in those whose condition is unnatural it is the intermingling of certain humours that causes them to get unnatural impressions from the external objects. Our reply to this would be that it is possible that the external objects actually are in reality such as they appear to those who are said to be in an unnatural state; and that since persons in a state of good health

also have mixed humours, it may be that it is these humours that
make the objects appear different to them. For it would be a
fabrication to attribute to the humours of sick people a power to
to change external objects, and to deny this power to the humours
of the healthy. After all, it is natural for the healthy to be in a
healthy state, and unnatural for them to be in a sick state. By the
same token it is unnatural for the sick to be in a healthy state, but
natural for them to be in a sick state. Consequently, the sick warrant credence also, since they too are in some respect in a natural
state. Whether one is in a sleeping or a waking state also makes a
difference in the sense-impressions, since our manner of perception while awake differs from the perception we have in sleep; and
our manner of perception in sleep is not like our waking perception.
As a result, the existence or non-existence of our sense-impressions
is not absolute but relative, since they bear a relation to our sleeping or waking state. It is probable, therefore, that although our
dream-images are unreal in our waking state, they are nevertheless not absolutely unreal, for they do exist in our dreams.[3] In the
same manner the realities of the waking state, even if they do not
exist in dreams, nevertheless exist. Age also makes a difference.
Old men, for example, may think the air is cold, but the same air
seems mild to those who are in the prime of life. The same colour
appears dim to older persons but full to those in their prime. And
a sound, likewise the same, seems faint to the former but quite
audible to the latter. The matter of choice and avoidance of things
also provokes different reactions in people of different ages. Children, perhaps, take their ball-games and their hoops seriously, but
grown men have different tastes, and old men prefer still other
things. From this it follows that differences of age also can cause
the sense-impressions to be different where the external objects
are the same. Motion or rest may also be the determining factor
when objects appear different. For instance, things which we see
to be motionless when we are stationary seem to be moving when
we are sailing past them. Loving or hating may also make the

----

3. This belief has been much discussed by twentieth-century philosophers. See Norman Malcolm's little book, *Dreaming*.

difference. For example, there are those to whom pork is extremely repugnant, while others eat it with gusto. Hence also Menander's lines:

> And then what does his face look like,
> Since he has come to be like this? Why, he's a beast!
> Fair dealing makes us fair as well.

There are also many who have ugly mistresses and yet think them very beautiful. Hunger or satiety may also be the cause, as the same food can seem very tasty to the hungry and yet disagreeable to those who have had their fill. Drunkenness or soberness is another cause, since what we think shameful when sober does not seem shameful to us when we are drunk. Predispositions are another cause, since the same wine seems to be sour if you have eaten dates or dried figs beforehand, and sweet if you have eaten nuts or chick-peas. Also, the vestibule of the bath-house is warming to those who come in from the outside, but chills those who are coming out, if they tarry in it. Fear or confidence is also a cause, as a thing may seem fearful and terrible to the coward, yet not at all so to the man who is more daring. Being in a state of grief or joy would also be a factor, since the same matters are at once burdensome to those who are in grief and pleasant to those who are rejoicing.

Now, considering the fact that so much discrepancy is due to the states we are in, and that men are in different states at different times, it is easy, perhaps, to state the nature of each object as it appears to this or that person, but difficult to say further what its real nature is. This is because the discrepancy does not lend itself to judgement. In fact, whoever attempts to resolve this discrepancy will find himself either in one or the other of the aforesaid states or else in no state at all. But now to say that he is in no state at all, that he is neither healthy nor sick, neither in motion nor at rest, that he is not of any particular age, and that he is free from the other states, is perfectly absurd. On the other hand, the fact of his being in some state or other while attempting to pass judgement will make him a party to the controversy. And moreover, he will be confused by the states in which he finds himself, and this will prevent him from being an absolute judge[4] in the matter. A person, therefore, who is in the waking state cannot compare the impressions of a sleeping person with those of waking persons, and a healthy person cannot compare the impressions of sick people with those of the healthy. We do, after all, tend to give our assent to those things which are present and have a present influence over us rather than to things which are not present.

The discrepancy between such impressions is irresolvable on other grounds also, for if a person prefers one sense-impression to another, and one circumstance to another, he does so either without judging and without proof or by judging and offering proof. But he cannot do so without judgement and proof, for then he will be discredited. Nor can he do so even with judgement and proof, for if he judges the impressions, he must at all events use a criterion in judging them. And this criterion he will declare to be either true or false. If false, he will not be worthy of belief; but if he claims it is true, then his statement that the criterion is true will be offered either without proof or with proof. If without proof, again he will not be worthy of belief; but if he offers proof for his statement, the proof must in any case be a true one, otherwise he will not be worthy of belief. Now, if he says that the proof employed for the confirmation of his criterion is true, will he say this after having passed judgement on the proof, or without having judged it? If he has not judged it, he will not be worthy of belief, but if he has, obviously he will say he has used a criterion in his judgement. We shall ask for a proof for this criterion, and for this proof another criterion. For the proof always needs a criterion to confirm it, and the criterion needs a proof to show that it is true. A proof cannot be sound without the pre-existence of a true criterion, and a criterion cannot be true either without prior confirmation of the proof. And so both the criterion and the proof fall into circular argument,[5] in which both are found to be un-

---

4. The word "absolute" is important in this sentence. There are relative judges, or practical criteria—standards of action, as Sextus puts it in Ch. XI. In the area of action these judges (common-sense men) and criteria do have competence; they can help us live successfully amongst relative phenomena.

5. Actually, if one would be strict in classifying the modes of argu-

trustworthy. The fact that each expects confirmation from the other makes both of them equally untrustworthy. It is impossible, then, for a person to give the preference to one sense-impression over another. This being so, such differences in sense-impressions as arise from a disparity of states will be irresolvable. As a result, this mode also serves to introduce suspension of judgement with regard to the nature of external objects.

The Fifth Mode

The fifth argument is the one based on positions, distances, and places. Each of these can cause the same objects to appear different. Take a portico for example. When seen from either end, it appears tapered, yet the same portico viewed from the middle appears symmetrical on all sides. Also, the same boat appears small and stationary from a distance, and large and moving from close by. And the same tower appears round from afar but square from near by.

These differences are the result of the distances involved.[6] Then there are differences due to the places involved. For example, the light of a lamp appears dim in sunlight but bright in the dark, the same oar appears broken in the water but straight when out of the water,[7] and the egg is soft inside the bird but hard when exposed to the air. Amber is liquid when inside the lynx but hard when exposed to the air,[8] and coral is soft when in the sea but hard in the air. And a sound appears different according to whether it is produced in a pipe, a flute, or simply in the air.

Position also may be the cause of different appearances. The same picture appears smooth when inclined backwards, but seems to have hollows and prominences when inclined forward to a

---

ment, this one would appear in Ch. XV with Agrippa's five modes, specifically the one on circular reasoning.

6. In the example of the portico, both position and distance seem to be involved. Note also that Sextus' use of terms is not exact: "tapered" is not asymmetrical. (—Tr.)

7. Another example that was to be much used by subsequent philosophers seeking to prove the relativity of sense-knowledge.

8. *Lyngurion*, amber or a type of amber, thought to be the solidified urine of the lynx; from the Greek words for "lynx" and "urine." (—Tr.)

certain angle. Also, the necks of pigeons appear different in colour according to differences in inclination.

Thus all objects appearing to us are seen as being in some place or other, at a certain distance, and in a certain position, and each of these factors makes a great difference in the sense-impressions, as we have mentioned. Hence, by this mode also we shall be compelled to have recourse to suspension of judgement. In point of fact, anyone who wishes to give any of these sense-impressions the preference over the others will be undertaking an impossible task. For if he makes his judgement simply and without proof, he will be discredited; and if he wishes to employ a proof, then says his proof is false, he will be refuting himself; if he says the proof is true, he will be asked for a proof of its truth, and another proof for that one, and so on *ad infinitum*.[9] But it is impossible to present an infinite series of proofs; therefore he will not be able, even by the use of proofs, to prefer one sense-impression to another. And if a person is unable to pass judgement on the above-mentioned impressions either without proof or with proof, then the necessary result is suspension of judgement. Thus, while we are perhaps able to state of what nature each object appears to be in one particular position, at one particular distance, and in one location, it is not in our power, for the reasons just given, to declare what its true nature is.

The Sixth Mode

The sixth mode is the one based on admixtures. By this mode we conclude that, since none of the external objects appears to us singly but always in conjunction with something else, it is perhaps possible to state the nature of the mixture resulting from the conjunction of the external object and that other thing which we perceive together with it, but we are not able to say what the real nature of the external object is in its unmixed state. That no external object is ever perceived singly but in all cases together with something else, and that this causes it to have a different appearance for us, I take as evident fact. Our skin, for instance, shows a

---

9. Here again Agrippa's modes will cover the same point in Ch. XV.

different colour according to whether the air is warm or cold; and we cannot say what our true natural colour is, but only what it appears to be in conjunction with each of these conditions. And the same sound appears different according as it occurs in air which is rarefied or dense; and aromatic odours are rather more overpowering in the warm bath and in the sun than in chilled air; and if a body is enclosed by water, it is light, but if enclosed by air, it is heavy.

But to get away from external admixtures, the internal contents of our eyes consist of both membranes and fluid matter. Now, since visible objects, in order to be seen, require both of these, they will not be apprehended with accuracy. What we actually perceive is the mixture, and this is the reason why people sick with jaundice see everything yellow, and those with bloodshot eyes see everything blood-red. And since the same sound appears different according as it occurs in open places or in narrow and winding places, and according as the air is pure or foul, it is probable that our apprehension of the sound is not free from admixture. For the ears have winding, narrow passages and are fouled with vaporous discharges which are said to gather from various parts of the head. And since secreted matter is also present in the nostrils and in the places where the sense of taste is located, our apprehension of the objects of taste and smell is not without admixture but includes the apprehension of that matter as well. Consequently, the admixtures prevent our senses from apprehending with accuracy the true nature of external objects.

But neither can the intellect do this, the chief reason being that the senses, which are its guides, are deceived; though perhaps the intellect, too, produces some peculiar admixture of its own, which then also affects the reports communicated by the senses. For we can perceive the presence of certain humours in each place where the dogmatists think the ruling part of the soul is located, whether one wishes to regard it as located in the brain, in the heart, or in any part of the animal body whatever. We see, therefore, that according to this mode also we are unable to predicate anything about the nature of external objects. As a result, we are compelled to suspend judgement.

The Seventh Mode

The seventh mode, as we said, is based on the quantities and compoundings of the external objects. By their "compounding" we mean
in general their composition. And it is evident that this mode
too obliges us to suspend judgement as regards the nature of
things. For example, the filings from a goat's horn appear white
when they are seen by themselves and uncompounded, but when
they are compounded so as to constitute a horn they appear black.
And filings of silver appear black by themselves, but in conjunction
with the whole they are perceived as white. And pieces of the
marble of Taenarum look white when they are polished, but when
together in the rough stone they appear yellow. Grains of sand
appear rough when they are scattered apart, but when combined
as a heap they produce the impression of softness. Hellebore causes
suffocation if taken as a fine powder, but not if taken coarse.
Wine strengthens us if drunk in moderate amounts, but if more
than this is taken, it enervates the body. And with food the case is
similar, for the efficacy it exhibits varies according to the quantity
taken. For instance, taking food in large quantities often causes
the body to be purged through attacks of indigestion and diarrhoea.
Here also, then, we shall be in a position to state the nature of the
small bit of horn and of the whole composed of the many fine
parts, and the nature of the chip of Taenarean marble and of the
whole composed of the many small pieces. We may also be able
to state the nature, in relative terms, of the grains of sand, the
hellebore, the wines, and the food. Yet we shall not be able to go
further and state the absolute nature of the objects. This we are
prevented from doing by the discrepancy in our sense-impressions
caused by the varying compositions of things.

In fact, it seems generally true that even things beneficial to
us become harmful through their use in immoderate quantities,
and that things that seem harmful when taken in excessive quantity
are not injurious in very small quantities. The best argument
in support of this reasoning is the observation we make regarding
the action of medicines. Here we find that an accurate mixing of
the component drugs renders the compound beneficial, while
sometimes the slightest inclination of the balance, if overlooked,
can render the product not only ineffectual but often very harmful,

even poisonous. Thus the argument based on the quantities and compoundings makes the question of the real properties of external objects a confused issue. Therefore, since we are unable to state in absolute terms the nature of external objects, this mode also will bring us round naturally to suspension of judgement.

The Eighth Mode

The eighth mode is the argument from relativity. By this mode we conclude that, since all things are relative, we shall suspend judgement as to what they are absolutely and in themselves. But there is one qualification we must realize, both here and elsewhere. This is that we employ the word "are" in place of the word "appear," so that what we are saying amounts virtually to this: "All things appear to be relative." And our statement about relativity has a double sense; in the first place, there is a relationship to the thing judging (for the external object being judged appears to the thing judging it), and there is a relationship—in another way—to the things which are perceived along with it, such as the relationship of right to left. But we have considered the relativity of all things in the foregoing also. With respect to the thing which judges, for instance, we said that each object appears relatively to some particular animal or man or sense, and to such and such a circumstance. With respect to the things perceived along with it, each object appears relatively to some particular admixture or manner or composition or quantity or position.

But it is also possible to prove separately that all things are relative. This is done in the following manner. Do absolutes differ from relatives or not? If they do not differ, then they are themselves relative. But if they do differ, since all things which differ are relative (for it is in relation to that from which it differs that it is said to differ), then absolute things are relative. Also, the dogmatists divide all existent things into three classes,[1] the highest

---

1. The highest class, or *summum genus*, has meaning not only relatively to lower genera but also depends upon what sort of thing you are trying to classify. If you are talking about everything, then the *summum genus* would be "being" or "entity"; the *infimae species*, or lowest species, the one that cannot be subdivided further, would be the class that contains only one individual, say, "Socrates." In between are genera that are both species of higher genera and classes containing individuals,

genera, the lowest species, and the things which are both genera and species. But all these are relative; therefore all things are relative. A further statement which they themselves make is that some things are manifest, others non-evident; and they say that apparent things are significative and that it is the non-evident things that are made manifest by the apparent things, for according to them, "Things apparent are an aspect of the things not evident."[2] But that which makes manifest and that which is made manifest are relative; therefore all things are relative. In addition to this, existent things are divided into the similar and the dissimilar, and the equal and the unequal. But now these are relative; therefore all things are relative. But even he who denies that all things are relative confirms, by his opposition to us, the proposition that all things are relative; for he shows that the proposition itself (that all things are relative) is relative[3] to us, and not universal.

The result, however, is clear once we show in this manner that all things are relative. We shall not be able to say what each object is in its own nature and absolutely, but what it appears to be under the aspect of relativity. Hence follows the necessity of our suspending judgement concerning the nature of things.

The Ninth Mode

The mode concerned with frequency or rarity of occurrence, which we said was ninth in order, we expound as follows. The sun is surely a much more amazing thing than a comet. But the sun we see constantly, whereas we rarely see a comet. Hence our astonishment at the sight of a comet is such that we may even believe it to be a divine omen, while we are not at all astonished

---

like the genus "man," which is lower than "entity" but higher than "Socrates." However, if you are talking about these nine modes, for example, the *summum genus* is "relativity," and there are ten *infimae species*, as Sextus pointed out before he started to present them. See p. 44.

2. A dictum of Anaxagoras. (—Tr.)

3. The word "relative" is suffering various changes in meaning throughout this paragraph; he is equivocating, and so the "relativity" he is defending here is not as clear as the ten modes themselves make it out to be.

at the sight of the sun. If, however, we only imagine the sun as appearing rarely and setting rarely, illuminating everything at once and causing everything to be thrown suddenly into shadow, then we shall observe great astonishment at the occurrence. Earthquakes, also, do not cause a like degree of confusion in those who are experiencing one for the first time as they do in those who have become accustomed to them by habit. And how great is the astonishment the sea causes in a man who beholds it for the first time! But also the beauty of the human body, in a subject we see for the first time, and suddenly, excites us more than if the sight should become a common one. Rare things seem to be valuable; things familiar to us, and easily obtainable, not at all. For example, if we suppose water to be a rare thing, how much more valuable it will appear to us than all the things which are held to be valuable! Or if we ponder the thought of gold simply lying about in large quantities on the ground like stones, to whom shall we suppose it would be so valuable, or so much worth locking up? Since, therefore, according to the frequency or rarity of their occurrence, the same things seem sometimes to be astonishing or valuable, and sometimes not at all so, we conclude that we shall perhaps be able to say what the nature of each of these things appears to be in the context of its frequent or rare occurrence, but that it is not within our power to state the nature of each external object considered purely and simply in itself. And so this mode too causes us to suspend judgement concerning them.

The Tenth Mode

There is a tenth mode, this one concerned chiefly with ethics. This is the argument from disciplines, customs, laws, mythical beliefs, and dogmatic notions. Now, a "discipline" is a choice of a way of life or of some objective, made by one person or by many. A case in point would be Diogenes, or the Laconians. A law is a written covenant among men who live in organized states, the transgressor of which is punished. A custom or habit (there is no difference) is a common acceptance by many men of a certain thing. Here the transgressor is not punished at all. Examples: It is a law not to commit adultery, but a custom not to have intercourse with a woman publicly. Mythical belief is an acceptance of

unhistorical and fictitious events, such as—among others—the tales
told of Kronos (for there are many who are led to believe these
tales). A dogmatic notion is acceptance of a thing in so far as
the acceptance seems to be confirmed by a line of reasoning or
by some proof, for example, that atoms[4] are the elements of existing things, or homoeomeries, or minimal bodies, or something else.

Each of these we oppose sometimes to itself, sometimes to each
of the others. We oppose custom to custom, for instance, in this
way. Some of the Ethiopians tattoo their babies, while we do not.
And Persians think that the use of bright-coloured, dragging gar-
ments is seemly, while we think it is unbecoming. And the Indians
have intercourse with their women in public, whereas most other
peoples hold this to be shameful. We oppose law to law in the
following manner. With the Romans, he who relinquishes claim
to the property inherited from his father is not obliged to pay his
father's debts, but with the Rhodians one must pay them in any
event. And among the Tauri of Scythia there was a law that
strangers should be sacrificed to Artemis, while with us the ritual
killing of humans is forbidden. We oppose discipline to discipline
when we set the discipline of Diogenes in opposition to that of
Aristippus, or that of the Laconians to that of the Italians. We
oppose mythical belief to mythical belief when we say that in one
version Zeus is spoken of as the father of gods and men, while in
another version it is Oceanus. To quote:

Ocean, sire of the gods, and Tethys their mother.[5]

And we set dogmatic notions against one other when we say that
some declare that there is only one element, while others assume
that they are infinite in number. We do so also when we say that
some believe the soul to be mortal, others immortal; and that some
declare that human affairs are directed by divine providence,
while others claim providence has no hand in them.

We oppose custom to the other things, as for example to a

---

4. Democritus, Epicurus, and Lucretius the Epicurean held the first
view; Anaxagoras believed in the homoeomeries; and Diodorus Cronos,
whose school was absorbed into the Stoics, believed in the minimal
bodies.
5. Homer, *Iliad* XIV 201. (—Tr.)

law, when we say that with Persian men it is a custom to indulge in homosexual practices, while with the Romans this practice is prohibited by law. This is also the case when we say that with us adultery is forbidden, while with the Massagetae the custom is traditionally an indifferent matter, as Eudoxus of Cnidos records in the first book of his *Voyage*. And whereas intercourse with our mothers is prohibited by our laws, with the Persians it is a custom to marry thus if one possibly can. Among the Egyptians men marry their sisters, a practice which with us is prohibited by law. The opposition of custom to discipline is seen in the fact that whereas most men have intercourse with their wives in private, Crates did so with Hipparchia in public.[6] And Diogenes went about with only a one-sleeved tunic, while we dress as is customary. Custom is opposed to mythical belief when the stories have it that Kronos devoured his own children, since it is our custom to provide for our children. And while it is habitual practice with us to venerate the gods as being good and unaffected by evils, the poets represent them as getting wounded and being envious of one another. And custom is opposed to dogmatic notion when Epicurus says, in opposition to our custom of begging favours of the gods, that the Divinity does not pay any attention to us; and when Aristippus thinks that dressing in women's clothes is a matter of indifference, whereas we consider this a shameful thing.

We have discipline opposed to law when in the face of a law which forbids the striking of a freeman or a well-born man, pancratiasts strike each other because of the discipline of the life they follow; and when gladiators, for the same reason, kill each other even though homicide is forbidden. We oppose mythical belief to discipline when we say that the myths tell of Heracles that he

> carded wool and endured the lot of a slave,[7]

and that he did things that no one, exercising even a moderate choice, would have done, whereas Heracles' discipline of life was

---

6. While this seems to us the very opposite of what we call "discipline," the point is that Crates' "discipline," or way of life, permitted this. (—Tr.)

7. Homer, *Odyssey* XXII 423 (the passage in Homer does not refer to Heracles). (—Tr.)

a noble one. Discipline is opposed to dogmatic notion when athletes pursue glory as something good, and for its sake take upon themselves a laborious discipline of life, while many philosophers have the dogmatic notion that glory is a trivial thing. We oppose law to mythical belief when the poets portray the gods as committing adultery and practising paederasty, whereas with us these practices are forbidden by law. And we oppose law to dogmatic notion when Chrysippus says that having intercourse with mothers or sisters is a matter of indifference, while the law forbids this. And we oppose mythical belief to dogmatic notion when the poets tell of Zeus coming down and having intercourse with mortal women, while with the dogmatists it is believed that this is impossible. And the Poet says that Zeus, in his grief over Sarpedon, "poured down showers of blood to the earth,"[8] yet it is a dogma of philosophers that the Deity is impassive; and philosophers confute the story of the horse-centaurs, and offer us the horse-centaur as an example of non-reality.

Now, it would be possible to take up many other examples for each of the antitheses mentioned above, but for a brief account these will be sufficient. However, since this mode too points out how great the discrepancy in things is, we shall not be able to say what quality an object possesses according to nature, but only what quality it appears to possess with reference to a particular discipline, a particular law, a particular custom, and so on with each of the others. This mode also, then, compels us to suspend judgement regarding the nature of external objects. And so in this manner, through the ten modes, we end with suspension of judgement.

CHAPTER XV

The Five Modes[9]

THE later Sceptics, however, teach five modes of suspension. These are the following. The first is based on disagreement. The second is that which produces to infinity. Third, that based on relativity. Fourth, that from assumption. And fifth, the argument in a circle.

-----

8. Homer, *Iliad* XVI 459. (—Tr.)
9. Usually attributed to Agrippa, about whom virtually nothing is known.

That based on disagreement is the one in which we find that in regard to a proposed matter there has arisen in the opinions both of people at large and of the philosophers an unresolved dissension. Because of this dissension we are unable either to choose or to reject anything, and thus we end with suspension of judgement.[10] The mode based on the extension to infinity is the one in which we say that the proof offered for the verification of a proposed matter requires a further verification, and this one another, and so on to infinity, so that since we lack a point of departure for our reasoning, the consequence is suspension of judgement. That based on relativity is that in which, just as we have already said, the object appears thus or thus in relation to the thing judging and the things perceived along with it, while as to its true nature we suspend judgement. The mode from assumption exists when the dogmatists, in their *regressus ad infinitum*, take as their point of departure a proposition which they do not establish by reasoning, but simply and without proof assume as conceded to them.[11] The mode of argument in a circle arises when that which ought itself to be confirmatory of the matter under investigation requires verification from the thing being investigated; at that point, being unable to take either of them to establish the other, we suspend judgement about both.

That it is possible to refer every question to these modes we shall show briefly as follows. The object proposed is either an object of sense or an object of thought; but no matter which it is, it is a disputed point. For some say that the objects of sense alone are true,[1] some say only the objects of thought are true, while others say that some objects of sense and some objects of thought are true. Now, will they assert that the disagreement is resolvable, or irresolvable? If irresolvable, then we have the necessity of sus-

---

10. This is a summary of the ten modes of Aenesidemus.

11. In terms of modern logical systems, this is not a serious difficulty because any postulate or axiom or assumption in set A can be proved in set B when B is "equivalent" to A. And so, theoretically, any assumption can be proved in some other system. See H. N. Lee, *Symbolic Logic*, p. 264.

1. Notice that the *truth* of sense-experience is at issue here, not its practicality as Recollective Sign (see Introduction, p. 26) or cue for action.

pension granted; for it is not possible to pronounce on things when the dispute about them is irresolvable. But if the dispute is resolvable, then we ask from what quarter the decision is to come. Taking, for example, the object of sense (to fix our argument on this one first), is it to be judged by an object of sense or by an object of thought? If by an object of sense, then, seeing that our inquiry is about objects of sense, that object too will need another as confirmation. And if that other is an object of sense, again it will itself need another to confirm it, and so on to infinity. But if the object of sense will have to be judged by an object of thought, then, since objects of thought also are a matter of dispute, this object, being an object of thought, will require judgement and confirmation. Where, then, is the confirmation to come from? If it is to be confirmed by an object of thought, we shall likewise have an extension *ad infinitum*; but if by an object of sense, the mode of circular reasoning is introduced, because an object of thought was employed for the confirmation of the object of sense and an object of sense for the confirmation of the object of thought.

If, however, our interlocutor should try to escape from these conclusions and claim the right to assume, as a concession without proof, some proposition serving to prove the rest of his argument, then the mode of assumption will be brought in, which leaves him no way out. For if a person is worthy of credence when he makes an assumption, then we shall in each case also be not less worthy of credence if we make the opposite assumption. And if the person making the assumption assumes something which is true, he renders it suspicious by taking it on assumption instead of proving it. But if what he assumes is false, the foundation of what he it trying to prove will be unsound. Moreover, if assumption conduces at all towards proof, let the thing in question itself be assumed and not something else by means of which he will then prove the thing under discussion.[2] But if it is absurd to assume

---

2. Many critics of Aristotle's logic were to say this: If you have to make an assumption to prove a conclusion, then you have not thoroughly proved it. Say that you are trying to prove that Socrates is mortal. To do so you assume that all men are mortal, though you cannot be sure of this with the facts at hand—you may be the immortal one! But this

the thing in question, it will also be absurd to assume what transcends it.[3]

But it is evident that all objects of sense are also relative, for they exist as such in relation to those who perceive them. It is clear, then, that whatever sensible object is set before us, it can easily be referred to the five modes. Our reasoning concerning the intelligible object is similar. For if it should be said that it is the subject of an irresolvable disagreement, the necessity of suspending judgement on this matter will be granted us. But in the case of a resolution of the disagreement, if the resolution is reached by means of an object of thought, we shall have recourse to the extension *ad infinitum*; if by means of an object of sense, we shall have recourse to the mode of circular reasoning. For as the sensible again is an object of disagreement, and incapable, because of the extension to infinity, of being decided by means of itself, it will stand in need of the intelligible just as the intelligible also requires the sensible. For these reasons, whoever accepts anything on assumption will again be in an absurd position. But intelligibles are also relative, for they are relative to the intellect in which they appear, whence their name.[4] And if they really were in nature such as they are said to be, there would be no disagreement about them. Thus the intelligible too has been referred to the five modes, so that in any case we must suspend judgement with regard to the object presented.

Such are the five modes taught by the later Sceptics. Their purpose in setting them forth is not to repudiate the ten modes, but to provide for a more diversified exposure of the rashness of the dogmatists by combining these modes with the others.

---

assumption already "contains" your conclusion about Socrates' mortality, once you grant the obvious fact that Socrates is a man. Well, if your assumption already contains the conclusion, why go through this roundabout method? Why not assume the conclusion right off?

3. That is, if it is absurd to assume that Socrates is mortal, it is also absurd to assume the more general proposition that contains it, namely, "All men are mortal," as was pointed out in the preceding note.

4. *Noeta*, "objects of thought" or "intelligibles," is derived from *nus*, "mind" or "intellect." (—Tr.)

CHAPTER XVI

The Two Modes

THEY also teach two other modes of suspension. Since everything apprehended seems to be apprehended either through itself or through something else, they show us that nothing is apprehended either through itself or through another thing, thus introducing, as they think, doubt about all things. That nothing is apprehended through itself is clear, they say, from the disagreement existing amongst the physicists regarding, I believe, all sensibles and intelligibles.[5] Since we are not able to take either an object of sense or an object of thought as a criterion (any criterion we take, if there is disagreement about it, is unreliable),[6] the disagreement is of course irresolvable. Because of this they do not concede that anything can be apprehended through another thing either. For if that through which something is apprehended must itself always be apprehended through another thing, we fall into the mode of circular reasoning or into the mode of infinity. But if a person should wish to assume a thing (through which another thing is apprehended) as being apprehended through itself, an objection arises in the fact that, by reason of what we have said above, nothing is apprehended through itself.[7] And we are uncertain as to how that which conflicts with itself can be apprehended either through itself or through something else, since no criterion of truth or of apprehension appears, and since even signs apart from proof are rejected,[8] as we shall recognize in the next book. So much, then, for the modes of suspension. What we have said will be sufficient for the present.

---

5. This opaque remark assumes that disagreement about "all sensibles and intelligibles" is the case, and also assumes that this disagreement proves that nothing is apprehended through itself. These two points require much further discussion on the part of this critic of circular reasoning.

6. If there is disagreement about it, it is not a "criterion" at all. See p. 49, fn. 7.

7. This will not do, because of the unclarity or incompleteness of the "reason" he gave, as was mentioned in the preceding note.

8. In Bk. II, Ch. X, p. 102, fn. 1, "sign" is a broader concept than "proof," and includes the latter.

CHAPTER XVII

The Modes for Refuting the Aetiologists

JUST as we teach the modes of suspension of judgement, in like manner some Sceptics set forth modes which enable us to raise difficulties about the particular aetiologies[9] of the dogmatists and thus check them in their inordinate pride in these aetiologies. Thus Aenesidemus teaches eight modes by which he believes he can refute and declare fallacious every aetiology of the dogmatists. According to the first of these, he says, aetiology in general, because of its involvement in unseen things,[1] derives no confirmation from appearances, none at least about which there is agreement. The second is the frequent propensity of some to limit themselves to only one theory of causation for the thing in question,[2] although there may be abundant opportunity to account for it in a variety of ways. The third is, that to events which take place in an orderly manner they assign causes which exhibit no order.[3] Fourth, when they once understand how appearances come about, they think they also have an understanding of the genesis of things which are not appearances, although, while it is possible that non-apparent things come to pass in a manner similar to appearances, perhaps they do not, but have their own peculiar way. Fifth, that almost all of them carry on their investigations into causes according to their own assumptions about the elements, rather than employing certain methods which are common to all and agreed upon. Sixth, that they often admit only facts which are discoverable in the light of their own peculiar as-

---

9. Aetiology, "theory of causation." (—Tr.)

1. Things behind or beyond what appears in consciousness.

2. A defender of a materialistic sort of causation would say that Socrates sat in jail and refused to flee the hemlock because his muscles did, or failed to do, such and such, and his brain refused to send appropriate messages for flight to those muscles; but theorists of causation would say that the goal he had in mind, a future state of affairs envisaged by him, not a past state of affairs unknown to him, caused him to do or not to do certain things. Both ways of accounting for Socrates' action (or inaction) are inadequate, since each claims to be a full account, and the situation could be accounted for in a variety of ways with equal plausibility.

3. The orderly movements of the planets might be accounted for by pointing out various causes, causes which amongst themselves exhibit no interrelationships, no orderly pattern.

sumptions, dismissing opposing facts, even those that possess equal probability. Seventh, that they often assign causes that conflict not only with appearances but even with their own assumptions. Eighth, that when there are difficulties in the seemingly apparent things as well as in that which is the object of further search, the material out of which they construct their doctrines often shows difficulties equal to the difficulties of the things their doctrines are about. And it is not impossible, Aenesidemus says, that some will also fail in their theories of causation by reason of certain modes combined from and dependent on those mentioned above.

Perhaps, also, the five modes of suspension would be sufficient to take care of the aetiologies. For the cause which a person gives will either be in harmony with all the sects of philosophy, with Scepticism, and with appearances, or it will not. Perhaps, however, it is not possible for it to be in harmony with them, for both appearances and non-evident things have all been disputed. But if his cause is not in harmony with these, the cause of this cause will also be demanded of him. If for an apparent cause he assumes a cause which is apparent, or if for a non-evident cause he assumes one that is non-evident, he will be drawn out to infinity; and if he assumes one kind as cause of the other, he will be reasoning in a circle. And if he stops anywhere, he will either say that the cause holds good as far as the circumstances of the present discussion go, thus introducing the relative and abolishing the absolute point of view, or else he will make some unwarranted assumption and be stopped on this score. These modes too, then, would no doubt enable us to expose the rashness of the dogmatists in their aetiologies.

CHAPTER XVIII

The Sceptic Formulae

Now, our use of each of these modes, and of the modes leading to suspension, involves the utterance of certain expressions. These expressions are indicative of the Sceptic attitude and of our state of mind. Examples are "Not more" and "One must determine nothing." There are also some others, and our task will now be to discuss these in order, starting with the formula "Not more."

CHAPTER XIX

The Formula "Not More"

THIS formula we sometimes utter in the form given, sometime thus: "No more."[4] We do not, as some understand us to do, employ the formula "Not more" in specific inquiries and the formula "No more" in generic inquiries. Rather, we utter both the formula "Not more" and the formula "No more" indifferently, and in the present discussion we shall treat them as one.

Now, this formula is elliptical. For just as when we say "a double" our meaning is "a double hearth,"[5] and when we say a "broad" we mean a "broad way," likewise, when we speak the words "Not more" we mean to say, for example, "Not more up than down." Some of the Sceptics, however, understand the word "not" in lieu of a question of the form "(For) what one thing more than another," taking the word "what" in a causal sense here, to make it mean: "Why one thing more than another?" It is a common thing to use questions in place of positive statements, as for example:

What mortal knows not the man who shared his wife with Zeus?[6]

and to use positive statements for questions, such as "I am looking for where Dion lives," and "I am inquiring what it is one should admire in a poet."[7] Moreover, the word "what" in the sense of "why" is also used in Menander:

(For) what was I left behind?

The words "One thing not more than another" also reveal a state of mind we have, whereby because of the equal validity of the objects opposed we come in the end to a state of equilibrium.[8] By "equal validity" we mean what appears to us to be an equality of probability, and by "opposed" we mean, in a broad sense, conflicting. By "equilibrium" we mean an assent to neither. The formula

4. The famous formula *ouden mallon.*

5. This refers probably to a double house, or house for two families. (—Tr.)

6. Euripides, *Hercules* 1, referring to Amphitryon. (—Tr.)

7. Aristophanes, *Frogs* 1008, which is a direct question: "Tell me, what is it one should admire in a poet?" (—Tr.)

8. See above, pp. 32-34.

"No more," for instance, even though it exhibits the character of assent or denial, we do not use in this capacity. Rather, we employ it indifferently[9] and by a misuse of language either in lieu of a question or in lieu of saying, "I do not know to which alternative I ought to assent, and to which I ought not." For the task we have set ourselves is to make clear what appears to us; as to the formula we use to make this clear, it is a matter of indifference to us. This too must be understood, however, that in uttering the formula "No more" we make no positive statement that the formula is wholly true and certain, but merely state the matter, here as elsewhere, as it appears to us.[1]

---

9. In a very important way, Scepticism can be described as an "adverbial" philosophy, advocating no particular, absolute truth, but trying to induce a *way* of dealing with both claims about hidden things and claims about appearances; with respect to claims about hidden things the Sceptics, not entirely unlike the Stoics, advocate that we regard conflicting arguments "indifferently," that is, without denial and without affirmation; with respect to appearances, the practical criteria spoken about above (see pp. 39-40, and Introduction), they advocate that we act on our convictions concerning these things, but never as fanatically as we would if we believed these convictions to be the *absolute* truth about these things (see above, p. 41).

1. This typical phrase "as it appears to us" insists on the first-personal nature of a Sceptic's claim: he speaks for "me" or for "us." This first-personal relativity was beautifully exemplified in the "portrait" of himself that Montaigne drew in his *Essays*. The great French Sceptical polyhistor Pierre Bayle (1647–1706) de-emphasized this first-personal aspect of Scepticism and pointed up the *experimental*, impersonal aspect of "appearances"; David Hume, the Scottish Sceptic, analysed beliefs down to "impressions" which are relative to the mind that, "first-personally," has them, but are also capable of being used as objectively (that is, publicly) defensible data. The word "impression" meant "something had by an individual mind as its exclusive possession," but also it meant "the *given* that could be publicly repeatable or verifiable in somewhat the same way the data of an experiment could be repeatable or verifiable." Moreover, the "association of ideas," which allows us to associate, for example, the redness of the apple with its flavour even though redness is seen and not tasted and flavour is not seen and is tasted, this association was what he called "a gentle force, which commonly prevails" (*Treatise*, Bk. I, Sec. IV), a force involving "universal principles . . . uniform . . . in all times and places." This "common" or "universal" or "natural" force helped him give his impressions publicly defensible status. Since Sextus there have been two ways in which Sceptics have used "appearances"; one way is Montaigne's, which emphasizes the first-personal aspect of phenomena (they appear to *me*), and this might be called Personalistic Scepticism; and the other

CHAPTER XX

Non-Assertion

CONCERNING non-assertion we say the following. The word "assertion" has two senses, a general sense and a special sense. In the general sense it is understood as an expression indicating affirmation or negation, such as "It is day" and "It is not day." In the special sense it indicates affirmation only, and in this sense of the word negative statements are not called assertions. Non-assertion, then, is a disuse of assertion in the general sense in which, as we say, both affirmation and denial are implied. Hence non-assertion is a state of mind we are in, in consequence of which we declare that we neither affirm nor deny anything. From this it is clear that even non-assertion is not something we employ in the opinion that the nature of things is such as absolutely to call for it. On the contrary, our employment of it simply indicates that at the moment we utter it we find ourselves in this particular state regarding the problems of our inquiry. One must also remember that, as for dogmatic assertions about the non-evident, we neither affirm nor deny them; we yield our assent only to such propositions as move us emotionally or drive us under compulsion[2] to do so.

CHAPTER XXI

The Formulae "Perhaps," "It Is Possible," and "It Admits of Being"

THE formulae "Perhaps" and "Not, perhaps," "It is possible" and "It is not possible," and "It admits of being" and "It does not

---

way is that of Sextus, Bayle, and Hume, which might be called Experimental Scepticism. Obviously, it is this latter sort of Scepticism that flourished among physicians like Sextus. See Introduction, p. 27.

2. This compulsion involves habits, or habitual associations between phenomena or appearances: we habitually associate the word "dog" with the words "four-legged animal which is capable of barking" or with sights and sounds of a certain sort. This association of ideas, so similar to the association of ideas talked about by Locke, Berkeley, Hume, among others, can never be asserted to reveal the truth behind or beyond the ideas associated—it is something that holds only between what Sextus calls Recollective Signs; it is Hume's "gentle force" uniting appearances or phenomena, not "indicating" hidden truths beyond these phenomena. See Introduction, p. 16, pp. 25-26, and p. 101, fn. 8 below.

admit of being" we employ in lieu of "Perhaps it is and perhaps it is not," "It is possible that it is and it is possible that it is not," and "It admits of being and it admits of not being." As a result, for the sake of brevity, we use the expression "It is not possible" for "It is possible that it is not," and "It does not admit of being" for "It admits of not being," and "Not, perhaps" for "Perhaps it is not." But here again we do not dispute about words, nor do we inquire whether the formulae mean these things absolutely, but we use them, as I said, indifferently. Nevertheless it is evident, I take it, that these formulae are indicative of non-assertion. A person, for instance, who says, "Perhaps it is," by not stating positively that it is, affirms implicitly also the seemingly conflicting statement "Perhaps it is not." And the same applies also to the other formulae.

CHAPTER XXII

The Formula "I Suspend Judgement"[3]

WE use the formula "I suspend judgement" in lieu of "I cannot say which of the objects presented I ought to believe and which I ought to disbelieve." This usage makes it clear that as far as their credibility and incredibility are concerned the objects appear equal to us. And we make no positive claims as to whether they are equal, but merely state what our impression of them is at the time they come to our notice. We term this process "suspension" from the fact that the equal validity of the objects of investigation causes us to suspend our thinking so that it neither affirms nor denies anything about them.[4]

---

3. Another key Sceptical term: *epecho* (verb). Edmund Husserl (1859–1938) in his Phenomenology uses the term *epoche* (noun) to refer to the self-restraint the Phenomenologist has when tempted to believe in a world behind phenomena; to participate in his *epoche* is to put the world beyond phenomena "in brackets," outside of our area of belief or disbelief. *Epoche* involves being indifferent to a trans-phenomenal world. In these respects Phenomenology is close to Scepticism; in many other respects they are two very different philosophic movements.

4. Hence the balance-scale as the emblem of Scepticism.

CHAPTER XXIII

The Formula "I Determine Nothing"

ABOUT the formula "I determine nothing" we have the following to say. We believe that to determine means not simply to state something, but to bring forward and give assent to a view about a thing which is non-evident. From this one will perhaps discover that in determining nothing the Sceptic does not even determine the very formula "I determine nothing." It is not, in fact, a dogmatic notion, that is to say, an assent to something non-evident, but a formula expressive of a state of mind we are in. Thus, when the Sceptic says, "I determine nothing," he means this: "My state of mind at the present is such that I make no dogmatic affirmation or denial of anything falling under the present investigation."[5] And when he says this, he means that he is declaring in the manner of a reporter what his impression is of the things under discussion, and that he does so not with dogmatic confidence, but only to describe his own feelings in the matter.

CHAPTER XXIV

The Formula "All Things Are Undetermined"

INDETERMINATION is a state of mind in which we neither deny nor affirm anything falling within the realm of dogmatic inquiry, I mean the realm of the non-evident. So when the Sceptic says, "All things are undetermined," he takes the word "are" in the meaning that they "appear so to him." By "all things" he means not all existence but such non-evident matters investigated by the dog-

---

5. A common "refutation" of Scepticism involves pointing out that there is a contradiction at its heart: it says that no knowledge is possible, but at the same time affirms that *this* knowledge (that no knowledge is possible) is both possible and actual. The usual way that Sextus meets this "refutation" is to point out that the Sceptic never says that no knowledge is possible—he simply suspends judgement, letting the conflicting claims fight it out amongst themselves. He is not claiming to know anything about the possibility of knowledge—he is simply exhibiting conflicts, and letting the reader (as well as himself) suspend judgement on the whole matter. The "contradiction at the heart of Scepticism" dissolves, or at least must be found elsewhere, when one takes the language of Scepticism seriously and stops knocking down straw-men.

matists as he has examined. And by "undetermined" he means they are not superior, in the matter of credibility and incredibility, to whatever is opposed to them or in general conflicts with them. And just as when a person says, "I am walking about" he is virtually saying, "It is I who am walking about," so he who says, "All things are undetermined" means at the same time "in our view," or "as far as concerns me," or "as it appears to me." It would be equivalent to saying, "In all the investigations of the dogmatists I have come upon, their postulates appear to me to be such that none of them seems to be better, in point of credibility and incredibility, than that postulate which conflicts with it."

CHAPTER XXV

The Formula "All Things Are Non-Apprehensible"

OUR attitude is similar when we say, "All things are non-apprehensible." For we interpret the words "all things" and supply the additional qualification "to me" in a similar way as before. Consequently, what we say is this: "In all the dogmatic investigations I have inspected, the non-evident things they speculate about appear to me non-apprehensible." And this does not mean that the Sceptic is absolutely certain that the things which the dogmatists speculate about are of such nature as to be non-apprehensible, but simply that he is reporting his own state of mind about the matter. He expresses this state of mind when he says, "I suppose that because of the equal validity of the things opposed I have thus far not been able to apprehend any of those things; and for the same reason all arguments aimed at making us refute ourselves seem to me to be irrelevant to the things we report on."

CHAPTER XXVI

The Formulae "I Am Non-Apprehending" and "I Do Not Apprehend"

BOTH the formula "I am non-apprehending" and the formula "I do not apprehend" are indicative of a peculiar state of mind in which the Sceptic refrains, for the time being, from affirming or denying anything non-evident that may be the object of inquiry.

This is evident from what we have already said about the other formulae.

CHAPTER XXVII

The Formula "To Every Argument an Equal Argument Is Opposed"

IN our statement "To every argument an equal argument is opposed," the word "every" means every argument that we have examined. By "argument" we mean not a simple statement but the kind of statement which seeks to establish, in any way whatever (not necessarily by premises and conclusion), a point dogmatically, that is, some view touching on what is non-evident. By "equal" we mean equal in respect of credibility and incredibility. We take "is opposed" in the ordinary sense of "conflicts with," and we also supply the additional qualification "as it appears to me." Therefore, when I say, "To every argument an equal argument is opposed," my assertion is virtually this: "For every argument which I have examined, and which seeks to establish a point dogmatically, it appears to me that there is another argument opposed to it which seeks to establish a point dogmatically and is equal to it in point of credibility and incredibility." Uttered in this manner, our formula is not a dogmatic one, but a description of a human state of mind as it appears to the person experiencing it.

Some also utter the formula in this form: "To every argument an equal is to be opposed." They think it should have an admonishing turn, thus: "To every argument seeking to establish a point dogmatically, let us oppose an argument which investigates dogmatically, is of equal credibility and incredibility, and conflicts with it." They intend this to be addressed to the Sceptic, but they use the infinitive instead of the imperative: "to be opposed" instead of "let us oppose." They recommend this form to the Sceptic so that, in case he has been misled by the dogmatist, he will not renounce his investigation of him. If he does, his hastiness may cause him to fail to gain that mental tranquillity which is granted to them and which they believe goes hand in hand with a thoroughgoing suspension of judgement, as we have stated above.[6]

_____

6. This chapter, like some of the others immediately before it,

CHAPTER XXVIII

General Rules for the Sceptic Formulae

WE have gone through a sufficient number of formulae for the purposes of this outline, especially since one can discuss the remaining ones on the basis of what we have now said about these. In regard to all the Sceptic formulae it must be understood in advance that we make no assertions to the effect that they are absolutely true. We even say that they can be used to cancel themselves, since they are themselves included in those things to which they refer, just as purgative medicines not only remove the humours from the body but expel themselves together with the humours.[7] Also, we do not pretend that in setting up these formulae we are revealing the real nature of the things for which they are used. On the contrary, we use them indifferently and (if you will) loosely. For one thing, it is not like the Sceptic to be disputing over words, especially as it works to our advantage to say that even these formulae have no absolute significance, but are relative, that is to say, relative to the Sceptics.[8] In addition, one must also remember the fact that we do not say them universally about all things, but about the non-evident things which form the objects of the dogmatists' speculations. Remember also that we speak of things as they appear to us, and do not give any positive opinions as to the real nature of

---

repeats much of what has been already pretty carefully explained. The editor has left it in because it emphasizes the point that non-evident things are the things involved in doubt, not Recollective Signs, impressions, phenomena, or experiences.

7. Here is the famous metaphor, used by Sextus and later to be used by Montaigne in his "Apology for Raymond Sebond." It should be clear by now that Scepticism is a kind of therapy for curing rampant, fanatical dogmatism by allowing us to be indifferent to it in all its forms. And it does all this in much the same way and for the same purposes for which a physician administers an aperient: to eliminate the troublesome and to permit his patient to lead a normal, healthy, trouble-free life. Greek Scepticism is seen in the light of this metaphor as a therapeutic, happiness-enhancing philosophy, not as a paralysis-inducing drug or disease.

8. If you contradict the Sceptic, you play into his hands; he will show arguments opposing your own. Maybe after a while you will get tired enough to see his point: let us return to our customs, laws, instincts, habits, and to our loose, modest, common-sensical use of language.

external objects. I believe that on this basis every sophism brought against a Sceptic formula can be disposed of.

We have now exemplified the character of Scepticism by a review of its notion, its parts, its criterion, and its end, and by a discussion of the Sceptic formulae. Our next task, we believe, is to review briefly the distinction existing between Scepticism and those systems of philosophy closely related to it, in order to achieve a more accurate understanding of the "suspending" discipline. We start with the philosophy of Heraclitus.

CHAPTER XXIX

Differences between Scepticism and the Heraclitean Philosophy

Now, it is evident that this philosophy differs from our discipline, for Heraclitus expresses dogmatic opinions about many non-evident things, while we, as has been stated, do not. Aenesidemus and his followers used to say that the Sceptic discipline is a road to the Heraclitean philosophy.[9] Their reasoning was that the notion of the same object appearing to admit contrary predicates leads logically to the notion that the same object actually does admit contrary predicates. And they argue that the Sceptics say that the same object does appear to admit contrary predicates and that the Heracliteans, proceeding from this, also hold that it actually does admit them. To these our reply is that the notion of contrary predicates appearing to apply to the same thing is not a belief peculiar to the Sceptics. It is a fact that suggests itself not only to Sceptics but to other philosophers and to all mankind as well. No one, for instance, would venture the assertion that honey does not taste sweet to people in good health or that it does not taste bitter to people who have the jaundice. We conclude, therefore, that the Heracliteans start from a common preconception of mankind just as we do,[1] and just

---

9. See Introduction, pp. 26-27.

1. The Sceptic is not afraid to acknowledge such "common preconceptions," providing that they are customary or habitual, and providing that they are not contradicted. Husserl, the Phenomenologist (see above, p. 82, fn. 3), set out to present a "presuppositionless science." The Sceptic's philosophy is full of "common" presuppositions, and he is not

as perhaps the other systems of philosophy do also. For this reason, if the statement about contrary predicates belonging to the same subject were taken from one of the Sceptic sayings, such as the saying "All things are non-apprehensible" or "I determine nothing," or any one about like these, they would perhaps be able to prove what they assert. But since their point of departure is one which suggests itself not only to us but also to the other philosophers and to the ordinary man, why should anyone say that our discipline, any more than each of the other philosophies, or even life itself (since all of us make use of the same common raw materials), is a road to the Heraclitean philosophy?

On the contrary, not only does Sceptic thought contribute nothing towards a knowledge of the Heraclitean philosophy, but it is probably even a hindrance to it. After all, the Sceptic attacks all the dogmatic views of Heraclitus as being rash statements. He is opposed to his doctrine of world-conflagration, he is opposed to his idea that the same thing may admit contrary predicates, he ridicules the dogmatic rashness of every doctrine of Heraclitus and pronounces his "I do not apprehend" and his "I determine nothing" over them, as I said before. All this conflicts with the Heracliteans. But it is absurd to say that a conflicting discipline is the road to that system of philosophy with which it conflicts; therefore it is absurd to say that the Sceptic discipline is a road leading to the Heraclitean philosophy.[2]

CHAPTER XXX

How Scepticism Differs from the Democritean Philosophy

But the Democritean philosophy[3] too is said to be closely connected with Scepticism in that it seems to use the same material

---

ashamed of them. They are part of that healthy everyday life he is trying to restore us to.

2. For a brief summary of Heraclitus' philosophy, see Windelband, *A History of Philosophy*, Part I, Ch. 1. His was a philosophy of nature and mind that found change and law the basic forces in the universe.

3. See Windelband, Part I, Ch. 1, for remarks on Democritus' philosophy. Perceptions of qualities like sweetness and redness were false in his philosophy, because the only reality for him, underlying all appearances, was atoms and the void in which those atoms moved.

as we do. For they say that Democritus concludes, from the fact that it appears sweet to some but bitter to others, that honey is neither sweet nor bitter, and that this leads him to pronounce the formula "Not more," which is a Sceptic formula. However, the Sceptics and the Democriteans use the formula in different ways. While they prescribe the use of the formula for the case where neither of two things obtains, we prescribe it when we do not know whether both or neither of the appearances is real, so that in this respect we differ. However, the distinction between us becomes most evident in the saying of Democritus "In sooth, atoms and void." He says "in sooth" for "in truth." And so his statement that the atoms and the void are in truth existent, even if he does start out from the inconsistency of appearances, makes his position different from ours. It is even superfluous, I think, to point this out.

CHAPTER XXXI

How Scepticism Differs from the Cyrenaic School

SOME assert that the Cyrenaic doctrine is identical with Scepticism since it too claims that states of mind are the only things that can be apprehended. Nevertheless, it is different from Scepticism. According to their doctrine, the end is pleasure and a smooth motion of the flesh, while for us it is mental tranquillity, to which their end is in opposition. For whether pleasure is present or not, the person who positively maintains that pleasure is the end will have to submit to perturbations, as I have shown in the chapter "On the End."[4] Then again, we suspend judgement as to the essence of external objects, while the Cyrenaics[5] make a declaration to the effect that their real nature is inapprehensible.

---

4. See Ch. XII. There *all* positive beliefs are shown to be sources of perturbation, positive claims about pleasure included.

5. See Windelband, Part I, Ch. 2. Aristippus and the other Cyrenaics believed that emotions and bodily movements are closely related—so that indifference was intimately involved with bodily rest, pain was involved with violent motion, and pleasure, their goal, was involved with gentle motion.

CHAPTER XXXII

How Scepticism Differs from the Doctrine of Protagoras

PROTAGORAS,[6] on the other hand, claims that "Man is the measure of all things, of the existence of existing things, and of the non-existence of non-existing things." By "measure" he means the criterion, and by "things" he means objects, so that his statement virtually amounts to this: "Man is the criterion of all objects, of the existence of existing objects, and of the non-existence of non-existing objects." And this means that he posits only what appears to the individual, thus introducing relativity. Therefore he seems also to have a close relationship to the Pyrrhoneans; he still differs from them, however, and we shall know the difference when we have in due course explained the doctrine of Protagoras. Now, this man says that matter is in a state of flux. As it flows, continuous additions arise to take the place of the effluxions, and the senses undergo rearrangement and alteration in accordance both with one's age and with the other conditions of the body. He says also that the grounds of all appearances lie in matter, so that its power extends so far as to enable it to be all those things which appear to all. And men apprehend things differently at different times because the conditions they are in are different. The man who is in a natural state, he says, apprehends those material substances which can appear to those who are in a natural state, and a person who is in an unnatural state apprehends those things which can appear to those in an unnatural state. And the same reasoning applies as well to differences depending on one's age, one's sleeping or waking state, and every kind of condition. Therefore man becomes, according to him, the criterion of the existence of things. For all

---

6. See Windelband, Part I, Ch. 2. Protagoras (about 480–410 B.C.) believed that perception was the resultant or interaction of two motions, the motions of the perceiver's organism and the motion of the perceived object in its medium (air, etc.). What we perceived was neither one motion nor the other, but a mixture of both, a mixture we could not untangle or unmix in order to find out the nature of the object itself or of the mind itself. Upon this physiological theory of perception, Protagoras apparently built his relativistic philosophy of knowledge, ethics, and religion. It is important to see that Protagoras was talking about these hidden motions, even though he asserted we knew nothing about each in its purity; with such talk Sextus would have nothing to do.

things, in so far as they appear to men, also exist, while those things that appear to no man do not exist at all.

We see, then, that he dogmatizes both about the fluid state of matter and about the subsistence in matter of the grounds of all appearances, although these are non-evident things about which we exercise suspension of judgement.

CHAPTER XXXIII

How Scepticism Differs from the Academic Philosophy

SOME say, again, that the Academic philosophy is identical with Scepticism. It would therefore be appropriate to discuss this philosophy also. There have been, according to most authorities, three Academies, one of them, and the most ancient, being that of Plato and his followers. The second, or Middle, Academy was that of Arcesilaus, the pupil of Polemo, and his followers. The third, or New, Academy was that of Carneades and Clitomachus. Some authorities, however, add also a fourth, that of Philo and Charmidas, and some even count as a fifth the school of Antiochus.[7] Let us then begin with the Old Academy and see what differences there are between the philosophies mentioned above and ours.

Now, some have said that Plato is dogmatic, others have said he is dubitative, and still others that he is in one respect dubitative, in another dogmatic. For in his propaedeutic[8] discourses, where

---

7. We know very little about these later schools; they seem, especially under Antiochus, to have been eclectically dogmatic, seeking to bring together into one system Platonism, Aristotelianism, and Stoicism; but they seem to have emphasized ethical problems over metaphysical ones.

8. The most famous of the Platonic dialogues concerned with stimulating and guiding the mind of the beginning student of philosophy are the *Theaetetus, Euthyphro,* and the *Meno.* In these dialogues Socrates is acting the part of the midwife who perplexes his student into recollecting the truths that have been embedded in his soul, like the baby in a body; and like the woman in childbirth, who must suffer in the process of giving birth, the student must doubt, must be perplexed, must see his ignorance as far as his own sense-derived "knowledge" is concerned. The preliminary stages of instruction in philosophy involve, as Socrates puts it explicitly in the *Meno,* looking into our own immortal souls in order to find the eternal truths embedded there; but this in turn could not happen if we did not doubt or feel perplexed about the superficial, fleeting, falli-

Socrates is introduced either as jesting with others or as contending against sophists, Plato's character, they say, is both propaedeutic and dubitative. They say he is dogmatic, on the other hand, where through the mouth either of Socrates or Timaeus or some other such character he declares his views in all seriousness.

It would not be to the point to speak at present of those who say that he is dogmatic, or in one respect dogmatic and in another dubitative, for they themselves concede that he is different from us. But the question is whether he is a true Sceptic or not. This question we discuss at greater length in our *Commentaries*,[9] but for the purposes of the present outline we shall argue, against Menodotus[1] and Aenesidemus (these being the leading representatives of this position), that whenever Plato declares his opinion about Ideas or about the existence of providence or about the preferability of the virtuous life over the life of vice, he does one of two things. Either he is agreeing that these things are real, in which case he is dogmatizing, or he consents to this view on the grounds of greater probability. In the latter case he does not admit of being characterized as a Sceptic, since he gives preference to one thing over another on the basis of their credibility and incredibility, a procedure which is foreign to us, as is already evident from what has been said above. And even if he does make some

---

ble "knowledge" our senses and ordinary opinions gave us. It is in the greatest epistemological treatise of antiquity, the *Theaetetus*, that Socrates states, "I myself practice midwifery," and this involves "perplexity and travail" for those who are trying to bring to the light the truth that is within them; and he also states in this dialogue that he as a midwife must "abstract and expose" the "first-born" of his student, must deprive him of "a darling folly," of a changeling opinion in order to perform fully his function as a midwife. From this brief summary it should be clear how different Socratic propaedeutics is from Scepticism: the eternal truths waiting to be recollected *via* doubt, and the notion of doubt as the process of "stifling" what he calls "falsehood," involve a way of thinking quite alien to Scepticism, despite the many similarities between the two ways of doing philosophy.

9. This refers to the five books *Against the Dogmatists* (*Against the Logicians* I and II, *Against the Physicists* I and II, and *Against the Ethicists*). (—Tr.)

1. Menodotus of Nicomedia lived about 150 A.D., and was one of the first of the Sceptics doing research in medicine. He was an "Empirical" medical Sceptic. See Introduction, p. 27.

statements in the Sceptic manner in the course of what they call his propaedeutic discourses, he will not on that account be a Sceptic. For a man who dogmatizes on a single subject, or gives preference to one sense-impression over another wholly on the basis of credibility and incredibility, or declares an opinion about a non-evident matter, assumes the character of a dogmatist.

Timon[2] makes this clear in his remarks about Xenophanes. For after having praised him generously, even to the point that he dedicated his *Lampoons* to him, he represented him as making this lamentation:

> Would that I had attained my share of shrewdness,
> To look two ways at once; on a treacherous path
> I was led astray, an old man, and still innocent
> Of Doubt! For wherever I turned my mind,
> All was resolved into one and the same, and all that exists,
> However weighed, was always of one same nature.

It is on this account, I suppose, that he speaks of him also as [only] "half-befogged" rather than as perfectly free from arrogance, in these verses:

> Xenophanes, half-befogged mocker of Homer's deceit,
> Ha! made him his god spherical, far from men,
> Unmoved, unscathed, abstracter than thought.

He spoke of him as "*half*-befogged" because in a way he *was* free from arrogance, and called him a "mocker of Homer's deceit" because he ridiculed the deceit found in Homer. But Xenophanes was a dogmatist in that, contrary to the preconceptions of other men, he held that the All is one, and that the Deity is organically present in all things, and is of spherical form and without feeling and unchangeable and rational. From this it is easy to prove that Xenophanes differs from us. But in any case it is already evident from what has been said that even if Plato does raise doubts about some things, this still will not make him a Sceptic, since in other places we see him either making assertions about the existence of non-evident things or giving the preference to non-evident things on grounds of probability.

---

2. See Introduction, pp. 15-17.

The philosophers of the New Academy,[3] even if they say that all things are inapprehensible, are distinguished from the Sceptics perhaps even by this very statement that all things are inapprehensible,[4] for they make it as a positive statement, while the Sceptic supposes it possible also that some things may be apprehended. The distinction is already evident, however, in the matter of their judgement of what is good and what is evil. The Academics do not speak of a thing being good or bad as we do, but with the conviction that when they call a thing good, there is more probability[5] of its really being so than of its being the opposite. And they speak of evil in the same way. We, however, do not speak of a thing as being good or evil with the belief that what we say is probable. We simply follow ordinary usage undogmatically, in order to avoid inactivity.[6] And we say that sense-impressions, as far as their essence is concerned, are equal[7] in respect of credibility and incredibility, while they assert that some are probable and others improbable.

They also make distinctions among the probable ones. They believe that some are probable, and probable only, others probable and tested, and others probable, tested, and irreversible.[8] For example, there is a certain length of rope lying coiled up in a dark room. When a man enters suddenly, the sense-impression he gets from it is the simply probable one that it is a snake. But when a person has looked round carefully and investigated all the circumstances, for instance that it does not move and that its colour is such and such, and so on, it appears to him, in accordance with his probable and tested sense-impression, as a rope. One which is also

---

3. See Introduction, p. 17. We have called them Academic Sceptics in general, without discussing all the Academies with their different shades of dogmatism (or scepticism).

4. Outside of this passage, we have little evidence that this sort of negative dogmatism was characteristic of the famous Academic Sceptics.

5. See Introduction, pp. 19-24, for the two notions of "probability," or belief short of absolute certainty.

6. See the Practical Criterion, p. 40. Actions here are said to have no metaphysical or "natural-law" basis; they are performed not because they are absolutely right, but because living happily apparently involves living actively.

7. For the notion of "equality of force," see p. 34, fn. 1.

8. See Introduction, pp. 23-24.

irreversible is like the following. The story goes that when Alcestis had died, Heracles brought her back again from Hades and showed her to Admetus, who received a sense-impression of Alcestis that was probable and tested. However, since he knew that she was dead, his mind was distracted from giving its assent and inclined towards disbelief.[9] The philosophers of the New Academy, therefore, prefer the probable and tested sense-impression to that which is simply probable, and to both of these the probable and tested and irreversible.[1]

And even if both the philosophers of the Academy and those of Scepticism admit that they believe certain things, the differences between their philosophies is evident in this case also. For the word "believe" has different senses.[2] It has the meaning, first, of not resisting but simply following, without strong inclination or attachment,[3] as a boy is said to "mind" his tutor. But sometimes it means to assent to something by choice and with a kind of affinity that comes from desiring it strongly, as the profligate believes the man who advocates extravagant living. Now, Carneades and Clitomachus[4] and their followers affirm that both when they believe a thing and when they assert its probability their action is accompanied by a strong inclination[5] to do so. We, on the other hand,

---

9. I see no reason to mark a lacuna after "disbelief" with the editors of the Greek text. Admetus had the impression, which was "irreversible" to him, that Alcestis was dead. Cf. *Against the Logicians* I, 254–56. (—Tr.)

1. The Academics are pointing out here that belief does not involve only present and future sense-experiences or Recollective Signs; they are saying that belief is founded on past experience, and on beliefs derived from that experience. Generalizations previously held are touchstones for testing new beliefs, especially if those touchstones have endured close scrutiny. A new belief must be consistent with them just as they must be consistent with each other, if we are to have "irreversible" knowledge. The Academics, then, were not "radical empiricists" but believed in the logical structure of science as well as in some experience. They believed in using hypotheses.

2. Greek *peithesthai*, "be persuaded," "believe," "obey," "mind," has more senses than are exploited here. The verbal ambiguity cannot be reproduced adequately in English. (—Tr.)

3. Not only without strong passions, but without purportedly final reasons.

4. See Introduction, p. 20.

5. Throughout, Sextus and the others offer a psychological descrip-

do so as a matter of simple yielding, without attachment. Therefore our position would be different from theirs in this respect as well.

But we also differ from the New Academy in our views regarding the end. For the men who claim they are representative of this school use the probable as a guide in the dealings of ordinary life. Our life, on the other hand, is unprejudiced by opinions.[6] We simply follow the laws and customs and our natural feelings. And we should have had more to say in regard to the distinction if we were not aiming at conciseness.

Arcesilaus,[7] however, who as I said was the president and founder of the Middle Academy, seems to me to have been quite in agreement with the arguments of Pyrrho, so that his discipline and ours are practically identical. For one thing, we do not find him declaring any opinion about the existence or non-existence of anything. Also, he does not give the preference to any one thing over another in point of credibility and incredibility, but suspends his judgement in regard to all things. He also says that suspension of judgement is the end; and as we said, mental tranquillity goes hand in hand with suspension. And he also speaks of particular cases of suspension as being good things, and of particular cases of assent as being bad things. The only objection might be that while on our part these statements are based on what appears to us, and are not made positively, he means them as true statements of reality, so that he also asserts that suspension is in itself good and that assent is in itself bad. And if there is any reliance on what is related of him, they claim he had the appearance, at first glance, of being a Pyrrhonean, but was in reality a dogmatist. He seemed to be a dubitative philosopher, they say, because he used to make trial of his pupils by the method of doubt. However, he did this in order to see whether they were naturally suited for the reception

---

tion of the attitude of believing, and one that prefigures Hume's notion of belief in his *Treatise* (p. 96), where he says that belief is "a lively idea related to or associated with a present impression."

6. This is not an easy passage to understand. How can one live without some opinions regarding probabilities? Is it not plainly more likely that a cart will hit you if you stand in its way than if you stay off the street? And don't our funded empirical beliefs constitute "opinions"? One wishes for less of Sextus' "conciseness" at this important point.

7. See Introduction, pp. 18-20.

of the Platonic dogmas, and to those pupils who were thus naturally suited he communicated the doctrines of Plato. Hence also the saying of Aristo about him:

Plato his head, Pyrrho his tail, Diodorus his middle.[8]

This was because, although he was an out-and-out Platonist, he employed the dialectic of Diodorus.

Philo says,[9] however, that as far as the Stoic criterion is concerned, that is to say the "apprehending sense-impression," objects are inapprehensible, but as far as their nature is concerned, they are apprehensible. And Antiochus actually tried to transfer the Stoa to the Academy, so that it was even said of him that he was teaching Stoic philosophy in the Academy. This was because of his attempt to show that the dogmas of the Stoics are already found in Plato. This makes quite evident the differences existing between the Sceptic discipline on the one hand and both the fourth and fifth Academies, so-called, on the other.

CHAPTER XXXIV

Is Medical Empiricism Identical with Scepticism?

Now, there are also some who assert that the Sceptic philosophy is identical with the Empiric[1] school in medicine. Here we must realize that inasmuch as that form of Empiricism strongly maintains that non-evident things are not apprehensible, it cannot be identical with Scepticism. Neither would it be fitting for a Sceptic to take up study with that school. He would do better, I should think, to follow the so-called Methodic school.[2] This is the

---

8. This is a parody of Homer's description of the chimera as "lion the head of her, dragon the tail of her, her trunk a she-goat." Diodorus was a dialectically astute fourth-century metaphysician. Its point is: Plato did the thinking or the originating; Diodorus supplied the method, or means, for doing what Plato said; and both wagged poor Pyrrho, the appendage.

9. Philo of Larissa was a successor of Carneades in the Academy, and he gave up the belief that we have no absolute knowledge, turning the Academy back in the direction of dogmatizing.

1. See Introduction, p. 27.

2. If Sextus got the name "Empiricus" from his allegiance to the Empiric school of medical thought, then this defence of the rival medical school is queer. See Introduction, p. 27.

only one of the schools in medicine which seems not to involve itself in reckless and arrogant speculation about the apprehensibility or non-apprehensibility of things in the sphere of the non-evident. On the contrary, in conformity with the Sceptics, they follow the appearances and take from these whatever seems expedient.[3] For as we said before, everyday life—to which the Sceptic also is subject—is fourfold. One part consists in the guidance of nature, another in the compulsion of the feelings, another in the tradition of laws and customs, and another in the instruction of the arts. Now, just as the Sceptic, in accordance with the compulsion of the feelings, is guided by thirst to drink and by hunger to food, and in like manner to various other objects, so also the Methodic physician is led by the feelings of the patient to the corresponding remedies. By constipation he is led to the remedy of relaxation, just as the contraction due to intense cold causes a person to take refuge in a warm spot. By a flux[4] he is led to the suppression of it, just as persons in a hot bath, dripping all over with sweat and becoming faint, see that they must put a stop to it, and hence seek the relief of the cold air. It is also evident that feelings naturally alien to us compel us to proceed to their removal, seeing that even a dog, when a thorn is stuck in him, goes about removing it.

I do not wish to overstep the outline character of this treatise by a discussion of details, but I think we can say that all the cases thus described by the Methodics can be classified as falling under the compulsion proceeding from the feelings, both the natural and the unnatural feelings. In addition to this, the unprejudiced and indifferent use of terms is another common feature of the two disciplines. For just as the Sceptic employs the formulae "I determine nothing" and "I apprehend nothing" without prejudice, as stated, so also the Methodic uses the terms "generality" and "pervade"[5] and the like without any subtlety of meaning. So it is also with

---

3. A summary of the positive thrust of Scepticism, as has been pointed out.

4. An abnormal flow of any sort, but here gastro-intestinal.

5. These two quoted words are used synonymously: the more general pervades the less general or the special; that is, animality pervades all horses.

his use of the term "indication."[6] He uses this term without prejudice to mean that the feelings, both natural and unnatural, which appear in the patient point the way to what seem to be the corresponding remedies, just as I mentioned in the case of thirst, hunger, and the other feelings. Hence we must say that, to judge from these and similar characteristics, the system of the Methodics in medicine has a certain affinity with Scepticism; and speaking not absolutely but in terms of a comparison with the other schools of medical theory, it has more affinity than they.

So much, then, for our discussion of those schools which are thought to be closely connected with that of the Sceptics. With this we conclude both our general account of Scepticism and the First Book of our *Outlines*.

---

6. This word will be used later (p. 101) to label a sign (an Indicative Sign) which indicates the inner nature or constitution of something beyond all experience. Here "indication" is used purely within the realm of observables, or experience.

from BOOK TWO

CHAPTER X

Concerning Sign

ACCORDING to the dogmatists, then, some objects are self-evident and others are non-evident. Of the non-evident ones, some are absolutely non-evident, some are temporarily non-evident, and some are naturally non-evident. Things that come to our knowledge of themselves, they say, are self-evident. An example of this is the fact that it is day. Things that are not of such a nature as to fall within our apprehension are absolutely non-evident—for example, that the stars are even in number. And things that are of a visible nature but are rendered obscure to us from time to time by certain external circumstances are temporarily non-evident, as the city of Athens now is to me.[7] And things that are not of such a nature as to fall within our clear perception are naturally non-evident. An example would be the intelligible pores. These never become apparent of themselves. If they are to be thought of as being apprehended at all, it is through the medium of other things, such as perspiration or something of that sort. Now, they say that the self-evident objects do not require a sign, for they are apprehended of themselves. But the absolutely non-evident objects do not require one either, since of course they are not even objects of apprehension in the first place. The temporarily non-evident objects and the naturally non-evident, they say, are apprehended by means of signs, though not, to be sure, by the same signs. Temporarily non-evident objects are apprehended by means of "recollective" signs, and naturally non-evident ones by means of "indicative" signs.

According to them, then, some signs are recollective and some indicative. They call a "recollective sign" one which has been

---

7. Scholars have used this remark to support their claim that Sextus wrote all this while away from Athens; but it is possible that he is at the time of writing in a room in Athens, a room that does not look out upon the streets and people of that *plein air* society. The "external circumstances" then would be a wall.

associated in our observation with the thing signified and which
by its clearness at the time of perception—although that thing remains hidden—reminds us of the thing which in our observation
has been associated with it and which is not now clearly perceived.
This is the case with smoke and fire. An "indicative sign," they say,
is that which signifies its object not through having been clearly
associated in our observation with the thing signified, but by virtue
of its own nature and constitution,[8] just as bodily movements are

---

8. This distinction between Recollective and Indicative Signs, usually
attributed to Aenesidemus, is of central importance if one would see
Scepticism as a subtle philosophy. Every empirical philosophy that arose
after the publishing of these outlines (and some philosophies, like Plato's
and Aristotle's, before this time) distinguished experience from what is
beyond all experience, and this is exactly what is being distinguished by
the above distinction. The sight of smoke is a Recollective Sign of the
sight of fire; the British Empiricists after Locke developed the notion of
the "association of ideas" to analyse the sign-relationship between two experiences, like the sight of smoke and the sight of fire. But even Locke
did not confine himself to Recollective Signs, or experience; in his Essay,
Bk. II, Ch. 8, Sec. 15, he wrote that "ideas of primary qualities of bodies
[their number, shape, motion—in short, measurable qualities] are resemblances of them, and their patterns do really exist in the bodies themselves." When Locke used Aristotle's, Galileo's, Hobbes's, and Descartes'
distinction between experiences that *do* reveal the inner, unexperienced
constitution of things and experiences that *don't* (their distinction between
ideas of primary qualities and ideas of secondary qualities), he was leaving the realm of Recollective Signs and was using Indicative Signs.
    To summarize the distinction between these two deeply different
signs, Recollective Signs, or associated ideas, are two experiences, or
images of experiences, "that in themselves are not at all of kind" (to use
Locke's phrase), but which get bound together by habituation (like the
sight of smoke and the sight of fire, or the sight of smoke and the smell
of smoke); Indicative Signs, on the other hand, involve one experience
(or a copy or image of an experience) and something that is itself beyond all experience; moreover, these two entities, far from being "not at
all of kind," are said (in the case of primary qualities) to *resemble* each
other. Here we do not have two habitually concomitant copies of experience; we have one such copy whose inner structure, or shape, is said to
resemble something beyond all immediate experience, just as the visible
shape of an apple is said to resemble the inner nature and constitution,
the non-evident shape of it.
    Locke had introduced the association of ideas in the *Essay* (Bk. II,
Ch. 28) in order to attack prejudice and fanaticism as the product of
blind habit binding together otherwise disparate ideas. What the Sceptics before Locke and the British Empiricists after him did was to throw
out all claims for knowledge concerning a material world "indicated" by

signs of the soul. Hence they also define this sign in these terms: "An indicative sign is an antecedent proposition, in a sound hypothetical syllogism, serving to reveal its consequent proposition."[9] Now, our arguments are not directed against every sign, but (signs being of two kinds, as we said) only against the indicative type, because it seems to be a fabrication of the dogmatists. For the recollective sign enjoys the confidence of the world at large, since when a man sees smoke he infers fire, and when he looks at a scar he says that there has been a wound. Hence not only do we not fight against the world at large, but we even fight on the same side by giving our undogmatic assent to that sign which it relies on and by opposing the private fabrications of the dogmatists.

It was fitting, perhaps, to premise these remarks in the interest of making clear the object of our inquiry. It remains for us to proceed to our refutation, not that we are eager to show that the indicative sign is wholly non-existent, but we wish to mention the fact that the arguments adduced both for its existence and for its non-existence appear to be of equal validity.

CHAPTER XIV

On Syllogisms

FOR that reason it is perhaps also superfluous to go through and discuss their much talked-of "syllogisms." For one thing, they are included in our refutation of the existence of "proof."[1] It is of course plain that if proof does not exist, there is no place either for demonstrative argument. Secondly, we have implicitly con-

---

experience in favour of knowledge-claims *within* the circle of Recollective Signs. Here again we see how Classical Scepticism, far from having anything to do with anaesthesia, or unawareness of experience, was a precursor of philosophies totally devoted to experience, and was itself such a philosophy.

9. In modern logic this little operation is called *modus ponens*: If A, then B; A is true, therefore B is true. An example Sextus might attack would read like this: If sweat passes through the skin, then we have intelligible (non-evident) pores; sweat passes through the skin; therefore, we have intelligible pores. He would try to crack such inferences because they go beyond the association of experiences.

1. "Proof" had been shown in the preceding chapter (not included here) to be "no more" existent than non-existent. Redundancy (immediately below) had also been discussed in the preceding chapter. (—Tr.)

tradicted them in our statements above, where we discussed redundancy. There we mentioned a certain method by which it can
be shown that all the demonstrative arguments both of the Stoics
and of the Peripatetics are inconclusive. But for good measure,
perhaps we may as well treat of them separately also, considering
the pride they take in them. Now, there is much we could say to
suggest their unsubstantiality, but for the purpose of an outline it
is sufficient to use the following method against them. And I shall
be speaking now of the non-demonstrable syllogisms, for if these
are destroyed, all the rest of their arguments are also overturned,
since it is from these that they derive the proof for their deductions.

Now, this premiss "Every man is an animal" is established by
induction from the particular instances. For Socrates, since he is a
man, is also an animal, and Plato and Dion and each of the particular instances likewise. From this fact they think it is possible to
affirm that every man is an animal, with the result that if even a
single one of the particular instances should appear to be in opposition to the others, the universal premiss is not sound. Take a case
like this. Since most animals move the lower jaw and only the
crocodile moves the upper jaw, the premiss "Every animal moves
the lower jaw" is not true. So when they say, "Every man is an
animal, but Socrates is a man, therefore Socrates is an animal,"
their intention is to deduce from the universal proposition "Every
man is an animal" the particular proposition "therefore Socrates is
an animal." This particular proposition is actually what establishes
the universal proposition, and it does so (as we mentioned) by the
inductive method. Hence they fall into circular reasoning, since
they are using each of the particular propositions to establish the
universal proposition inductively, and deducing each of the particular propositions from the universal by means of the syllogism.
And in the case of such an argument as this, "Socrates is a man, but
no man is four-footed, therefore Socrates is not four-footed," they
do about the same thing. They wish to establish the proposition
"No man is four-footed" by induction from the particular instances, and they wish to deduce by the syllogism each of the
particulars from the proposition "No man is four-footed." And so
they are caught in the embarrassment of circular reasoning.

In like manner we must examine also the rest of the arguments

called "non-demonstrable"[2] by the Peripatetics, and also those of
the type "If it is day, it is light." The proposition "If it is day, it is
light" is capable, as they say, of proving the fact that "it is light,"
while the fact that "it is light," together with the fact that "it is
day," is confirmatory of the proposition "If it is day, it is light."
For the hypothetical proposition above stated would not have been
considered sound were it not for the fact that previously the fact
that "it is light" had always been observed to coexist with the fact
that "it is day." If, therefore, in order to construct the hypothetical
premiss "If it is day, it is light," it is necessary to have premised
the fact that if it is day it is assuredly light also, while it is by
means of this hypothetical premiss that the fact is deduced that
when it is day it is light; and if at the same time the premiss "If it
is day, it is light" proves, as far as the non-demonstrable argument
in question is concerned, the coexistence of the fact of it being
day and the fact of it being light, and the coexistence of the facts
referred to above is what serves to establish the premiss, then
here also the circular character of the question upsets the substance of the argument.

It is the same with arguments of this type: "If it is day, it is
light; but it is not light; therefore it is not day."[3] For from the fact
that day is not observed without light the hypothetical premiss
"If it is day, it is light" might be considered to be valid, just as it
would be said to be false if day (let us suppose) should once really
appear without light. But, as far as the non-demonstrable argument
stated above is concerned, the non-existence of day in the absence
of light is deduced by means of the premiss "If it is day, it is light."
Consequently, each of these statements requires for its confirmation that the other be firmly taken for granted, so that in accordance with their method of circular reasoning it may become credible
by means of the other. Also, from the fact that some things are
incapable of coexistence with each other, such as day, for instance,
and night, both the negative conjunctive proposition "It is not both

---

2. Aristotle's categorial syllogisms are referred to here. Some of these
are not of the "If . . . then . . ." form, but use phrases like "All . . .
are . . ." and "Some . . . are . . . ."

3. Modern logic describes this operation as *modus tollens*, still a
basic pattern of human reasoning.

day and night" and the disjunctive proposition "Either it is day or it is night" might be thought valid. But they believe that it is the negative conjunctive and the disjunctive which establish their non-coexistence. They put it thus: "It is not both day and night; yet indeed it is night; therefore it is not day," and thus: "Either it is day or it is night; yet indeed it is night; therefore it is not day." From this we conclude again that if for the confirmation of the disjunctive and negative conjunctive propositions we need to apprehend in advance the fact that the propositions contained in them are incompatible with each other, while they, on the other hand, think that it is by means of the disjunctive and the negative conjunctive propositions that their incompatibility is deduced, then the mode of circular reasoning is introduced. For we are unable either to believe the aforesaid premisses without having apprehended the incompatibility of the propositions contained in them, or to maintain positively this incompatibility prior to our propounding the syllogisms based on those premisses. Therefore, since owing to the circular nature of the argument we can gain no foothold for our belief, we shall declare that, as far as these statements are concerned, neither the third nor the fourth nor the fifth of the non-demonstrable syllogisms has any foundation.

So much for the present, then, on syllogisms.

CHAPTER XV

Induction

It is also easy, I think, to dispose of their method of induction. They claim that the universal is established from the particulars by means of induction. If this is so, they will effect it by reviewing either all the particulars or only some of them. But if they review only some, their induction will be unreliable, since it is possible that some of the particulars omitted in the induction may contradict the universal. If, on the other hand, their review is to include all the particulars, theirs will be an impossible task, because particulars are infinite and indefinite.[4] Thus it turns out, I think, that induction, viewed from both ways, rests on a shaky foundation.

---

4. In many cases Sextus is right; to check up conclusively on "All men are mortal" and see whether the generalization is true, is indeed to

Definitions

ALSO, the dogmatists take great pride in what they are pleased to call their "systematic treatment" of definitions. This they assign to the logical division of their so-called philosophy. Well, then, let us see now what few remarks we can make about definitions.

Now, the dogmatists believe that definitions have many uses, but you will probably find that the main heads which they say comprise all their essential uses are two. They point out that in all cases it is either for apprehension or for instruction that definitions are necessary. Now, if we suggest that they are useful for neither of these, we shall, I think, upset all the vain labour that the dogmatists have expended on them.

To begin with, then, the man who does not perceive the object of definition is not capable of defining it because it is not perceived by him. And the man who does perceive it and then defines it has not apprehended the object from the definition but has merely framed his definition upon the object he has already apprehended. If this is so, then definition is not necessary for the apprehension of objects. For since the wish to define all things, because of the extension to infinity involved, will lead to our defining absolutely nothing, and since to agree that some things can be apprehended even apart from definitions is to declare that definitions are not necessary to apprehension (since we can apprehend all things apart from definitions in the same way as the undefined objects

---

engage in an "infinite and indefinite" task, since even if we include all known particulars, and our checker is a machine presiding over a dead human race and checking for life in their bodies, there may be other human beings yet to come, and they may not be mortal. (We could win a victory by definition, an empty victory, by calling these creatures not "men" but "gods," but this is obviously question-begging.) Sextus here, however, does ignore what is called "perfect induction": such a case is one wherein we are trying to see whether the claim "There are two men in this room" is true. This is finitely and definitely verifiable or falsifiable. Sextus, it seems, would accept this type of induction as conclusive, but would dismiss it as unimportant to his attack upon dogmatic inductive claims to the truth.

were apprehended), then we shall either define absolutely nothing or we shall declare that definitions are not necessary.

And for the same reasons we shall find that they are not necessary for instruction either. For just as the first man to perceive an object has perceived it without the aid of definition, so also the man who is being instructed about it can do without the aid of definition about equally well. Besides, it is by the objects defined that they judge their definitions, and they declare that those definitions are unsound which embrace any qualities not belonging either to all or to some of the objects defined. Hence, whenever a person makes the statement that man is "a rational, immortal animal," or "a rational, mortal, and literary animal," whereas no man is immortal and some are not literary, they say the definition is unsound. But it may also occur that definitions cannot be judged because of the infinity of the particulars from which any judgement of them must proceed. Further, they would not convey apprehension and instruction regarding those particulars by which they are judged, as these have been known and apprehended, if at all, beforehand.

And how could it be anything else but absurd to assert that definitions are useful for apprehension or instruction or for any clarification at all, seeing that they bury us in so much obscurity? Thus for example—to allow ourselves the jest—what if a person wished to inquire of someone whether he had met a man riding a horse and leading a dog, and conducted his interrogation like this: "O rational, mortal animal, receptive of thought and knowledge, have you met an animal capable of laughter, flat-nailed, receptive of political science, with his rounded portions resting upon a mortal animal capable of neighing, and leading a four-footed animal capable of barking?" What else could we call him but ridiculous, when in so familiar a subject-matter he strikes the man dumb with his definitions?[5]

---

5. This sort of humour reminds one of Timon's *Silloi*, or *Lampoons* (see Introduction, p. 16). Sceptics are traditionally unsympathetic towards those who leave plain talk and plain living behind in order to use blabbermouthed circumlocutions. They do not look lovingly on those who talk their way out of living experience.

Definition, then, so far as this enables us to say, is useless, whether one calls it "a statement which by means of a brief reminder leads us to form a notion of the objects underlying the terms," as they clearly do (I think it is clear from what we have just now said), or "a statement which sets forth the essence,"[6] or what you will. As a matter of fact, their desire to give a definition of "definition" plunges them into an endless controversy which I now pass over as being inconsistent with the scope of my treatise, inasmuch as what we said here about the uselessness of definitions seems to do away with them as well. And I think that for now this account of definition will suffice.

CHAPTER XXI

On Common Properties

WE can apply about the same arguments to the "common properties." For supposing that vision is one and the same property in Dion and Theon, if Dion perishes while Theon survives and continues to see, either they will say that the vision of the perished Dion remains uncorrupted, which is an incongruity, or they will say that the same vision has both perished and not perished, which is absurd. Therefore Theon's vision is not identical with that of Dion. If anything, each man's vision is peculiar to himself. And further, if breathing is a common property in Dion and Theon, it is impossible for Theon's breathing to be existent while Dion's breathing is non-existent. But it is possible—when the one has perished and the other survives him. Therefore it is not the same.[7]

---

6. The definition of "man"—"rational animal"—was believed by Aristotle to reveal the absolute "essence" manhood. The essence was a form or set of traits that not only appeared in experience, but that also preceded and limited that experience. It is not only what we see of men's rationality and animality; it is also the set of rational and animal *possibilities* that are in all men whether we see them or not, and that determine and limit what we do see. It is these possibilities beyond all experience that the Sceptics suspend judgement on; and what they are suspending judgement on is definitions used as indicative signs of entities beyond experience.

7. The word "same" is ambiguous: a colour can be the "same" as another colour—that is, similar to it, but residing in a different place; but when John is the same person as Smith, there is no possibility of their being in different places at the same time. That is, there is qualitative

Now, on this subject these short remarks will suffice for the present.

from CHAPTER XXII

On Sophisms

IN the case of sophisms which might profitably require exposure, the dialectician[8] will have nothing to say. The arguments he puts to us are like the following: "If it is not so that you have shapely horns and you have horns, you have horns; but it is not so that you have shapely horns and that you have horns; therefore you have horns." "If anything moves, either it moves in the place where it is, or where it is not; but it moves neither in the place where it is (for it would remain there) nor where it is not (for how could anything be active in a place where it does not even exist to begin with?); therefore nothing moves." "Either the existent becomes or the non-existent; now, the existent does not become (for it exists); but neither does the non-existent (for whatever becomes undergoes something, but the non-existent does not undergo anything); therefore nothing becomes." "Snow is frozen water; but water is black; therefore snow is black."

And when he has made a collection of such claptrap as this, he

and there is numerical identity or similarity. What Sextus is suspending judgement on here is the claim that there is a numerical identity in all cases where there is a qualitative identity; he is saying that just because two people are healthy it does not follow that the "universal" or pure form of health is physically or metaphysically present in both people at the same time.

Actually, in this passage he is not suspending judgement—he is asserting that universals do not subsist or exist in two places at the same time; and so he may be accused of being a rival dogmatist or metaphysician, and lacking that delicate touch required for the suspension of judgement on these matters. But before levelling this accusation against Sextus, one should remember that he always states the opposing case as strongly as he can so as to bring about the suspension of judgement; and he leaves it to us to let the two conflicting views ("There are universals in different places at the same time" and "There are no universals in different places at the same time") cancel each other out.

8. The Stoics held that dialectics is "the science of things true and false and neither true nor false," in fact, the universal science, the practice of seeking and the results of seeking the absolute, universal truth about all things.

knits his eyebrows, gets his dialectic ready, and undertakes very solemnly to prove to us by syllogistic demonstrations that something becomes, that something moves, that snow is white, and that we do not have horns. And yet it is probably sufficient to hold up against this stuff the palpable facts. Then a positive affirmation of any such nonsense will be shattered by the equally valid counter-evidence of appearances. And that is why a certain philosopher, when the argument against motion was put to him, without a word proceeded to walk about. And people who follow the ordinary pursuits of life go on journeys by land and across the sea, and they build themselves ships and houses and beget children in neglect of the arguments against motion and becoming.[9] There is also recorded an elegant little story told by Herophilus, the physician. This man was a contemporary of Diodorus, who showed his bad taste in dialectic by expounding sophistical arguments against motion and many other things as well. Once when Diodorus had dislocated his shoulder and had come to Herophilus to receive treatment, the latter said to him in jest: "Your shoulder has been dislocated either in the place where it was, or where it was not; but it has been dislocated neither where it was nor where it was not; therefore it has not been dislocated." So the Sophist besought him to let such arguments be and apply the treatment suitable to him from the point of view of the medical art.—For it is sufficient, I think, to pass one's life empirically and undogmatically in accordance with the commonly accepted observances and preconceptions, suspending judgement about statements grounded on dogmatic subtlety and furthest removed from the business of life.[1]

If, therefore, dialectic cannot do away with those sophisms

---

9. By now we need not emphasize the typicality of this remark, especially of its emphasis upon "the ordinary pursuits of life." Montaigne was to use a similar observation about ships in his great Sceptical essay "Apology for Raymond Sebond."

1. Notice how the Sceptic here reduces the dogmatists' claims to absurdity in much the same way that dogmatists and dramatists (like Molière) have tried to reduce him to absurdity. The Sceptic thrives on such reductions, and wishes them to continue on all sides until we get tired of getting excited about the legerdemain of this rogue reason and go back to plain talk and plain living.

which might usefully be confuted, while it would serve no purpose for dialectic to do away with those sophisms which one might grant it capable of doing away with, then as far as confuting sophisms goes, dialectic is useless. . . .

from BOOK THREE

In the following pages Sextus tries to show how that rogue reason leads us into conflicting cosmological or metaphysical claims when we let it operate without universal criteria, far away from plain talk and plain experience. Sextus is not being a rival metaphysician here; rather, he is letting the rival theories speak up well for themselves, and by letting them contradict each other he is letting them cancel each other out.

The casual reader may wish to skip this section. But the student who has read Augustine's *Confessions*, or is interested in Kant's *Critique of Pure Reason*, will find some striking affinities between the Sceptics and these later philosophers. Kant's four Antinomies in particular, which use what he calls the "Sceptical Method," have some interesting relationships to the following chapters, whether or not Kant read Sextus. The careful student of his Sceptical Method might compare the first Antinomy in the *Critique* with the chapters that follow, even though Kant himself sharply but carelessly distinguished his Sceptical Method from "scepticism" (Kant, *Critique of Pure Reason*, p. 395). Consider Kant's definition of the Sceptical Method.

> [It is the] method of watching, or rather provoking, a conflict of assertions, not for the purpose of deciding in favour of one or other side, but of investigating whether the object of controversy is not perhaps a deceptive appearance which each vainly strives to grasp, and in regard to which, even if there were no opposition to be overcome, neither can arrive at any result.

Especially in this last phrase do we see a hint of the dogmatism of Kant, as against the delicate balance of Sextus and the Sceptics (and indeed, as Kant says, his Sceptical Method "aims at certainty," while the antitheses of the Sceptics and Sextus do not). But despite this important difference, the above-quoted passage points up the similarities between Kant's antinomies and Sextus' antitheses. To read the following pages is to see more detailed similarities. The upshot of all these similarities is that despite real differences both philosophies sought to humble what have been called "the proud pretensions of dogmatic Reason" by "watching, or rather provoking," a conflict between those pretensions.

—Ed.

CHAPTER V

Is Anything the Cause of Anything?

IT is probable that cause exists. For how else could there be growth, diminution, generation, corruption, and motion in general? And how else could the particular effects, both physical and mental, be brought about, and the ordering of the whole universe, and everything else, but by some cause? For even if none of these things has any real existence, we shall say that it must be due to some cause, certainly, that they appear to us such as they are not. And if cause did not exist, we should even have all things being produced from all things, and that at random; for instance, horses would be begotten from flies, if you like, and elephants from ants. And if there were no cause why the southern regions should be stormy and the eastern regions dry, there would be on occasion violent rains and snow-storms at Thebes in Egypt, and the southern regions would not have their rain-storms. Moreover, whoever declares that there is no cause is even refuting himself. For if he asserts that his declaration is made absolutely and without any cause, he will be disbelieved. But if he says there is some cause for his assertion, he is positing cause in his wish to abolish it, since he is giving us a cause why cause does not exist.

These arguments, then, make it probable that cause exists. But that it is also plausible to say that nothing is a cause of anything will be evident after we have set forth, for the purpose of mentioning this view, a few of the many arguments for it.[2] One of these is, for instance, that it is impossible to conceive of a cause before we apprehend the effect of this cause qua its effect. For it is only when we apprehend the effect qua effect that we realize that the cause is causative of the effect. But neither can we apprehend the effect of the cause qua its effect unless we apprehend

---

2. Observe the device of antithesis, or equally weighty conflicting arguments, being used quite mechanically throughout this chapter.

the cause of the effect qua its cause. For it is only when we apprehend its cause qua its cause that we think we know that it is its effect. If, therefore, it is necessary to recognize the effect first in order to conceive the cause, and necessary, as I said, to understand the cause first in order to know the effect, the circular character of the problem shows that both are inconceivable, as neither can the cause be conceived qua cause nor the effect qua effect. For since each of them needs the confirmation of the other, we shall not know which of them we are to take as a starting-point for our thinking. Therefore we shall also be unable to declare that anything is the cause of anything.

But even granted that cause can be conceived, it will be regarded as inapprehensible because of differences of opinion,[3] some saying that there is some cause of something, others denying this, while others suspend judgement. For he who says that there is some cause for something either claims that his statement is made absolutely and is not based on any rational cause, or else he will say that there were certain causes leading him to give his assent to it. If he says his statement is made absolutely, he will be no more worthy of credence than the man who states absolutely that nothing is the cause of anything. But if he says he has causes for believing that there is some cause of something, he will be attempting to prove the question at issue by means of the question at issue. For whereas we are inquiring whether there is some cause of something, he takes the existence of a cause for the existence of cause as grounds for asserting that cause exists. And besides, since we are inquiring about the existence of cause, it will be absolutely necessary for him also to produce a cause for the cause why any cause exists, and for that cause he must produce another, and so on *ad infinitum*. But it is impossible to produce causes to infinity.

---

3. The student of the history of philosophy should read Hume's famous Section in his *Treatise*, entitled "Of the Idea of Necessary Connexion" (Bk. I, Sec. XIV). There are wide dissimilarities between these two little essays, but the upshot of them both is to return us to experience and to the effects upon us of custom or habituation; both, in short, seek to deflate such terms as "cause" and "effect" of all arbitrary or imaginary meanings that leave behind the Recollective Signs which are the core of our practical knowledge.

Therefore, it is impossible to make the positive declaration that there is any cause of anything.

In addition to this, when the cause produces the effect, the cause either exists and subsists already qua cause or it does not exist qua cause. And if it does not, it cannot produce the effect. But if it exists qua cause, it must subsist and exist as a cause previously, before it thus brings on the subsequent effect, which is said to be accomplished by it on the assumption that it already exists qua cause. But since cause is relative, that is to say, relative to the effect, it is clear that it cannot, qua cause of this effect, be prior to the effect. Therefore not even its quality as a cause can enable the cause to bring about that of which it is cause. But if it brings about nothing, either in its quality as non-cause or in its quality as cause, it brings about nothing at all. Hence it will not be a cause. For without the idea of bringing about something cause cannot be conceived as cause.

Hence some also adduce the following argument. The cause must either subsist simultaneously with the effect or subsist before it or exist after the effect comes about. Now, to say that the cause is brought into existence after the production of its effect would, I fear, border on the ridiculous. But it cannot subsist before the effect either, for it is said to be conceived in relation to it, and they themselves declare that relatives, in so far as they are relative, coexist and are conceived together with each other. But neither does it subsist simultaneously with the effect, for if it is causative of it, and that which is brought about must be brought about by something already existent, the cause must be a cause before it thus produces the subsequent effect. If, then, the cause neither subsists before its effect nor simultaneously with it, and there is no effect before the cause either, it probably has no substantial existence at all. And it is probably clear that the idea of cause is again overturned by the following argument too. For if cause, inasmuch as it is relative, cannot be conceived before its effect, while in order to be conceived as cause of its effect it must be conceived before its effect, and if it is impossible for anything to be conceived before that before which it cannot be conceived, it is impossible for cause to be conceived.

From all this, then, we conclude finally that if plausibility attaches both to the arguments by which we have shown that one must predicate the existence of cause and to those which prove that it is not proper to declare the existence of any cause, and if it is not admissible to give preference to any of these arguments over the others (since we admittedly have neither sign nor criterion nor proof, as we have stated above),[4] then we must necessarily suspend judgement regarding the existence of cause also, and say that as far as the statements of the dogmatists are concerned there is "no more" any cause existent than non-existent.

CHAPTER XV

On Physical Change

SOME[5] also state that there is no foundation in fact for "physical change," so-called. This they attempt to prove with arguments such as the following. If a thing changes, the thing changing is either corporeal or incorporeal. But each of these is a matter of dispute; therefore the theory of change will also be disputable. If a thing changes, it changes in accordance with certain activities of a cause, and by being acted upon. But this is impossible, for the reality of cause is overthrown, and with it the thing acted upon, since it has nothing to act upon it. Therefore nothing changes at all. If a thing changes, what changes either exists or does not exist. Now, that which does not exist is unreal and can neither suffer nor do anything, and thus does not admit of change either. If the thing changing exists, it changes either in so far as it exists or in so far as it does not exist. In so far as it does not exist, it does not change, for it is not even existent. But if it changes in so far as it exists, it is other

---

4. Again this is the crucial question Sceptics pose to the dogmatists: where is the (universally acceptable) criterion that will help us to make a *decisive*, conclusive choice between conflicting claims? Bring it forth, or do not speak as if you have made a conclusive choice for all of us. Neither denial nor affirmation is the heart of Scepticism; this question and this request are alone at the heart of Sceptical doubt.

5. See Windelband, *A History of Philosophy*, Part I, Ch. 1. The Greek Eleatics, led by Parmenides, put forth such claims about there being a solid-block universe, and they were opposed by Heraclitus and his followers, who believed in a changing, flowing universe.

than existent; that is to say, it will be non-existent. But it is absurd to say that the existent becomes non-existent, therefore the existent does not change either. And if neither the existent nor the non-existent changes, and there is nothing else besides these, it remains only to say that nothing changes.

Some give this further argument. That which changes must change in some time or other. But nothing changes either in the past or in the future, nor for that matter in the present, as we shall point out. Therefore nothing changes. Nothing changes in past or future time because neither of these is present, and it is impossible to do or suffer anything in time which is not real and present. But then nothing changes in the present either, for the present time is probably also unreal. However, to pass over this point for the present, it is certainly indivisible. And it is impossible to believe that iron, for example, undergoes the change from hardness to softness in an indivisible point of time, or that each of the other changes takes place in this time, for they appear to require extension in time. Therefore, if nothing changes either in past time or in future time or in the present, we must say that nothing changes at all.

A further argument is that if change exists at all it is either sensible or intelligible; but it is not sensible, for the senses are of specialized passibility,[6] whereas change is considered to possess "concurrent recollection"[7] both of that from which it changes and of that into which it is said to change. And if it is intelligible, since there exists (as we have often mentioned already) among the ancients an unsettled difference of opinion concerning the reality of intelligibles,[8] we shall not be able to say anything about the reality of change either.

---

6. Literally, "are unipassible," i.e., each sense is capable of being acted on only by the class of objects to which it is suited. (—Tr.)

7. The Stoics used this phrase to refer to the fact that in thinking about fire as a cause and smoke as an effect, both the fire and the smoke must in some manner be in our consciousness—we must be aware of them both, even if that awareness is the last link in a causal chain the first link of which (the object in itself apart from all awareness of it) we cannot grasp.

8. According to Gorgias, the Sophist, the intellect does not exist, nor does any of its objects; according to Heraclitus, the dogmatist, all things exist, and so does the intellect that perceives the rational patterns of this changing world.

Becoming and Perishing

Now, both becoming and perishing are refuted along with addition and subtraction and physical change, since there can be no becoming or perishing of anything apart from these. Examples would be, as they put it, that the becoming of the number nine is consequent upon the perishing of the number ten, by the subtraction of one, and that the number ten becomes in consequence of the perishing of the nine, by the addition of one; and that the becoming of rust is consequent upon the perishing of bronze, by change. If, then, the aforesaid motions are abolished, the result will probably be that becoming and perishing are also of necessity abolished.

Nevertheless, some add these arguments. If Socrates was born, Socrates became either when Socrates was not or when Socrates already was. But if he should be said to have become when he already was, he would have become twice; and if when he was not, Socrates both was and was not at once. He "was" by virtue of having become, and "was not" by virtue of our stipulation. And if Socrates died, he died either when he was living or when he had died. But he did not die when he was living, since the same person would be both living and dead. And he did not die when he had died either, since he would have died twice. Therefore Socrates did not die. And by applying this argument to each thing which is said to become or perish, one can dispose of becoming and perishing.

Some also use this argument. If a thing becomes, it is either the existent or the non-existent that becomes. But the non-existent does not become, because since nothing can happen to what is non-existent, becoming cannot happen to it either. Nor yet does the existent become. For if the existent becomes, it becomes either in so far as it is existent or in so far as it is non-existent. Now, in so far as it is non-existent it does not become. But if it becomes in so far as it is existent, since they assert that becoming involves becoming something different, that which becomes will be something different from the existent, that is to say, something which is not. That which becomes, then, will be something which is not, an absurd proposition. If, therefore, it is neither the non-existent nor the existent that becomes, nothing becomes at all.

For the same reasons, nothing perishes either. For if anything perishes, it is either the existent or the non-existent that perishes. Now, that which is not does not perish, for what perishes must have something happen to it. But the existent does not perish either. For when it perishes, it must be either remaining in its existent state or not so remaining. And if when it perishes it remains in its existent state, the same object will be both something which is and something which is not. For since it does not perish in so far as it is non-existent but in so far as it is existent, it will be, in so far as it is said to have perished, something different from the existent and hence something which is not; and it will be, in so far as it is said to perish while remaining in its existent state, something which is. But it is absurd to say that the same object is both something which is and something which is not. Therefore the existent does not perish while remaining in existence. But if the existent does not perish while remaining in existence, but first passes over into non-existence and then perishes in that state, it is no longer the existent that perishes but the non-existent. This, as we have shown, is impossible. And so if neither the existent nor the non-existent perishes, and there is nothing else besides these, nothing perishes at all.

Now, these observations concerning the motions will suffice for the purposes of an outline. It follows from them that the physical science of the dogmatists is unreal and inconceivable.

CHAPTER XVII

On Rest

CONSEQUENTLY, some have also raised doubts about absolute rest. Their argument is that what is in motion is not at rest, whereas according to the assumptions of the dogmatists everything that is body is constantly in motion, since they say that being is in a state of flux and always creating effluxions and additions. Thus Plato, they say, does not even speak of bodies as "being" but rather calls them "becoming," and Heraclitus likens the mobility of our matter to the swift flow of a river. Therefore no body is at rest. That which is nevertheless said to be at rest is thought to be enclosed by the things surrounding it. But that which is enclosed is acted upon, and nothing acted upon exists, since not even cause exists, as we have shown. Therefore nothing is at rest.

Some frame also this argument. That which is at rest is acted upon, and that which is acted upon is in motion. Therefore that which is said to be at rest is in motion. But if it is in motion, it is not at rest. But from this it is evident that the incorporeal does not admit of rest either. For if that which is at rest is acted upon, and being acted upon is peculiar to bodies, if anything, and not to incorporeals, no incorporeal thing can either be acted upon or be at rest; therefore nothing is at rest.

So much then for rest also. But since none of the things we have mentioned is conceived apart from place or time, we must proceed to our inquiry into these. For if a person proves these to be unreal, each one of the others will be proved unreal also. Let us begin with place.

CHAPTER XVIII

Place

"PLACE," then, is used in two senses, a strict sense and a loose sense. In the loose sense it is "place" understood broadly, as "my city," and in the strict sense place is that which confines precisely—by which I am precisely enclosed. Now, our inquiry is concerned with place in the precise sense. The reality of place in this sense has been affirmed by some, but denied by others, while some have suspended judgement about it. Those who assert its reality appeal to the data of experience. Who, they say, would assert that place does not exist when he sees the parts of place, such as right and left, up and down, before and behind, and when he is in different places at different times, and when he sees that where my teacher was talking, there I am talking now, and when he finds that the place of things naturally light is different from that of things naturally heavy, and also when he hears the ancients declaring, "For verily, first of all was Chaos"?[9] For they call place "chaos"

---

9. Hesiod, *Theogony* 116. (—Tr.)

from its ability to contain the things in it.[1] And besides, if any body exists, they say, place also exists, for without it body would not exist. And if the "by-which" and the "from-which" exist, the "in-which"—namely, place—also exists. But the first clause in each of the two syllogisms is true; therefore the second in both is true.[2]

But those who deny place do not grant the existence of the parts of place. For place, they say, is nothing aside from its parts, and he who attempts to deduce the existence of place from the assumption that its parts exist is purposing to prove the matter in question by means of itself. They think equally silly the arguments of those who assert that it must be in some place or other that a thing becomes or has become, when place in general is not admitted, and who take for granted the existence of body, although it is obviously not admitted. And they say that the "from-which" and the "by-which"[3] can be shown to be unreal in much the same manner as place. Also, Hesiod is not a trustworthy judge of philosophical matters. And not only do they fend off thus the arguments tending to prove the existence of place; they also make their proof of the non-existence of place more diversified by making use, additionally, of what are thought to be the more weighty opinions of the dogmatists about place. These opinions, which are those of the Stoics and the Peripatetics, they make use of in the following way.

The Stoics say that "void" is that which, while capable of being occupied by an existent, is not so occupied, or an extension empty of body, or an extension not taken up by body, and that "place" is an extension occupied by an existent and coextensive with that which occupies it ("body" is here denominated "existent"). "Space," they say, is an extension partly occupied by body and partly unoc-

---

1. *Choretikos*, "able to contain," derived from *chora*, "space," is falsely connected with "chaos." (—Tr.)

2. In each of the two hypothetical syllogisms (beginning with "And besides . . .") the first member (the if-clause) is true; therefore, in both the conclusion is true (that place, and the "in-which," exist). In both syllogisms the minor premiss is understood: "But some body does exist," and "But the by-which and the from-which exist." (—Tr.)

3. The "by-which" is the efficient cause of an entity, the hand of the sculptor, for example, being the efficient cause by which the statue is moulded; the "from-which" is the material cause of the statue—the materials (marble, etc.) from which the statue is made. These are Aristotle's notions, most succinctly stated in his *Metaphysics*, Bk. I, Ch. 3.

cupied. Some of them, however, say that space is the place of a large body, so that the difference between place and space would depend on size. The argument against them, then, is this. When they say that place is an extension occupied by an existent, in what sense, further, do they call it an "extension"? Do they mean in respect of the length of the body or its breadth or its depth only, or in respect of the three dimensions? If they mean one dimension, the place is not equal to that of which it is the place, plus the fact that what encloses is only a part of what is enclosed. This is quite absurd. And if the three dimensions are meant, since there subsists in what they call place neither a void nor another body possessing dimension, and since the body which (they say) exists in place is all but composed of the dimensions (for it actually is these: length, breadth, depth, and solidity, of which the last is said to be a property of the aforesaid dimensions), then body itself will be its own place, and the same object will be at once enclosing and enclosed, which is absurd. Therefore there exists no dimension of an existing place, and from this it follows that place does not exist at all either.

This argument is also set forth. Since we do not observe a double set of dimensions for each of the objects said to exist in place, but only one length, one breadth, and one depth, do these dimensions belong to the body only or to the place only, or to both? If they belong only to the place, the body will not have any length or breadth or depth of its own. Consequently the body will not even be body, which is absurd. But if they belong to both, then, since the void has no reality over and above the dimensions, if the dimensions of the void subsist in the body and go to make up the body itself, the components of the void will also be components of the body. It is not possible, as we have shown, to make any positive statements concerning the reality of solidity, but since the only dimensions appearing in body, so-called, are those which belong to the void and are identical with the void, body will be a void, which is absurd. And if the dimensions belong only to the body, there will be no dimension of place, and hence no place either. Accordingly, if in none of the ways referred to above we find dimension of place, place does not exist.

An additional argument is that when the body comes over the void and becomes place, the void either remains or withdraws or perishes. But if it remains, the same thing will be both full and empty. And if it withdraws by a movement involving change to another place, or perishes by undergoing a change, the void will be body, for these processes are peculiar to body. But it is absurd to say that the same thing is both empty and full, or that the void is body. Therefore it is absurd to say that the void can be occupied by body and become place. For this reason we find that the void too is unreal, since it cannot be occupied by body and become place, for "void" was said to be that which is capable of being occupied by body. And space also is refuted along with these. For if "space is the large place," it is cancelled along with place, while if it is "partly occupied by body, and partly empty extension," it is destroyed together with both of these.

These arguments, then (and more besides), are advanced against the views of the Stoics on place. The Peripatetics say that place is the limit of the enclosing medium, in so far as it encloses; so that my place would be that surface of the air enfolding my body. But if this is place, the same thing will both be and not be. For when the body is to be in a certain place, inasmuch as nothing can be in what is non-existent, the place must be pre-existent in order for the body thus to be in it. Hence the place will exist before the body in the place is in it. But in so far as it is produced when the surface of the surrounding medium enfolds the thing surrounded, place cannot subsist before the body is in it, and for this reason will at that time not exist. But it is absurd to say that the same thing both is and is not. Therefore place is not the limit of the enclosing medium in so far as it encloses.

Another argument is that if place is anything, it is either created or uncreated. Now, it is not uncreated, for it is produced, they say, by its being fitted round the body which is in it. But it is not created either. For if place (in which the thing in place is already said to be located) is created, it is created either when the body is located in it or when it is not located in it. But it is not created when the body is in it, for it is already the place of the body located in it. Nor is it created when it is not in it, since, as they assert, the enclosing medium becomes place only when it enfolds the thing enclosed, and nothing can be fitted round that which is not within it. But if place is generated neither when the body is in place nor when it is not in place, and we can conceive no other possibilities than these, then place is not created at all. And if it is neither created nor uncreated, it does not exist.

These arguments can also be stated in more general terms. If place is anything, it is either corporeal or incorporeal. But each of these concepts is a matter of doubt, as we have shown. Therefore place also is disputable.—Place is conceived together with the body of which it is the place. But the doctrine about the reality of body is disputable; therefore that about place is also.—The place of each thing is not eternal, but is said to become. But as becoming is unreal, we find place to be unreal also.

There are many other arguments we might advance, but—not to be prolix—we must bring forward the one point that, while the Sceptics are put to shame by the arguments, they are also put out of countenance by the data of experience. Therefore we side with neither party in this matter of the dogmatist doctrine, but suspend judgement regarding place.

CHAPTER XIX

Time

WE are confronted with the same state of affairs in our inquiry about time also. For as far as appearances go, time seems to be something, but when we come to the arguments about it, it appears unreal. Some say that time is "the extension of the motion of the whole" ("whole" meaning the universe). Others say it is "the very motion of the universe." Aristotle (or Plato, according to some) says it is "the number of the prior and posterior in motion." Strato (or Aristotle, according to some) says it is "the measure of motion and rest." Epicurus (according to Demetrius, the Laconian)[4] says it is "an accident of accidents, concomitant with days and nights and seasons and affections and impassibilities and motions and states of rest." And as to its substance, some have said it is corporeal, as Aenesidemus and his followers (for their

---

4. A follower of Epicurus, who believed that atoms and the void are the basic stuff of the universe—solid stuff and space—and therefore that time is an epiphenomenon, or an incidental side-effect of the ultimate real entities.

view is that it is in nothing different from being and the prime body),[5] and others have said it is incorporeal. Now, either all these views are true, or all false, or some true and some false. But they cannot all be true (most of them are conflicting),[6] nor will all be admitted to be false by the dogmatists. And besides, if it should be granted that both assertions—that time is corporeal and that it is incorporeal—are false, the unreality of time will be granted at once, for besides these alternatives there is nothing else it can be. Nor can we tell by apprehension which of these views are true and which false, because of the fact that the different views are evenly matched and because there is embarrassment in the matter of the criterion and the proof. As a result we shall for these reasons be unable to make any positive assertions about time.

Next, since time seems not to subsist without motion or even rest, if motion is done away with, and rest likewise, time is done away with. Nevertheless, some do advance the following arguments against time. If time is anything, it is either limited or unlimited. If it is limited, it began at a certain time and will end at a certain time. Therefore there was once a time when time did not exist[7] (before it began), and there once will be a time when time will not exist (after it stops), which is absurd. Therefore time is not limited. But if it is unlimited, since part of it is said to be past, part present, and part future, the future and the past either exist or do not exist. But if they do not exist, since there remains only the present, which is momentary, time will be limited and there will follow the perplexities we had at first. And if the past exists and the future exists, each of them will be present. But it is absurd to say that the past and the future are present. Therefore time is not unlimited either. But if time is neither unlimited nor limited, it does not exist at all.

Another argument. If time exists, it is either divisible or in-

---

5. The basic stuff of the universe, thought of as not having any particular form or shape.

6. The heart of the definition of the term "conflicting" is that claims to which the term applies cannot all be true.

7. St Augustine, in his *Confessions* (Bk. XI, Chs. XIII, XIV), was to try to resolve this problem, and he was to resolve it in a very modern manner in Ch. XXX by saying that the question of whether there was time before time is empty, nonsensical.

divisible. Now, it is not indivisible, for as they themselves say, it is divided into present and past and future. Nor is it divisible. For each divisible thing is measured by some part of itself, the measure coinciding with each part of the thing measured, as when we measure a cubit by fingers. But time cannot be measured by any part of itself. For if the present, say, measures the past, it will coincide with the past and will therefore be past, and likewise, in the case of the future, it will be future. And if the future should measure the other parts, it will be present and past, and the past in the same way will be future and present, which is absurd. Therefore time is not divisible either. But if it is neither indivisible nor divisible, it does not exist.

Again, time is said to be tripartite, and partly past, partly present, partly future. Of these the past and the future do not exist. For if past and future time exist now, each of them will be identical with the present. But the present does not exist either. For if present time exists, it is either indivisible or divisible, Now, it is not indivisible, for things which change are said to change in present time, but no change takes place in indivisible time;[8] that of iron into softness does not, for example, nor anything else. Consequently present time is not indivisible. But it is not divisible either. For a division into "presents" would be impossible, since on account of the swift flux of the things in the universe the present is said to change imperceptibly into the past. And it cannot be divided into past and future, for in that case it will be unreal, having one part of itself no longer existent and the other not yet existent. For this reason the present cannot be the end of the past and the beginning of the future, as then it will both exist and not exist. It will exist qua present but again will not exist, inasmuch as its parts do not exist. Therefore it is not divisible either. But if the present is neither indivisible nor divisible, it does not exist. And if the present does not exist, nor the past either, nor the

---

8. Aristotle, in *Physics*, Bk. VI, Ch. 6, shows that motion or change cannot take place in an indivisible moment: if the moment cannot be divided, then there is rest at that moment, motion requiring a change of state, and a change of state requiring at least two different, distinguishable moments.

future, then time is not anything either. For that which is composed of unreal things is unreal.

The following argument is also advanced against time. If time exists, it is either generated and perishable or ungenerated and imperishable.[9] Now, it is not ungenerated and imperishable, since one part of it is said to be past and no longer existent and another part to be future and not yet existent. But it is not generated and perishable either. For, according to the assumptions of the dogmatists themselves, things being generated must be generated from something existent, and things perishing must perish into something existent. Now, if time perishes into the past, it perishes into a non-existent, and if it is generated out of the future, it is generated out of a non-existent, for neither of these exists. But it is absurd to say that a thing is generated out of a non-existent or that it perishes into the non-existent. But if time is neither ungenerated and imperishable nor generated and perishable, it does not exist at all.

In addition to this, since everything that becomes seems to become in time, if time becomes, it becomes in time. Therefore either time itself becomes in itself, or one time becomes in another. But if time itself becomes in itself, the same thing will both exist and not exist. For since that in which a thing becomes must exist before that which becomes in it, the time which becomes in itself, in so far as it becomes, does not yet exist, while in so far as it becomes in itself, it already exists. And so it does not become in itself. But neither does one time become in another. For if the present becomes in the future, the present will be future, and if it becomes in the past, it will be past. And the same is to be said of the other times. Thus it is not so, either, that one time becomes in another. But if neither time itself becomes in itself nor one time becomes in another, time is not generated. And it was shown that it is not ungenerated either. Therefore, since it is neither generated nor ungenerated, it does not exist at all. For each existing thing must be either generated or ungenerated.

---

9. According to Plato's *Timaeus*, time was generated, or came into existence; according to Aristotle's *Metaphysics*, time was not generated, did not come into existence.

CHAPTER XXXII

Why the Sceptic Sometimes Deliberately
Propounds Arguments Weak in Plausibility

THE Sceptic wishes, from considerations of humanity, to do
all he can with the arguments at his disposal to cure the self-
conceit and rashness of the dogmatists. And so just as healers of
bodily ailments keep remedies of various potency, and administer
the powerful ones to those whose ailments are violent and the
lighter ones to those with light complaints, in the same manner
the Sceptic too propounds arguments differing in strength. In the
case of those suffering from violent attacks of rashness he uses
those arguments which are weighty and capable of forcibly removing the condition of dogmatist self-conceit. But in those cases
where the condition of conceitedness is superficial and easily cured,
and can be removed by a lighter application of plausibilities,[1] he
uses the lighter arguments. This is why the man who is at home in
Scepticism does not hesitate to propound at one time arguments of
weighty plausibility and at another time arguments which may
even appear rather feeble. He does this on purpose, as these are
often sufficient for the accomplishment of his object.

---

1. Notice the medical metaphors, and remember that the basic metaphor is that of the laxative, or aperient, which washes itself away with
the waste materials it works on. It is important to see here that the previous passages on time, etc., are simply presented, without sceptical
comment, allowed to work on each other to secure our suspension of
judgement, or to weaken each other, and then all the cures and ills are
left behind, our mind being now clear to face living experience itself.
    This notion of philosophy as therapy, or cure, is elaborated in depth,
and with results similar to those of the Classical Sceptics, by Ludwig
Wittgenstein, especially in his *Philosophical Investigations,* where he too
talks of "different therapies," *verschiedene Therapien* (p. 51).

PART TWO: *On Man*

from AGAINST THE LOGICIANS, BOOK ONE

from BOOK ONE

On Man

LET us, then, go on to examine first in order the agent "by whom," that is to say, man. I believe that, if the difficulty which it involves is raised first, it will no longer be needful to say anything further about the other criteria.[1] For these are either parts or actions or affections of man. If, then, this criterion is apprehensible, it is bound to be conceived long before, inasmuch as a conception logically precedes every apprehension. But up to now man has turned out to be inconceivable, as we shall show; therefore at all events he is not apprehensible. From this it follows that knowledge of the truth is indiscoverable, since he who knows it is inapprehensible. For of those who have examined the conception, Socrates, for example, found himself embarrassed: he remained in doubt and declared that he was ignorant both of his own nature and of his relationship to the universe. "For I do not know," he says, "whether I am a man or some other kind of beast more complex than Typhon."[2] And Democritus, who likened himself to the voice of Zeus when he said, "These things I declare about the universe,"[3] did indeed attempt to give an explanation of the conception, but was not able to come up with anything more than a vulgar statement. He said, "Man is that which we all know." In the first place, we all know "dog" too, but the dog is not man. And we all know "horse" and "plant," but none of these is man. Next, he has also begged the question; for no one will readily grant that the nature of man is known, seeing that the Pythian god[4] has set

---

1. Sextus has been discussing in this Book the various criteria by which we decide whether a given belief is a true belief; he has said that some philosophers think we decide this by reason alone, some by means of the "irrational senses," and others by way of reference to the nature of man, or the knowing agent.

2. Plato, *Phaedrus* 230 A. (—Tr.)

3. This oracular statement was apparently the opening sentence of one of Democritus's major works. (—Tr.)

4. Apollo. (—Tr.)

before man as his principal object the injunction "Know thyself." And even if a person grants this, he will not allow that all philosophers have a knowledge of man, but only the most exact of them. Epicurus believed that the conception of man could be shown by pointing. He would say, "Man is *this* sort of shape in conjunction with animation." But he did not recognize that if what is pointed out is man, that which is not pointed out is not man.[5] And again, the object of such pointing out is either a man or a woman, an older man or a youth, snub-nosed or hook-nosed, straight-haired or curly-haired, and so on with the other differences. And if the one pointed at should be a man, womankind will not be "man," and if a woman, the males will be excluded, and if a young man, the other ages of life will be expelled from the concept of "man."

Some philosophers used to give an explanation of man in general by means of a definition, in the expectation that from this the conception of particular men would emerge. Of these philosophers some have defined man thus: "Man is a rational, mortal animal, receptive of thought and knowledge." So these too have given us not man but the attributes of man. But the attribute of a thing differs from the thing of which it is an attribute, since if it does not differ, you see, it would not be an attribute but the thing itself. Then too, of course, some attributes are inseparable from the things of which they are attributes, as length, breadth, and depth are from bodies (for without their presence it is impossible to conceive of body), while others can be separated from the things to which they belong, that thing remaining when they are removed. It is in this sense that running, conversing, sleeping, and waking are attributes of man, for all these things happen to us, but not continuously, as we remain the same persons when we are not running and when

---

5. In this and what follows until the end of the paragraph, Sextus is choosing to ignore the phrase "sort of" in the previously quoted statement of Epicurus. Epicurus was not pointing out one particular person, nor even one particular sex, but one *general* sort of being, and Sextus' doubts are valid only if we ignore the general reference of the assertion of Epicurus. Of course, Sextus in response to all this would say that the phrase "sort of" begs the whole question—which is: What *is* the sort of being that man is? And *this* would be a serious objection to Epicurus' assertion.

we are silent, and the same applies in the case of the other attributes.

Now, although there are two different kinds of attributes, we shall find that neither kind is identical with the thing which is the underlying substance, but always different from it. Accordingly, those too are foolish who define man as "a rational, mortal animal," and so on. For instead of defining man, they have recounted his attributes. And of these, "animal" is one of his permanent attributes, for it is impossible to be a man without being an animal. But "mortal" is not even an attribute, but something which occurs subsequent to man. For when we are men, we are alive and not dead. As for "reasoning" and "possessing knowledge," these are attributes, but not permanent ones. For there are some who are men and yet do not exercise reason, as for instance those who are "held fast by sweet sleep," and there are some who, though not possessing knowledge, are not on that account excluded from the concept "man," as for instance madmen. And so while we were seeking one thing, they have produced another.

Further, "animal" is not "man," as otherwise every animal will be a man. And if "rational" is to stand for "exercising reason," then the gods too will become men when they reason, and perhaps some of the other animals too. But if it stands for "uttering significant sounds," we shall be saying that crows and parrots and their like are men too, which is absurd. And moreover, if one should say that "mortal" means "man," it will follow that even irrational animals are men, since they are mortal. Our understanding of the words "receptive of reasoning and knowledge" must be similar. For in the first place, these attributes apply to the gods also. And secondly, even if man is receptive of them, man is not these things; on the contrary, man is he who is receptive of these things but whose nature they have failed to explain.

Nevertheless, some of those of the dogmatic school who are reputed to be wise say in reply to this that it is not each of the attributes enumerated that is "man," but all of them in conjunction that go to make up "man"—the sort of situation we observe in the case of parts and a whole. For just as neither a hand by itself is a man, nor a head, nor a foot, nor any other such part, but it is the whole made up of them that is so conceived, so too man is neither merely "animal" nor only "rational" nor exclusively "mortal," but the aggregate of all these, that is to say, at once animal and mortal and rational. But to this also the answer is obvious. In the first place, if each of these things by itself is not man, how can they be united so as to constitute man without either exceeding what he is or falling short of what he implies or taking some other false turn? And next, they cannot all come together to begin with—to the end that in the aggregate they should become man. Thus, for instance, when we are men, "mortal" is not an attribute of ours, but is taken for granted on the basis of concurrent recollection. For when we consider that Dion and Theon and Socrates,[6] and in general individuals similar to ourselves, are dead, we reason that we too are mortal, even though death is not yet present with us—for without doubt we are alive. Moreover, reasoning too is sometimes present with us, sometimes not present; and possessing knowledge, again, is not one of the constant attributes of man, as we have already shown. We must say, therefore, that not even a combination of all these is "man."

Plato's definition of man is even worse than the others. He says, "Man is a featherless, two-footed, flat-nailed animal, receptive of political science."[7] It is obvious what our reply to him ought to be. For, once more, it is not man he has expounded; on the contrary, he has enumerated what are and what are not his attributes. For "featherless" is a negative attribute, while "animal," "two-footed," and "flat-nailed" are positive attributes; and "receptive of political science" is sometimes a positive attribute, sometimes a negative one. Consequently, he gives us something quite different from what we were seeking to learn.

Well then, let us take this as proof that man is incapable of forming a ready conception of himself. Next, we must declare also that the apprehension of man is an impracticable thing, especially as this has already been partially agreed upon. For that which is not conceived is not of such a nature as to be apprehended either; and man has been shown to be inconceivable, at least as far as the

6. I.e., "Smith, Jones, and Robinson." (—Tr.)

7. This is from the post-Platonic *Definitions* (415 A), where the text, however, is "receptive of rational knowledge." (—Tr.)

conceptions of the dogmatists are concerned; therefore he is also inapprehensible. Nevertheless, it will be possible to establish this point in another way. If man is apprehensible, it is either he in his entirety that seeks and apprehends himself throughout, or he in his entirety that is the object sought and coming under apprehension; or, he partly seeks and apprehends himself, partly is the object sought and coming under apprehension. It is just as if one were to suppose that the sense of sight sees itself; either it will be wholly seeing or seen, or partly seeing itself and partly seen by itself. But if it should be man in his entirety throughout that is seeking himself, and he should be associated in thought with this (with the fact that it is he in his entirety and throughout that conceives of himself), there will no longer be anything to be apprehended, which is absurd. And if he in his entirety should be the object sought and should in his entirety be linked in thought with this (with the fact of being sought for), again there will be nothing left to do the seeking and make the apprehension. Moreover, it is not possible for him to change sides, to be sometimes in his entirety the thing seeking, and sometimes in his entirety the thing sought. For when he in his entirety is seeking and in his entirety is associated in thought with this (with the fact that he in his entirety is seeking), there will be nothing left for him to seek; and conversely, when he in his entirety throughout is the thing sought, the thing seeking will not exist.

There remains, then, the alternative that he does not in his entirety apprehend himself, but effects the apprehension of himself with some part of himself. This, again, is an impracticable thing. For man is nothing more than his mass, his senses, and his intellect. Consequently, if he is to apprehend himself with some one of his parts, either he will get to know his senses and his intellect with his body, or contrariwise, he will apprehend his body with his senses and his intellect. Now, it is impossible to get to know one's senses and one's intellect with one's body, for it is irrational and senseless and unsuited by nature for suchlike investigations. And besides, if the body is able to perceive the senses and the intellect, in the process of apprehending these it is bound to become like them, that is, it must be assimilated to their condition and become both sense and intellect. For when it perceives sight, it will, in so far as it sees, be sight, and when it apprehends taste in the act of tasting it will become taste, and so on analogously with the other senses. For just as whatever perceives a hot thing as hot perceives it by being heated, and by being heated is at once hot, and as whatever gains knowledge of a cold thing as cold by growing cold is at once cold, so also if the fleshy mass perceives the senses as senses, it has sense-perception, and if it has sense-perception it will at all events become sense, and thus that which seeks will no longer exist but will be the thing sought. Add to this the fact that it is perfectly ridiculous to say that the body does not differ from the senses and the intellect when nearly all of the dogmatic philosophers have explained the difference between them.

The same argument applies to the intellect also. For if the body perceives it as intellect, that is, as thinking, the body will be intellect, and since it is intellect it will not be the thing seeking but the thing sought. The body, therefore, is not capable of apprehending man.

Nor are the senses, for that matter. For these are only passive and receive impressions like wax,[8] and know not so much as a single thing else, since if we ascribe to them a seeking for something they will of course no longer be irrational, but faculties that are rational and possessed of an investigative nature. But this is not the case, for if receiving impressions of whiteness, blackness, sweetness, bitterness, fragrant odours, and being affected in general is a characteristic of theirs, then seeking actively will not be one of their characteristics.

Next, how is it possible for the bodily mass to be apprehended by these when they do not have the same nature? Thus the sense of sight, for example, is able to perceive form and size and colour, but the mass of the body is neither form nor size nor colour but, if anything, that of which these are attributes. Hence, sight is not able to perceive body, but sees only the attributes of body, such as its form, size, and colour. "Yes," someone will say, "but that which is made up of the joint contributions of these is the body." But

---

8. An Aristotelian doctrine, based on certain passages in Plato, but belied by Plato's notion in the *Timaeus* that the eye, at least, actively emits energy in perceiving objects.

this is a silly thing to say. In the first place, we have shown that
not even the union of all the attributes of a thing is that thing of
which they are attributes. And further, even if this is so, it is again
an impossibility for the body to be apprehended by the sense of
sight. For if the body is neither length merely, nor form by itself,
nor colour separately, but the compound made up of them, it will
be necessary for the sight which perceives the body to combine
these singly on its own account and thus to call the general aggregate of them all "body." But the combining of one thing with
another, and the apprehending of such and such a size in conjunction with such and such a form, belongs to a rational faculty.
But the sense of sight is irrational, therefore it is not its function
to perceive the body. And indeed, not only is it unfitted by nature
to apprehend the general aggregate as body, but it is also in-
capacitated for the apprehension of each of the body's attributes.
Take length, for example. It is by passing over its parts that length
is naturally apprehended, as we start from one part, pass through
another, and end up at another part. This an irrational nature cannot do. And then depth: sight can wander right over the surface,
but does not enter into depth. Thus copper coins that are gilded
over escape its detection. And it was stated in our confutation of
the Cyrenaic position[9] that sight is unfitted for the recognition of
colour as well. Hence, if the sense of sight is not even perceptive
of the properties of body, much less will it be able to perceive
body itself. Nor indeed is this a task for the sense of hearing or
smell or taste or touch, for each of these understands only the
percept directed to itself, and this will not be the bodily mass.
Hearing is perceptive only of sound, but the mass of the body is
not sound. And smell is a criterion only of what is odorous or malodorous. But no one is so foolish as to assign the substance of our
body to the classification of things odorous or malodorous. And to
make a long story short, the same must be said of the other senses
also. Consequently, these do not apprehend body.

And indeed they do not even apprehend themselves. For who
has seen the sense of sight with his sight, or who has heard the

---

9. The section "Concerning the Criterion" of *Against the Logicians*
I has this discussion.

sense of hearing with his hearing? And who ever tasted the sense of taste with his taste, or smelt smell with his smell, or touched touch with his touch? It is inconceivable. Accordingly, we must say that the senses are not even perceptive of themselves, nor even, it follows, of one another. For sight cannot see hearing in the act of hearing, and conversely hearing cannot, from its nature, hear sight seeing, and with the other senses it would be the same sort of undertaking—since, of course, if we say that hearing qua hearing (that is, in the act of hearing) is perceptible by sight, we shall be granting that sight is homogeneous with the former, so as to be no longer sight but hearing; for how can it recognize hearing in the act of hearing unless it itself possesses a nature capable of hearing? And conversely, in order also for hearing to perceive sight seeing, it must itself long since have become sight. Yet a greater absurdity would seem to be impossible. We must say, therefore, that the senses do not perceive either the body or themselves or one another.

"Yes," say the dogmatists, "but the intellect takes cognizance of both the bodily mass and the senses and itself." But this too is an impracticable thing. For when they claim that the intellect is perceptive both of the whole body and of the things in it, we shall inquire whether in making the apprehension it throws itself upon the whole of the bodily mass at once, or upon its parts, and then by combining these apprehends the whole. That they would not maintain that it throws itself upon the whole will be evident from what follows. And if they should say that it combines the parts and from that apprehends the whole, they will be harassed by a greater difficulty. For some of the parts of the bodily mass are irrational, and the irrational ones affect us irrationally. Accordingly, the intellect, as it is affected irrationally by these, will become irrational. But if it is irrational, it will not be intellect. Consequently, the intellect will not apprehend the body.

And indeed, in the same way, it cannot discern the senses either. For just as it cannot apprehend the body because of the fact that it has itself a share in a rational faculty while the body is irrational, so again it will be unable to apprehend the senses, since they are irrational and therefore affect irrationally whatever apprehends them. Furthermore, if it perceives the senses it will in any case be a sense itself. For in order to perceive the senses qua senses (that is, in the act of sense-perception), it will itself become of like kind with them. For if it apprehends sight in the act of seeing, it will, much sooner than that, become sight; and if it perceives hearing in the act of hearing, it will become no different from hearing. And the same argument holds for both smell and taste and touch.—But if the intellect that apprehends the senses is found to have passed over into their nature, there will no longer be anything identified as that which is seeking after the senses. For that which on our assumption was to be seeking has turned out to be identical with the senses being sought for, and consequently requires something to apprehend it. "Yes," they say, "but one and the same thing is both intellect and sense, though not in the same respect, but in one respect intellect, in another, sense. And just as the same drinking-cup is said to be both concave and convex, though not in the same respect, but in one respect concave (the inside part), and in another respect convex (the outside), and just as the same road is conceived of both as an uphill one and a down-hill one—an uphill one for those going up it, a downhill one for those going down it—so also the same faculty is in one respect thought, and in another respect sense. And being the same does not preclude it from the aforementioned apprehension of the senses." But—perfect simpletons that they are—they can respond only with inane replies to the difficulties set forth. For we assert that, even if the existence of these different faculties in connexion with the same substance is conceded, once again the difficulty we raised a moment ago remains. For as to this thing which is said to be in one respect thought and in another respect sense, how, I inquire, can it by its aspect as thought perceive its aspect as sense? Since it is rational and is apprehending an irrational thing, it will be affected irrationally, and being affected irrationally it will be irrational, and if it is this it will not be apprehending but apprehended. This, again, is absurd.

These arguments, then, should be enough to show that man is unable to perceive either the senses by means of the body, or on the other hand the body by means of the senses, since these cannot perceive either themselves or one another. Next we must show that intellect is not a judge of itself either, as the dogmatic philosophers claim it is. For if the mind apprehends itself, either it will be the whole of it that apprehends itself, or it will do this not as a whole but by employing some part of itself for this end. And it will not be able as a whole to apprehend itself; for if it is the whole of it that apprehends itself, the whole of it will be apprehension and apprehending, and since the whole is apprehending there will be nothing left to be apprehended. But it is a most absurd idea that a subject of apprehension should exist without the existence of an object of apprehension. Nor indeed can the mind employ any part of itself for this end. For how can the part itself apprehend itself? If as a whole, there will be nothing to be sought after, and if with some part, how will that part know itself? And so on *ad infinitum.* The result is that apprehension is without beginning, as there is either nothing to be found to make an apprehension in the first place, or nothing there to be apprehended.—Again, if the mind apprehends itself, it will also apprehend simultaneously the place in which it exists; for everything that is apprehended is apprehended in connexion with some place. But if the mind apprehends, simultaneously with itself, also the place in which it exists, this place ought not to be a matter of dispute with the philosophers, some of whom say it is the head, some the breast, and in particular some the brain, some the *pia mater*,[1] some the heart, and others the portal fissure of the liver or some such part of the body. But the dogmatic philosophers do disagree on this point; therefore the mind does not apprehend itself.

So much, then, for the problems raised by the inquiry about the criterion in so far as they relate more generally to every man. But the dogmatists, conceited as they are, do not yield the judgement of the truth to others but claim truth as their own exclusive discovery. All right, let us base our argument on them[2] and show that not even in this way can any criterion of truth possibly be discovered.

Now, each one of those who claim to have discovered the truth either declares this by mere assertion only or else uses a proof.

---

1. A soft membrane enveloping the brain and spinal cord.
2. I.e., on their arguments. (—Tr.)

But he will not say it by mere assertion, for one of those on the opposing side will bring forward an assertion that claims the contrary, and in this way the former will be "no more" credible than the latter, one bare assertion being equal to another. If, on the other hand, he has proof for his declaration of himself as the criterion, it must in any case be a sound one. But in order to ascertain the soundness of the proof he uses in declaring himself the criterion, we must have a criterion, and moreover one that is agreed on beforehand. But we possess no generally accepted criterion, that being what is sought after. It is impossible, therefore, to discover a criterion.

Again, since those who call themselves criteria of the truth derive from different philosophical schools, and for this reason disagree with one another, we need to have at our disposal some criterion which we can use to decide their dispute for the purpose of giving our assent to some and withholding it from others. Now, this criterion is either in disagreement with all the parties disagreeing or it is in agreement with one only. But if in disagreement with all, it will itself also become a party to the disagreement, and as a party to it will not be a criterion but will itself be in need of judgement, like the disagreement as a whole. For it is an impossibility for the same thing to be at once both the examiner and the thing examined. And if it is not in disagreement with all views but is in agreement with one of them, this one with which it agrees, since it is involved in the disagreement, has need of an examiner. And hence the criterion agreeing with that view will require judgement, as it is no different from it; and if it requires judgement it will not be a criterion.

But—what is most important of all—if we say that any one dogmatist is the judge of truth and that he alone is the repository of truth, we shall be saying this either because we fix our gaze on his age, or not on his age but on his hard work, or not on this but on his sagacity and intellect, or not on his sagacity but on the testimony of the multitude. But it is not appropriate in an investigation concerned with the truth to pay attention either to age or industry or any other of the factors mentioned, as we shall show. One should not, therefore, say that any one of the philosophers is

the criterion of truth.[3] Indeed, the consideration of age is excluded
by the fact that most of the dogmatists were more or less equal in
age when they declared themselves criteria of the truth. For they
were all old men—Plato, for example, and Democritus and Epicurus
and Zeno—when they attributed to themselves the discovery of
the truth. Also, it is not unreasonable to suppose that, just as in
ordinary life and common intercourse we observe that young men
are often more intelligent than older men, so also in philosophy
young men may be shrewder than old men. For some, among them
Asclepiades, the physician, say expressly that old men fall far short
of the intelligence and shrewdness of young men, though owing
to the false opinion of the more hasty multitude the opposite is
assumed to be the case. Because of the great experience of the old,
younger men are thought to lag behind them in intelligence,
whereas the opposite is the case. For while the aged have, as I
said, greater experience, they are not more intelligent than the
young. Therefore one must not say that any one dogmatist, by reason of his age, is the criterion. Nor indeed by reason of his industry
either: for all are equally industrious, and there is none whose
behaviour is sluggish once he has entered the contest for truth
and claims to have found it. And when equality in this respect
is ascribed to all, it is an injustice to incline towards one only.

And likewise one could not very well select one philosopher as
superior to another on account of his intelligence. In the first place,
they are all intelligent; they are not classed as dullards and non-
dullards. Further, men who are considered intelligent often are
advocates not of truth but of falsehood. For example, we call those

---

3. This is a typical form of Sceptical argument against such notions
as that of the Sage, or Wise Man, who is the arbiter of all knowledge and
value to the Stoics. We met it in various places in *Outlines of Pyrrhonism*
I (above, pp. 50, 57). Nowadays this seems like a rather obvious "conclusion," but in the Middle Ages, for instance, it was to be by no means obvious, and this little sequence of arguments is one of the most potent attacks upon the notion of one-man authoritarianism to be found in Western
civilization. The authority in question is an authority on intellectual matters, but this attack could be and was to be also extended to political
authority. Neo-Sceptics like Petrarch, Erasmus, and Montaigne were to
knock down the authority of the Philosopher, Aristotle, toward the end of
the Middle Ages, but they were also to invade political thought, with arguments similar to the ones given by Sextus here and in the *Outlines*.

orators powerful and intellectual who nobly come to the aid of the false and raise it to a level of credibility equal to the true; and conversely, those who are not of this class we call dull and unintelligent. Perhaps in philosophy too, then, those inquirers after truth who are the most ingenious seem to be convincing even if they plead the cause of falsehood, because they are naturally gifted, while the untalented are considered unconvincing even if they are allied with the truth. Therefore neither by reason of age nor of industry nor of intelligence is it proper to give the preference to any one person over anybody else and say that this man has discovered the truth and that man has not.

There remains, then, the alternative of listening to the agreement of the majority, for possibly someone will say that he is the best judge of truth whom the majority agree in approving. But this is foolish, and would be a worse criterion than those we have already discredited. For—to pass over all else—those who controvert any given set of facts are equal in number to those in agreement about the same facts. The Epicureans, for example, are equal to the Aristotelians, and the Stoics to the Epicureans, and so on with the others. If, then, a discerner of the truth is the best one when all those who derive from him are of the same opinion as he, how shall we say that this one rather than that one is the best, and the criterion of truth? For example, if we say Epicurus is the best because of the great number of those who agree that it is he who has discovered the truth, why Epicurus rather than Aristotle, seeing that his adherents too are no less numerous? Nevertheless, on the other hand, just as in the affairs of daily life it is not impossible for one intelligent person to be better than many unintelligent ones, so also in philosophy it is not unreasonable to suppose that there is one man who is sensible, and hence reliable, and many who are like geese and for this reason unreliable, even if they are in agreement in their testimony in favour of somebody; for the intelligent man is rare, while the thoughtless are common. Also, even if we do give heed to agreement and to the testimony of the majority, we are brought round again to the opposite of the end in view, for of necessity those disagreeing about a thing outnumber those who agree about it.

What I mean will become clearer when we have set up an

appropriate example. Let us suppose, for the sake of the argument, that the followers of the Stoic school of philosophy are more numerous than the followers of each of the other schools. Let us also suppose that they agree in declaring that Zeno alone, and nobody else, has discovered the truth. The Epicureans will then, of course, contradict them, the Peripatetics will call them liars, and the Academics, and in general all the members of other schools, will oppose them. The result, again, is that those who are agreed in their preference for Zeno, when compared with those who are agreed in declaring that Zeno is not the criterion, are found to be by far the fewer. And for this very reason, even if one ought, when they are numerous, to give credence to those whose declared opinions on a given matter are in agreement, one must say that no one has discovered the truth, because for every man applauded by one group there are many from the other schools who speak up against him. But the most conclusive argument of all is this. Those who are in agreement that a certain person is the discoverer of the truth are led to agree either by different states of mind or not by different ones at all but by one and the same state of mind. But by no means will they be in different states of mind, for otherwise they must at all events disagree; and if they are in one state of mind, they are brought round to a status of equality with whoever states the opposite opinion. For just as the latter is led by only one state of mind to oppose them, so also the state of mind of the former is merely equal to his, because from that point on their numerical superiority is redundant as far as proof is concerned. For that matter, if there were, let us say, only one of them saying this, his word would be equal to that of the whole group.

But now if the discoverer of truth in philosophy is said to owe his success either to his age, or his industry, or his intelligence, or to the fact that he has large numbers to speak for him, while we, on the other hand, have shown that one can for none of these reasons say that he is the criterion of truth, then it is manifest that the criterion in philosophy is undiscoverable.

Also, the philosopher who declares himself to be the criterion is saying nothing more than what appears to himself. Therefore, since each of the other philosophers also says what appears to himself, and what is contrary to the statement of the former, it is plain that, as he is on an equal basis with all the others, we shall not be able to say definitely that any one of them is the criterion. For if this man is trustworthy because it appears to him that he himself is the criterion, the second man too will be trustworthy, since it appears to him also that he himself is the criterion, and so on with the third and all the rest. From this it follows that no one is definitely[4] the criterion of truth.

In addition to this, it is either by mere assertion that a man claims to be the criterion, or it is because he is using a criterion. But if it is by mere assertion, he will be checked by mere assertion, and if he is using a criterion, he will refute himself. For this criterion either disagrees or agrees with him. And if it disagrees it is untrustworthy, since it is in disagreement with him who believes himself to be the criterion, while if it agrees it will have need of a judge. For just as this man who declares himself the criterion was seen to be untrustworthy, so also the criterion which agrees with him, since it is in a way possessed of the same function[5] as he, will require some other criterion. And if this is so, then we must not say that each philosopher is the criterion, for everything that requires judging is of itself untrustworthy.—Again, whoever declares himself the criterion makes this claim either by mere assertion or by virtue of a proof. He cannot, for the reasons already urged, do so by mere assertion. And if he does so by virtue of a proof, it must at any rate be a sound one. But his declaration of the soundness of this proof is made either by assertion or by virtue of proof, and so on *ad infinitum*. And so this is one reason more why we must declare that the criterion of truth is undiscoverable.

Another argument is this. Those who profess to be able to judge the truth are bound to have a criterion of truth. Now, this criterion is either untested or tested. And if it is untested, how can it be trustworthy? No subject of dispute is without judging trust-

---

4. This does not necessarily mean that all of them are speaking falsely; it means only that we have no way of deciding whether one and one only is speaking truly. Sextus is here suspending judgement, not making an adverse judgement on the basis of the previous argument.

5. The man and the criterion are both personal standards for making a decision about truth and falsity.

worthy. But if it is tested, then that which adjudges it is in turn either untested or tested. And if untested, it is untrustworthy; if tested, that which tests it is again either tested or not tested, and so on *ad infinitum.*—Again, since the criterion is a subject of dispute, it requires some proof. But since some proofs are true and some false, the proof employed for confirming the criterion must itself be confirmed by means of some criterion. The result is that we fall into the mode of circular reasoning, since the criterion is awaiting confirmation by the proof while the proof is waiting for confirmation from the criterion, and neither of them is able to show confirmation by the other. Besides, the same thing becomes both trustworthy and untrustworthy. The criterion is trustworthy because it judges the proof, and the proof because it proves the criterion; and the criterion is untrustworthy because it undergoes proof at the hand of the proof, and the proof because it undergoes judgement at the hand of the criterion.

Well, these are the many arguments with which the Sceptics raise objections to the obscurity of the first criterion, the agent "by which." Our argument in regard to their second criterion, I mean the instrument "by means of which," is also easily expounded. For if man discovers the truth, he discovers it by the use either of the senses only, or of the intellect, or of both the senses and the intellect in combination. But he is able to find the truth by using neither the senses only, nor the intellect by itself, nor the senses and the intellect in common, as we shall show. Therefore it is not in man's nature to find the truth. Now, he is not able to apprehend the truth by the senses alone, as we have pointed out in the foregoing and shall now briefly explain. For they are by nature irrational, and as they are incapable of anything more than receiving impressions from the objects presented to the mind, they are altogether unfit for discovering the truth. After all, that which is to perceive the truth in the real objects must not simply have a sensation of whiteness or sweetness but must also be led to have an impression of such an object that "this thing is white" or "this thing is sweet."[6] And the same goes for the other senses. But the

---

6. Many modern philosophers, especially C. I. Lewis, have similarly insisted that our sense-experience "neat," or pure of any thinking, involves no knowledge, but is "irrational," or empty of meaning; only when

perception of such an object is no longer a function of the sense. From its nature, sense can only apprehend colour and flavour and sound, while the judgement "This thing is white," or "This thing is sweet," being neither colour nor flavour, is not within the province of sense. In many cases, too, the senses deceive us and are in disagreement with one another, as we showed when we went over the Ten Modes of Aenesidemus.[7] But that which is in disagreement and confusion is not the criterion; rather, it is in need of a judge itself. Therefore the senses are not able by themselves to judge of the truth.—There is need also of both a power of combination and memory if real objects such as man, plant, and the like are to be perceived. For man is a combination of colour together with size and shape and certain other peculiarities, while sense is unable to combine anything by power of memory because of the fact that the combination is neither colour nor flavour nor sound, and it is these alone that sense can apprehend.

And in fact the intellect will not do, either. For if the intellect can recognize the truth, it ought sooner to recognize itself. And just as a master-builder cannot distinguish the straight and the crooked without apprehending the structure of his criteria, that of his line and his rule, so too the intellect, if it is able to distinguish the true and the false, ought much sooner to apprehend its own nature—for example, the substance out of which it is made, its natural place of abode, and all its other features. But it can hardly become aware of such things, inasmuch as some, like Dicaearchus, say that it is nothing but a certain condition of body, while others say that it exists, though not all of them say it is contained within the

---

sense-experience is shot through and through with judgement or thinking does sense-experience become knowledge. As C. I. Lewis put it in *Mind and the World Order*, Ch. 2, "There is no knowledge merely by direct awareness." He goes on to say that "the given" (or the "simple ideas" or "impressions") of the British Empiricists "is a fiction." Pure, passive experience of a thing does not occur in our conscious life—we are always using terms we have learned, are always thinking with some degree of explicitness. And he summarizes this point against so many philosophers, especially Locke, Berkeley and Hume, as follows: "We do not see patches of color, but trees and houses; we hear, not indescribable sound, but voices and violins." In making the claims Sextus has made, Lewis has suggested a subtler analysis of experience than the British Empiricists gave us, whether or not it is truer than their analyses.

7. See above, pp. 42-72.

same place. Some of these place it outside the body, like Aenesidemus following Heraclitus, others in the whole of the body, as some
do following Democritus, and others in a part of the body, the
opinions of these latter being again much divided. Also, some—
the majority—say that it is different from the senses, while others
say it actually is the senses, and that it peeps out through the
sense-organs as if through openings of a sort—a position originated
by Strato the physicist and Aenesidemus. Therefore the intellect
is not the criterion.—Intellects are also many in number, and since
they are many in number they are in disagreement, and being in
disagreement they have need of something to pass judgement
upon them. Now, this is either intellect again or something other
than intellect. And it will not be intellect, for as it will be a party
to the disagreement and will require judging, it will no longer
be the criterion. On the other hand, if it is something other than
intellect, it proves that intellect is not the criterion. It will be
allowed, too, in this connexion, to use as evidence the conclusions
stated by these men;[8] but then there is no need, for our part, of
repeating them here.—Moreover, since according to most philosophers there exists in us not only an intellectual part, but in addition to this a sensitive part also, which is set before the intellectual
part, this sensitive part, being set before the other, will of necessity
prevent the intellect from perceiving the external objects. For as
a body lying between the eyes and the object of sight prevents
the eyes from perceiving the object of sight, so if the sense of sight,
which is irrational, lies between the intellect and the external object of sight, the sense of sight will prevent the intellect from perceiving the external object of sight; and if the sense of hearing is
between the intellect and the external object of hearing, it will not
allow the intellect to become acquainted with the object of hearing. The same applies to the other senses. The intellect, then, being
shut up inside, and being kept in the dark by the senses, will not
be capable of perceiving any external object. Therefore we cannot
say here either that, taken by itself, it is the criterion.

It remains, then, to say that both of them are the criterion: that
is, the intellect, using sense as its assistant, perceives external

---

8. I.e., the diversity of their conclusions as a whole is an argument
for distrusting the intellect. (—Tr.)

objects. But this, again, is impossible. For the faculty of sense does not deliver the external objects to the intellect, but reports its own peculiar affections. Touch, for example, when warmed by a fire, does not send up to the intellect the external and burning fire but the warmth from it, which is its own peculiar affection. Yet even this statement must be qualified. For if thought receives the affection of sense, it will be sense. For that which is receptive of visual affection is visually affected, and that which is visually affected is the sense of sight. And that which is receptive of acoustic affection is acoustically affected, and what is acoustically affected is the sense of hearing. The same holds good for the other senses.

Therefore the intellect, too, if it takes up the affection of each sense, is affected like sense, and as it is affected like sense, it is sense; and since it is sense, it is irrational, and being irrational it ceases to be thought any longer, and not being thought it will not, as thought, receive the affection of sense. But even if it does receive the affection of the senses, it will not know external objects. For external objects are dissimilar to our affections, and the sense-impression is far different from the thing presented, as the sense-impression derived from fire, for example, is different from fire, for the latter burns, while the former cannot burn. And besides, even if we grant that external objects are similar to our affections, it does not necessarily follow that by receiving our affections the intellect will apprehend external objects. For things similar to others are different things from those to which they are similar. Hence, if the intellect knows things similar to external objects, it knows not the external objects but the things that are similar to them. And just as a man who does not know Socrates does not know, when he sees a likeness of Socrates, whether Socrates is similar to the likeness shown him, in the same way the intellect, as it perceives the affections but does not behold the external objects, will know neither the real qualities of the latter nor whether they are similar to the affections. And if it does not know the things that appear, neither will it understand the non-evident things which (it is claimed) are known by inference from them.[9] But if this is so, neither will it be the criterion of truth.

---

9. This argument would be very damaging to Locke's assertion, for instance in his *Essay Concerning Human Understanding*, Bk. II, Ch. 8,

But some of the dogmatists keep repeating in this connexion the rejoinder mentioned above. They contend that these different parts of the soul, that is, the rational and irrational, are not separated. On the contrary, just as honey, as a whole and throughout, is both liquid and sweet at once, so the soul as a whole and throughout possesses two faculties which are coextensive with each other, of which one is rational and the other irrational. And the rational faculty, they say, is affected by objects of thought, while the irrational is perceptive of objects of sense. For this reason it is also to no purpose to say that the intellect, or the soul in general, is unable to apprehend one of these two kinds of objects. For since it has a different apparatus for each, naturally it is also capable of apprehending both kinds. But they are quite silly. For these faculties, even if they seem ever so much to be united in the same substance and to be coextensive with each other and to permeate the whole of the soul, do none the less differ in kind from each other, and are in fact two distinct things. And this is easily understood from what are rather obvious facts. There are many things, in point of fact, which though observed to be connected with the same matter, do not have the same nature. For instance, weight and colour, both connected with the same body, are distinct from each other. And again, shape and size are attributes of the same substance but have each their separate nature, size being conceived of as one thing, shape as another. In this way, then, even though the aforesaid rational faculty subsists in admixture with the irrational faculty, again it will also be different from it. From this it follows further, for the reasons enumerated above, that the one cannot be affected in like manner as the other and cannot have similar affections, since otherwise both will necessarily become one, the rational irrational if affected irrationally, and the irrational rational is affected rationally.

But even if we suppose that the intellect peeps out through

Sec. 15, that "the ideas of primary qualities of bodies are resemblances of them, and their patterns do really exist in the bodies themselves." After all, how can we compare two distinct things one of which is in our consciousness but the other of which is "non-evident," outside of all our experience? Moreover, Berkeley was to criticize Locke by insisting in the ninth section of his *Principles* that "An idea can be like nothing but another idea." Here again the Sceptics have gone beyond at least the first great British Empiricists.

the passages of sensation—through peep-holes, so to speak—and impinges upon the external objects independently of the senses located in front of it, even so their theory will be found none the less impossible. For an intellect which perceives real objects in this way must perceive the real objects as self-evident. But nothing is self-evident, as we shall establish; therefore it is not possible to find out the truth in the real objects. For the self-evident, as our opponents maintain, is "that which is perceived of itself and requires no other thing to prove it." But nothing is naturally fitted to be perceived of itself; rather, all things are perceived through an affection, and this is something different from the object of presentation causing it. For when I am affected with a sensation of sweetness after the application of honey, I conjecture that the external real object "honey" is sweet, and when I am warmed after the application of fire, I infer from my own condition that the external real object "fire" is hot, and the same argument applies in the case of the other sense-objects. Since, therefore, what is perceptible through another thing is by universal consent non-evident, and since all things are perceived through our affections although different from them, all external objects are non-evident and for this reason for us unknowable. For the knowledge of things non-apparent requires the presence of some self-evident fact, and if this is not present, the apprehension of those things is also absent.

It is likewise impossible to say that, while on the strength of this argument those things are non-evident, yet they are apprehended by us because the inference derived from the affections is dependable. After all, my being affected with a sensation of sweetness at the application of honey to my sense of taste does not necessarily mean that honey is sweet, and if I have a feeling of bitterness at the application of wormwood, it does not mean that wormwood is bitter, as if the feelings belonging to us were of necessity bound to adhere also to the causes which produce them. For as the lash that falls on the flesh pains the flesh without itself being pain, and as food or drink pleases the man who is eating or drinking without actually being pleasure, so also fire can warm without being itself necessarily hot, and honey can sweeten without itself being sweet.[1]

---

1. This argument, that the sensation of pain does not resemble its cause—say, a sharp edge of a sword—was to remain one of the crucial arguments amongst philosophers for proving that sense-experience need

The same argument holds for the other objects of sense also. But since the existence of something self-evident is a prerequisite to our knowing the truth, and it has been shown that all things are non-evident, we must concede that the truth is unknowable.

And how can disagreement on the part of the philosophers regarding the highest matters fail to obstruct the knowledge of the truth? For if some of the physicists, like Democritus, have denied all appearances, and others, like Epicurus and Protagoras, have posited all, and others have denied some and posited others, like the Stoics and Peripatetics, it is in the first place altogether and in any case necessary that either something apparent or something non-evident be employed to decide between them. And this is so whether one assumes as the criterion the intellect, or the sense, or both together. But to use an apparent thing is impossible, for being derived from the disputed matter it will be disputable and on this account not the criterion. And if a non-evident thing is used, things are turned upside down, since that which is supposed to be known is being confirmed by that which is not known —an absurd procedure.

However, in order that the claim of the dogmatists may proceed, let the substantial existence of man, the senses, and the intellect be taken as conceded. But for anything to be known even by means of these, it is necessary to agree about the third criterion, that is, presentation,[2] as neither sense nor thought can perceive things without undergoing alteration in connexion with the presentation. But this criterion too is replete with great difficulties, as we may see by taking the arguments in their proper order right from the beginning. For since some of those who measure things by the rule of presentation turn to the "apprehensive"[3] presentation and

---

not necessarily resemble the causes in the external world of those sensations.

2. That which is "presented" to or occurs in consciousness, like the impression or experience of a red apple.

3. The Stoics are at issue here. See Introduction, pp. 18-21. What follows is another attack upon the Empiricists' notion of "impressions," or "simple ideas," or experience as a set of passively received, "given" sense data, imprinted upon our minds as a seal is upon wax. What Sextus is trying to do here is find out what in the world the metaphor "impression" or "presentation" *means* for human knowledge.

others to the "probable" presentation, we shall select the form common to both, I mean presentation itself, and destroy that. For once this is abolished, the specific kinds of presentation are also abolished. And just as, if no animal exists, man does not exist either, so if presentation does not exist, neither is there any such thing as an "apprehensive" or "probable" presentation. For if presentation is "an impression in the soul," it is either an impression of elevations and hollows, as with Cleanthes, or one that is mere alteration, as it is for Chrysippus. And if it is one of elevations and hollows, the following absurdities, which Chrysippus mentions, will result. If the soul, when affected by a presentation, is impressed like wax, the last impression will always obscure the previous presentation, just as the imprint of a second seal tends to obliterate the first. But if this is so, memory, the "treasury of presentations," is abolished, and every art is abolished, since art is "a system and aggregate of apprehensions"; and it is not possible for a large number of different presentations to subsist in the ruling part of the soul when the impressions in it are conceived of as being different ones at different times. The impression, therefore, in the proper sense of the term, is not a presentation.

Besides, if "things apparent are an aspect of the non-evident things,"[4] and we observe that there are bodies of things apparent which are of much denser parts than breath[5] is, and yet are unable to retain any impression whatever upon them, it is reasonable to

---

4. This is the dictum of Anaxagoras quoted above, p. 68. (—Tr.)
5. The Stoics' key technical term *pneuma* is sometimes translated as "fire," sometimes as "warm, moist breath." It is the basic stuff of the world and of God, and it functions in two ways: its active function is divine; indeed, it works as a creative force in the world; as such a force it *is* God; its passive function is to become matter, partly water and partly earth. But the *pneuma* is one substance permeating all there is, God and matter, and making the universe pantheistic. God is the universe regarded as an active intelligent principle which regulates everything providentially and correspondingly; the universe is inwardly directed by its active soul. God, through the universe, also contains the passive principle, matter. This one term *pneuma* is one of the richest terms in the history of philosophy, deriving aspects of its meaning from the philosophies of Aristotle, Heraclitus, Anaxagoras, and Democritus. This versatile basic stuff of the universe is like breath only with respect to its warmth and moistness, and like fire with respect to its speed and power. But whatever it is, it functions as God and as matter in the Stoic's universe.

suppose that breath also does not preserve even so much as a single impression of any presentation made on it. And water, in fact, is of denser parts than breath, but when a finger has been pressed upon it, it appears never to preserve the imprint made by the pressure. Yet why speak of water, when even very soft wax (which is actually firm by comparison), because of its pliancy, can take an impression in no time at all, and yet does not keep the impression? And so if this body—which is solid in comparison with water—is quite incapable of preserving any impressions made on it, surely it is manifest that breath is not possessed, any more than they are, of a nature suitable for this purpose.

"Yes, but the presentation is not an impression in the strict sense, but a mere alteration of the intellect." This, again, is worse than the first definition. For there are two kinds of alteration, one an alteration of affection and the other a kind of change in the substance. It is an alteration of affection, for instance, if a statue which remains materially the same in substance and shape should by turns at one time be warmed by the sun shining on it and at another time, at night, cooled by the falling dew. It is a kind of change in the substance, on the other hand, if this statue should be melted and become a brazen ball. If, then, presentation is an alteration of the soul, either it is merely an alteration of affection or it represents a change in the substance. And if it is one of affection, since affection is different in the different presentations, the new affection changes the older one, and thus there will be no retention of anything in the intellect, which is absurd. If, on the other hand, it is a kind of change in the substance, then no sooner will the soul receive a presentation of something than it will desist from being a soul and will be destroyed, just as the statue, when melted into a sphere, at that time also desisted from being a statue. Therefore presentation is not an alteration of the soul either. Add to this the fact that the difficulty they have with change is chafing to them. For if a thing changes and is altered, it is either what remains or what does not remain that thus changes and is altered. But neither is it what remains that is altered and changes, for it remains in its previous state of existence; nor is it what does not remain, for this has been destroyed and has been changed, but does not change. For example, if white changes, it changes either while remaining white or while not so remaining. But it neither changes while remaining white, for it remains white, and in so far as it is white it does not change; nor does it change while not remaining white, for it has been destroyed and has been changed, but does not change. Therefore white does not change. Hence, also, if presentation is a kind of change and alteration of the soul, it is non-existent.

Also, even if alteration is granted, the actual existence of presentation will not be forthwith conceded. For it was said to be an impression of the ruling part,[6] but whether this ruling part exists, and if so in what place, is not agreed upon. Some, like Asclepiades, say that there is no such thing at all as a ruling part, while others believe that it exists but do not agree about the place enclosing it. On this account, in so far as this disagreement is unresolved, one must remain in suspension on the ground that it is not conceded that presentation is an impression of the ruling part.

But let even this point be granted, that it is an impression of the ruling part. Still, since this impression is not communicated to the ruling part otherwise than through the sense, as for example sight, hearing, or any other such faculty, I ask whether the alteration that comes over the ruling part is of the same sort as that in the sense, or different.

If it is the same, then since each one of the senses is irrational, the ruling part when altered will also be irrational and no different from sense. But if it is different, it will not receive the object of presentation as it really is; rather, the real object will be one thing, and the presentation that takes shape in the ruling part will be a different thing. This again is absurd. Therefore one cannot say in this way, either, that presentation is an impression and alteration of the ruling part.

In addition to this, the presentation is an effect of the object presented, and the object presented is the cause of the presentation and is capable of making impressions on the faculty of sense; also,

---

6. A Stoic, but also a Platonic and Aristotelian, notion that the soul of man is sovereign over the other aspects of man. Sextus does not at all believe in this doctrine himself; on the contrary, it makes little sense to him or to most of the other Sceptics. See the ten modes of Aenesidemus, pp. 45-72.

the effect is a thing different from that which causes it. Hence, since the mind apprehends the presentations, what it receives will be the effects of the objects of presentation rather than the external objects. And if anyone should argue from the feelings and affections present to the mind that it apprehends the external objects, we shall adduce the difficulties stated in the foregoing.[7] For the external objects either are identical with our presentations, or they will be not identical but similar. But no—for how can the same thing be conceived both as cause and as effect of itself? But if similar, since what is similar to a thing is something other than that to which it is similar, what the intellect knows will be things similar to the objects presented but not the objects of presentation themselves; and this too, incidentally, raises difficulties. For how will the intellect know that the objects presented are similar to the presentations?[8] Even this it will know either without presentation or by means of some presentation. And without presentation it is impossible, for it is in the nature of the intellect to receive nothing except by having presentations. But if by means of a presentation, then this presentation, in order that its own similarity to the presented object causing it may become known, ought at all events to perceive both itself and the presented object it represents. Well, it will probably be able to perceive the presented object it represents, as it is a presentation of it; but how will it perceive itself? For in order for this to happen, it will be necessary for the same thing to become both presentation and object presented. And since the presented object is one thing (the cause) and the presentation another (the effect), the same thing will be other than itself, and be cause and effect at once; but both conclusions are contrary to reason.

Now that these doubts have been raised, let us pass on and consider other difficulties which arise even with agreement that presentation is the sort of thing the dogmatists hold it to be. Certainly, if we must admit that presentation is the criterion, we must say either that every presentation is true, as Protagoras said, or that every one is false, as Xeniades of Corinth asserted, or that

---

7. See above, pp. 154-55.
8. Again, the refutation of Locke's doctrine of Primary Qualities.

some are true and some false, the assertion of the Stoics and
Academics, and also of the Peripatetics. But we can say neither
that every one is true nor that every one is false, nor that some
are true and some false—as we shall establish. We must not, therefore, say that presentation is the criterion. Now, that every presentation is true, no one can assert, because of the contradiction involved, as both Democritus and Plato taught in opposition to
Protagoras. For if every presentation is true, the proposition "Not
every presentation is true," which exists in presentation, will be
true also, and thus the proposition that every presentation is true
will become false.—But even apart from this self-refutation, it is
contrary to what is apparent and to evident fact to say that every
presentation is true, when many are quite false. For we do not at
this present moment react in the same way to the statements "It
is day" and "It is night," or to "Socrates is alive" and "Socrates is
dead," nor do these ever offer equal self-evidence; rather, "It is
now day" and "Socrates is dead" seem to be credible, while "It is
night" and "Socrates is alive" are not in like manner credible but
seem unreal.

The same argument also applies to cases where sequence and
conflict are inherent in certain things. For "It is light" plainly
follows from "It is day," and "You are in motion" from "You are
walking about," while "It is night" is obviously in conflict with
"It is day," and "You are not in motion" with "You are walking
about," and the affirmation of the one is the denial of the other;
and certainly, if a thing follows from a thing, then what is in
conflict is certainly also one thing as against another. But if there
is anything in conflict with anything, not every presentation is
true. For where there is a conflict with anything, it is either a
conflict of the true with the false or of the false with the true.

Also, if it so happens that all presentations are true, nothing
is non-evident to us. For it is when there is something true and
something false, and it is not known which of them is true and
which false, that we have what is non-evident; and when a man
says, "It is non-evident to me whether the stars are even or odd in
number," he is virtually saying that he does not know whether it
is true or whether it is false that the stars are even or odd. Consequently, if all things are true and all presentations are true, nothing

will be non-evident to us. And if nothing is non-evident to us, all things will be self-evident. And if all things are self-evident, there will be no inquiring and doubting about anything, for a man inquires and has doubts about a thing which is non-evident to him, but not about what is clear to him. But it is absurd to deny that there is inquiry and doubt. Therefore not every presentation is true, nor are all things true.

Moreover, if every presentation is true and all things are true, there is no such thing as veracity or freedom from error, no instruction, no learning, no art, no proof, no virtue, nor anything else of this sort. Let us look into this statement. Now, if every presentation is true, nothing is false; and if nothing is false, there will be neither lying nor erring nor lack of skill nor worthlessness. For each of these things borders on falsehood and derives its origin from that quarter. And if there is no liar, there will be no one who speaks the truth either, and if there is no one who errs, neither will there be anyone who is unerring.[9] Similarly, if there is no unskilled person, with this the skilled craftsman is also abolished, and if there is no thoughtless person, the wise man also is abolished. For these things are conceived in conjunction, and just as, if no right exists there exists no left, and if no down exists there exists no up—in this way if one of two opposites does not exist, the other will not exist either. Also, both proof and sign will disappear. For the former is proof that the true exists rather than the false. But if no falsehood exists, there is no need for anything that is supposed to teach us that falsehood does not exist. And sign and token, it was claimed, tend to reveal what is non-evident; but if all things are true and in themselves clear, we have no need of a thing that is supposed to inform us whether something unknown is true or false.

---

9. This is a very important modern notion as far as so-called "analytic" philosophies, like that of Wittgenstein, are concerned. Such a notion involves the assertion that before a term can be descriptively useful, clear, or even meaningful, it must have what Wittgenstein called an "antithesis"; there must be something to which it does *not* apply. If it applies to everything, it cannot be used as a term of distinction or description, is useless, and empty of meaning, at least according to some modern philosophers. Many words used in metaphysics—like the word "matter" as it is used in materialism—are thus meaningless, or unclear, or useless for describing anything.

And yet why expound all this, when neither animal nor universe in general will exist if it is conceded that all presentations are true? For if all things are true, all things will be self-evident to us, and if this is so, it will also be a valid and true proposition that all things are non-evident to us, this being one of the whole number of things. And if it is true that all things are non-evident, we shall not admit that either animal or plant or universe appears to us—which is absurd. For all these reasons, then, we must say that not all presentations are true and credible, and indeed we must for similar reasons add that not all are false. For the statement "All are false" is equal in force to the statement "All are true." Hence it will also be possible to bring all our previous arguments to bear against this position. For if all the presentations are false and nothing is true, a true thing exists; and it was in this way that Xeniades was brought round to conclude the opposite of what he intended. He had said that all presentations are false and that there is nothing true at all in the real world. In fact, generally speaking, it is impossible to declare any particular thing false without also laying down a truth. For example, when we say that A is false, we are predicating the existence of that very thing, the falsity of A, and we are making the affirmative statement "A is false," so that we are virtually declaring something like this: "It is true that A is false." And so no sooner do we declare a thing false than we necessarily declare the existence of truth. In the same way it is possible to show here also that the differences in presentations are more or less palpable—the differences which cause some presentations to attract our assent and others to repel it, and neither all of them together to attract nor all collectively to repel, since of course if there were no difference, but instead all were equally untrustworthy or trustworthy, there would never be either art or lack of art, there would be no praise, no censure, no deceit. For art and approbation and non-deceit are conceived through true presentations, but deceit and blame through false presentations. Therefore one may say neither that all are true and trustworthy nor that all are false and untrustworthy.

It remains, then, to hold that some are trustworthy and some untrustworthy, as the Stoics and the Academics say, the Stoics admitting the "apprehending" presentations, and the Academics those

which seem to be "probable." But even this view, on careful examination, looks to us more like wishful thinking than like the
truth. For an apprehending presentation[1]—to begin with this one
—is one which "bears the stamp and character of having come
from a real object and of representing that object itself, and is such
as would not originate from something not real." Carneades, however, says that although he will concede to the Stoics the other
points of the definition, the clause "such as would not originate
from something not real" is not to be conceded. For presentations
arise from things not really existent as well as from real objects.
And a sign of their indistinguishability is the fact that they are
found equally clear and striking, and a sign of their being equally
striking and clear is the fact that the corresponding actions are
joined to them. For just as in the waking state the thirsty man
feels pleasure as he draws off his drink, and the man who is fleeing
from a wild animal or some other dreadful thing calls and cries
out, so also in dreams joyful relief is had by those who are thirsty
and dream that they are drinking from a spring, and similarly
those who are frightened feel fear:

> Amazed, Achilles started up,
> Clapped his hands together, and spoke a word of lament.[2]

And just as in a sound condition we trust and give assent to very
clear appearances and deal with Dion, for instance, as Dion and
with Theon as Theon, so even in madness some have much the
same experience. Heracles, for instance, when he was mad, took a
presentation of his own children as coming from those of Eurystheus, and followed up this presentation with the corresponding
action. The logically correct thing to do was to destroy his enemy's
children, which he did. If, therefore, presentations are "apprehending" in so far as they lead us on to an assent and to following
them up with the corresponding action, then, since false ones too

---

1. See Introduction, pp. 18-21. Clarity and distinctness were proposed
by Descartes too as criteria for judging presentations, but he meant "intuitively or mathematically evident," something somewhat different from
what Sextus seems to be saying. See Descartes, *Discourse on Method*,
Part II.

2. Homer, *Iliad* XXIII 101 f. (—Tr.)

are obviously like this, we must declare that the non-apprehending presentations are indistinguishable from the apprehending ones. Moreover, the hero's presentation of his own children as being children of Eurystheus was received in the same way as that of his bow and arrows. For in each case the identical presentation existed previously in his mind, and he now received both while in the same condition.[3] Yet that of the bow and arrows was true, while that of the children was false. Therefore, since both affected him equally, we must admit that the one is indistinguishable from the other. And if that of the bow and arrows is called "apprehending" because it was followed up with the corresponding action when he made use of them as bow and arrows, let it be said that that of the children is no different from it, inasmuch as it too was followed up with the corresponding deed, that is, he had to kill the children of his enemy.

Well, certainly this form of indistinguishability of "apprehending" and "non-apprehending" presentations—in respect of the characteristic of vividness and intensity—is proved. But their indistinguishability in respect of stamp and impression is also no less

---

3. This sentence, because of its brachylogy, is difficult. It runs literally: "For one and the same presentation existed previously, and for one in the same condition." With the second clause one must understand "existed now." Werner Heintz's lengthy treatment of it (*Studien zu Sextus Empiricus*, pp. 142–146) seems overly subtle. He takes the words "one and the same presentation" to mean that the presentation of the bow and arrows and that of the children are coalesced into one presentation, then inconsistently spoken of as two in the next sentence. Rejecting this, he changes the text.

The sentence means substantially that, just as his present presentation of his bow and arrows corresponded with his previous presentation of them, so his present presentation of the "children of Eurystheus" corresponded with his previous presentation of them, which of course he must have had in order to "recognize" them now. This is the first point. The second is that both present presentations are experienced by him while he is in the same condition (mad), and hence are on the same footing in respect of the state of the individual experiencing them. Thus they are received in the same way, and should both be equally valid; "yet," he goes on, "one is true and the other is false." For evidence that Sextus actually has in mind the notion that Heracles must have had a previous real presentation of the children of Eurystheus, see *Against the Logicians* II 67, where he says the presentation in this case was derived from real objects, but "distorted" or misapplied. (—Tr.)

proved by the Academics. They summon the Stoics before the bar of the sense-data. For in the case of things alike in shape but different in substance, it is impossible to distinguish the apprehending presentation from the false and non-apprehending. For example, if of two eggs that perfectly resemble each other I give each in turn to the Stoic for examination, the "wise man" will not thereupon be able to say infallibly whether he is being shown one egg, or one and then another. And the same argument also applies in the case of twins. For their "good man" will receive a false presentation, even though the presentation "bears the stamp and character of being derived from a real object and of representing that object itself," if he has a presentation of Castor as being that of Poly-deuces. This fact is also the source of the "Veiled Argument": when a snake has stuck its head out and we wish to examine the object now presented to our view, we shall fall into great embarrassment and shall not be able to say whether it is the same snake as the one that stuck its head out previously or another one, since there are many snakes lying coiled up in the same hole. The apprehending presentation, then, possesses no characteristic feature differentiating it from the false and non-apprehending presentations.

Another point is that, if anything at all conveys apprehension of anything, the sense of sight does. But sight, as we shall show, is not apprehensive of anything. Therefore nothing is apprehensive of anything. For while sight does seem to perceive colours and sizes and forms and movements, it actually perceives none of these things, as will be apparent to us if we take colour as our starting-point. Now, if sight apprehends any colour at all, argue the Academics, it will apprehend that of man. But this it does not apprehend; therefore neither will it apprehend another colour. And that it does not apprehend it, is obvious. For it changes with seasons, ages, circumstances, diseases, health, sleeping, waking,[4] so that while we know the fact that it varies according to these factors, we are ignorant as to what it really is. And thus, if this colour is not capable of being apprehended, neither will any other become known. Moreover, in the case of form we shall find the

---

4. See the ten modes of Aenesidemus, above, pp. 44-72.

same kind of difficulty. For the same object can be perceived as both smooth and rough, as with pictures; as both round and square, as with towers; as both straight and bent, as with an oar when out of the water and in the water; and in the case of motion, as both in motion and at rest, as with persons seated in a ship and those standing on shore.

And besides, if the non-apprehending presentation is accommodated to the apprehending presentation, the apprehending presentation will not be the criterion of truth. For just as that which is accommodated to the crooked will not be the criterion of the straight, just so the apprehending presentation will not be the criterion if it is accommodated to false and non-apprehending presentations. But the apprehending is in fact accommodated to non-apprehending and false things, as we shall establish. Therefore the apprehending presentation is not the criterion of what is true and false. For in the case of the Sorites, when the last apprehending presentation is adjacent to the first non-apprehending one and is more or less difficult to distinguish from it, Chrysippus says that in the case of presentations where the difference is so small, the "wise man" will stop and be silent, but in cases where a greater difference makes its appearance he will assent to one of the two as true.[5] If, therefore, we show that adjacent to the appre-

---

5. The word "sorites" comes from *soros*, "heap," or "pile," in Greek. It refers (in the form "sorites") to a certain kind of syllogistic argument (see above, p. 104, fn. 2), as well as (in the form "Sorites") to a tricky, sophistical argument Carneades used to employ against the Stoics. Carneades was supposed to have had the following conversation with the Stoic Chrysippus:

Carneades: Is three few or many?
Chrysippus: Few.
Carneades: If I add one, is the group few or many?
Chrysippus: I shall hold back my horses, and rest here before I answer.
Carneades: Sleep, snore, if you wish, but if you know the answer to great questions, you should know the answer to this little one; and if you don't know the answer to little, clear ones involving little numbers, how can you presume to say you know the answer to deep, great questions?

The point of the argument is this: If you cannot tell the difference between a few and many (and you cannot if you go up step by step, unit by unit from a few) you should suspend judgement concerning the few and the many (or the small quantity and the heap). But if you have to

hending presentation are many false and non-apprehending things, it is plain that we shall have proved that one must not give assent to the apprehending presentation, lest by this approval we become involved in giving assent by proximity—no matter how great a difference may seem to show up between the presentations—to those as well which are non-apprehending and false. What is meant by this statement will be clear in an example. Let it be taken for granted that "Fifty is few" is an apprehending presentation. This is obviously widely separated from our other presentation, "Ten thousand is few." Therefore, since the non-apprehending presentation[6] "Ten thousand is few" is very far removed from the appre-

---

suspend judgement on such little matters, it is obvious you have to do so on darker, more complicated ones. And so it behoves us all to be Sceptics.

This argument from the sorites, or heap, was supposed to have been one of the most crushing arguments that the Sceptics, especially Carneades, used against the presumably all-knowing Stoics. It is quite similar, though not identical, to the one that Sextus gives in the following sentences. It is convincing only if one confuses such intrinsically or admittedly vague qualitative terms as "heap" with intrinsically or admittedly precise quantitative terms like "fifty." To ask that we establish a quantitatively precise boundary between a heap and a non-heap is like asking—and insisting—that the boundary between Athens and its environs be in millimetres, and in terms no less precise than terms involved in millimetre measurement. We know the difference between a heap of beans and a few scattered beans; we know the boundary between Athens and its environs. Why do we have to know these in terms of such precise numbers? Such words as "heap" function very well in our language without our having to try to make them perform other functions and then damning us and them when we cannot do so definitively. When you push a word like "heap" outside of its usual or legitimate use, you *do* get into trouble, but the trouble is the result of your own wilful causing; the trouble does not lie in the rational power of ordinary language or quantitative language. The difficulties with the heap refute bad or arbitrary uses of language; they do not refute reason or anything else. They are therefore "sophistical" difficulties when used as the Sceptics used them on the Stoics.

6. "Non-apprehending" means "doubtful" here. And the point is that if the difference between an obviously true claim (like "This is not a heap") and a doubtful one (like "This is a heap" when made about the same group you made the first claim about, but after you added one bean to it), if the difference between these two claims is as tiny as this (actually, there is no whole number between two successive numbers), then we must suspend judgement about both the claims, calling both of them "doubtful."

hending one "Fifty is few," the "good man" will not, since the
difference involved is great, suspend his judgement, but will
assent to the apprehending presentation "Fifty is few" and will
not assent to the non-apprehending one "Ten thousand is few."
But if the "wise man" will not assent to "Ten thousand is few,"
inasmuch as it is widely separated from "Fifty is few," it is, doubt-
less, evident that he will assent to "Fifty-one is few," for there is
nothing between this and "Fifty is few." But since "Fifty is few"
was the last apprehending presentation, "Fifty-one is few" is the
first non-apprehending one. The "good man," therefore, will give
his assent to the non-apprehending presentation "Fifty-one is few."
And if he assents to this as being not at all different from "Fifty is
few," he will assent also to the non-apprehending "Ten thousand
is few." For to a non-apprehending presentation every non-apprehending presentation is equal.[7] Now, since the non-apprehending
"Ten thousand is few" is equal to "Fifty-one is few," and this was
not at all different or separated from the apprehending "Fifty is
few," the apprehending "Fifty is few" will be equal to the non-
apprehending presentation "Ten thousand is few." And thus the
apprehending presentation, because of its indistinguishability, is
eliminated along with the false and non-apprehending.

Nor is it, for that matter, possible to assert that not every non-
apprehending is equal to every non-apprehending presentation,
but that one is more non-apprehending, another less so, since, in
the first place, the Stoics will be in conflict both with themselves
and with the nature of things. For just as man does not, in so far
as he is man, differ from man, nor stone from stone, in the same
way neither does non-apprehending presentation, qua non-apprehending, differ from non-apprehending presentation, nor false,
qua false, from false. This was the basis of Zeno's teaching that
"sins are equal." And yet let it be granted that one presentation
is more non-apprehending, another less so. How can this help
them? For it will follow that their "wise man" will not assent to
the more non-apprehending one, but will assent to the less. But

---

7. That is, all non-apprehending presentations are such that they do
not necessarily tell the truth, are either dubious or false, and in this
respect are all equally incapable of telling the truth with certainty. This
is discussed in the next paragraph, and is not entirely clear.

this is absurd, for according to them the "wise man" possesses an unerring criterion, and he is in all respects counted a god because never does he opine, that is, assent to falsehood—an act on which depends consummate unhappiness, and the failure of inferior men too.

Moreover, in order that a sense-presentation, such as one of sight, should occur at all, it is necessary, according to them, for five things to concur—the organ of sense, the object of sense, the place, the means,[8] and the intellect—since if one only is absent (as when the intellect is in an unnatural state), perception will not be kept intact, they say, even though the other factors are present. Hence some say that even the apprehending presentation is a criterion not generally but only when it has no physical obstacle. This, however, is an impossibility. For owing to differences in the sensory passages, to external circumstances, and on several other accounts, objects appear to us neither as the same nor in the same manner, as we have concluded earlier. Consequently, we may say that a thing appears before this particular sense and in this particular circumstance, but as to whether it is in reality such as it appears, or is otherwise than it appears, we cannot know authoritatively; and for this reason there is no presentation without an obstacle.

And then how will they avoid falling into the mode of circular reasoning? For when we inquire what the apprehending presentation is, they define it as "that which bears the stamp and character of having come from a real object and of representing that object itself, and is such as would not originate from something not real." Then again, since everything explained by definition is explained by things known, when we inquire further what, after all, the "real object" is, they invert it and say, "A real object is what causes an apprehending presentation." In other words, in order to understand the apprehending presentation we must first have perceived the real object, and in order to do this we must proceed to the apprehending presentation, and thus neither of them becomes clear because each awaits confirmation from the other.— And just as—some objects of presentation being both apparent and

---

8. Or "medium"—in this case, light. (—Tr.)

real, others apparent but not real—we need some criterion that will prove which are both apparent and real and which apparent and not real, in the same way, since some presentations too are apprehending and some not, we need a criterion that will ordain which are of this kind and which are non-apprehending and false. Now, this criterion will be either an apprehending presentation or a non-apprehending one. And if it is a non-apprehending one, it will follow that the non-apprehending presentation is the criterion even of all things in general, and that its function includes examining the apprehending presentation; and this they will not maintain. If, on the other hand, it is an apprehending one, in the first place this is foolish, for it was on this very one that we were seeking to pass judgement as to when it is apprehending. And secondly, if we employ the apprehending presentation as the criterion for distinguishing between the apprehending and the non-apprehending presentations, the presentation judging them will also have to be tested, by means of an apprehending presentation, as to whether it is really an apprehending one, and this again by means of another, and so on *ad infinitum*.

But perhaps someone will say that the apprehending presentation is the criterion both of the real existence of the object of presentation and of the fact that it is itself apprehending. This is no different from asserting the converse, that the object of presentation too is the test both of itself and of the presentation. For just as, when apparent things are in disagreement, our question is by what we shall judge of what is real and what not real, so also, when presentations do not agree, we consider the question by what we shall judge of the apprehending and the non-apprehending. Hence, as the things are similar, if the presentation, although at variance,[9] can be the criterion of itself, the object of presentation too will be of itself trustworthy, no matter how discordant it is—which is absurd. Or, if the latter, inasmuch as it is discordant, requires something to judge it, then the presentation also will re-

---

9. At variance with other presentations. This paragraph simply recapitulates the contention that the origin and fount of all Sceptical doubt is disaccord between claims to the truth, disagreement, dispute that has no universally cogent or acceptable way of being settled.

quire something to test it and show whether it is really an apprehending one.

And again, if (as they say) every conception had by a "fool" is ignorance, and only the "wise man" speaks the truth and has a sure knowledge of the truth, it follows that since the "wise man" has hitherto proved undiscoverable, the truth is also necessarily undiscoverable, and that for this reason all things are non-apprehensible, since as we are all "fools" we possess no certain apprehension of reality. And this being so, it remains for the charges made by the Stoics against the Sceptics to be made in turn by the Sceptics against the former. For since according to them both Zeno and Cleanthes and Chrysippus and the rest of the school are reckoned among the fools, and every fool is ruled by ignorance, Zeno was at all events ignorant of whether he was contained in the universe or himself contained the universe, and whether he was a man or a woman; and Chrysippus did not know whether he was a human being or some beast more complicated than Typhon.[1] Moreover, Chrysippus either knew this dogma, since it is a Stoic one (I mean the dogma "The fool is ignorant of all things"), or he did not know even this. And if he did know it, the dogma that the fool is ignorant of all things is false, for Chrysippus, although a fool, knew this very thing, that the fool is ignorant of all things. But if he did not even know this much, that he is ignorant of all things, how does he go on dogmatizing about many things, affirming that one universe exists, that it is ordered by providence, that its substance is liable to complete change,[2] and a whole multitude of other things? Of course, any opponent who wishes may bring up the other difficulties which they themselves usually advance against the Sceptics; however, as the character of our critique is now made clear, it is not necessary to draw out our discussion.

Against those who accept the "probable" presentations our

---

1. Plato's *Phaedrus* 230 A contains a remark by Socrates referring to the complexity of this creature, sometimes a hurricane, sometimes a fire-breathing, hundred-headed giant who wanted to rule the gods and men but who was subdued by Zeus. This whole essay on man opened with a reference to this saying by Socrates. See above, pp. 131-132.

2. The Stoics believed that the world would be resolved into fire, *pneuma*, the primary world-substance. See footnote on p. 153.

argument is a brief one. For these criteria are assumed by them as useful for one or the other of two purposes, either for the conduct of life or for the discovery of the truth in things constituting reality. And if they should specify the first alternative, they will be in an absurd position, as none of these presentations can, of itself, be of avail for the conduct of life. On the contrary, each one requires observation also, by which a particular presentation, for a particular reason, is seen to be "probable," and another for another reason "tested and irreversible." But if the discovery of the truth is the purpose intended, they will be wrong; for the probable presentation alone is not the criterion of truth. For the truth to be discovered it is far sooner necessary, rather, that the presentation be a "tested" one and that the tested one, again, be an "irreversible"[3] one, because in the course of going through each thing observed in connexion with the presentation we are sure to be brought back to a suspicion that something that ought to be tested in this connexion has been overlooked—and if a "reversal" occurs in the intellect, knowledge of the truth is destroyed. And in general, perhaps they are overcome by their own arguments. For just as, in their discrediting of the apprehending presentation, they kept saying that it is no criterion of truth because of the fact that adjacent to it there are other presentations indistinguishable from it which are false, in the same way it is not unlikely that in our examination of the probable presentation there are adjacent to the objects tested certain others which are false. The consequence might be, for example, that we seem to be in a sound condition of soul and body, but are not really so, or that the object of presentation appears to be seen from a moderate distance, but is not. However, the sum of the matter is that if neither all presentations are trustworthy nor all untrustworthy, nor some trustworthy and others untrustworthy, the presentation will not be the criterion of truth. From this it follows that no criterion exists, because neither that of the agent nor that of the means nor that "according to which" possesses a sure means of knowing.

But the dogmatists usually inquire, by way of rejoinder, "How

---

3. Irreversible knowledge is supposedly not only tested but consistent with other firmly held beliefs. See above, pp. 23-24.

in the world can even a Sceptic declare that there is no criterion?
For he says this either without judging or else with a criterion.
And if it is without judging, he will be discredited, while if it is
with a criterion, he will be refuting himself, and by saying that
there is no criterion he will be agreeing to the use of a criterion
for the proof of his statement." Again, when we propound the
argument "If a criterion exists, it is either judged or unjudged,"
and conclude from it one or the other of two things, either the
extension to infinity or the absurdity of a thing being said to be its
own criterion, they bring out the opposing argument that it is not
absurd to admit that a thing can be its own criterion. For the
straight is capable of testing both itself and other things, and the
balance is the measure both of the equality of other things and of
its own equality, and light appears to reveal both other things and
itself; hence also the criterion can be the criterion both of other
things and of itself. In reply to the first we must state that it is a
habit of the Sceptics not to plead the cause of things that are
believed, but to be satisfied, in the case of these things, with the
commonly held preconception as being sufficient in itself to establish them. Things which seem unworthy of belief, on the other
hand, we advocate; each of these we elevate to a position of equal
validity with the credence accorded those thought worthy of acceptance. Accordingly, in the present case too we are not abolishing the
criterion when we maintain the arguments against it; we only wish
to show that, since equal materials are given for the opposite view
also, the existence of a criterion is not by any means credible.[4]
Next, even if at the same time we really do seem to be abolishing
the criterion, we may for this purpose make use of whatever presentation comes to hand without thereby using it as a criterion; for

---

4. That is to say, the Sceptic is not denying anything: he is simply
putting arguments of equal weight in opposition to each other and
letting them cancel each other out, leaving us with the suspicion that
"the existence of a criterion is not by any means credible." The Sceptic
is not using an external criterion for judging the truth or falsity of beliefs:
he is only letting the plausibility of opposing arguments indicate that a
criterion is not apparently in operation or existence. He is (1) suspending judgement about the truth or falsity of any given belief, and (2)
stating that he has not yet found any evidence that there is a criterion
for judging non-evident matters of fact or value.

when we use it to state whatever probable arguments for the non-existence of a criterion occur to us, while we do state them, we do this without assent, because the arguments for the opposite view too are equally probable. "But by Zeus," they say, "a thing can also be its own criterion, as it was in the case of the rule and the balance." But this is puerile, for there exists for each of these some transcendent criterion, such as sense and mind, which is also the cause of our constructing them in the first place; but they maintain that there is no criterion above the one which is the subject of the present inquiry. It is untrustworthy, therefore, as it predicates something about itself without having anything to vouch for its truthfulness.[5]

So much, then, for the criterion . . .[6]

---

5. That is, one can *assume* one's judgements are true; but there is nothing that has been offered by the Stoics or the other dogmatists to *prove*, by reference to a transcendent, acceptable criterion, that these judgements are in fact true; and the non-existent Sage, or Wise Man, will not serve as a substitute for this universally acceptable criterion of truth, for reasons that have been given throughout this essay. One of those reasons is, of course, that he has not yet been found, and fools, not wise men, have been asserting that he will be found.

6. With such a sentence as this, the Sceptic rests his case. Find if you can a criterion, a universally acceptable, indubitable criterion that cannot be put in opposition to some other with equal plausibility, given enough ingenuity and time and passion. If you cannot, go back to the business of living amongst the practical "criteria" of everyday life, and do not seek the truth, but seek only happiness in living experience.

PART THREE: *On God*

from OUTLINES OF PYRRHONISM, BOOK THREE

and AGAINST THE PHYSICISTS, BOOK ONE

from Outlines of Pyrrhonism, *BOOK THREE*

CHAPTER III

On God

Now, since the majority have declared that God is the most efficient cause, let us first examine the question of God. We premise the remark that we conform to the ordinary view, in that we affirm undogmatically[1] the existence of gods, reverence gods, and affirm that they are possessed of foreknowledge. But in reply to the rashness of the dogmatists we have this to say.

When we form notions of objects, we ought to conceive of their substances[2]—for example, whether they are corporeal or incorporeal—and also of their forms, for no one would be able to conceive of a horse without first learning the form of a horse. And the object conceived must be conceived of as being somewhere. Now, some of the dogmatists assert that God is corporeal,[3] while others say he is incorporeal,[4] and some say he has human form,[5] while others deny it,[6] and some say he exists in a place, while others say he does not.[7] And of those who assert his existence in a place, some place him within the world and others outside it.[8] How then shall we be able to form a conception of God, when

---

1. "Undogmatically" means here: (1) without claiming something to be the non-relative, *absolute truth* for all men, (2) without *passionately* affirming something to be the truth, and (3) without passionately *denying* opposing beliefs.

2. Sextus is not saying that we can know the "substance" of anything, let alone God; he is simply introducing mutually conflicting dogmatic claims about the substance of God.

3. According to the Stoics, God is a fire-like being, and, by virtue of this similarity to fire, corporeal.

4. According to Aristotle, God is the incorporeal unmoved mover, pure of all matter.

5. The Epicureans thought of the gods as casual onlookers as far as human affairs are concerned.

6. The Stoics thought of God as a non-personal, non-human being.

7. The Epicureans and Stoics believed he had a place; and Aristotle thought of God as inhabiting no place.

8. The Stoics saw God as in the world; the Epicureans thought of him as outside the visible, everyday world.

neither his substance nor his form nor his whereabouts is agreed upon? Let them first reach agreement and harmony with themselves that God is of such and such a nature, and when they have presented us their sketch of that nature, then they can ask us to form a notion of God. But as long as their disagreement is unresolved, we have from them no agreed basis for forming a conception of God.[9]

But, they say, conceive of something imperishable and blessed,[1] and regard this as the Deity. But this is foolish. For just as the man who does not know Dion is also unable to conceive what properties belong to him qua Dion, so also when we are ignorant of the substance of God we shall be unable to learn and conceive of the properties belonging to him. And apart from this consideration, let them tell us what "the blessed" is, whether it is that which operates according to virtue and which takes thought for the things subject to itself, or that which is inactive and neither troubles itself about anything nor causes another any trouble. For by their unresolved disagreement on this head also, they have rendered inconceivable to us "the blessed" and therefore the Deity as well.

But granted that God can be conceived, it is necessary, as far as the dogmatists are concerned, to suspend judgement on the question of his existence or non-existence. For the existence of God is not self-evident. If the impression of him proceeded from himself, the dogmatists would have been in harmony with one another as to who he is, what he is like, and where he stays. But their unresolved disagreement has caused him to seem to us non-evident and in need of demonstration. Now, he who demonstrates the existence of God does so either by means of the self-evident or by means of the non-evident. He certainly cannot do so by means of the self-evident. For since that which is proved is conceived together with that which proves it,[2] and hence is also apprehended

---

9. Notice again the logical form of this whole argument: putting arguments in opposition and letting them counteract or cancel out each other.

1. Both the Stoics and the Epicureans believed this.

2. To *prove* that Socrates is mortal, one must conceive of man or all men as *mortal*, and one must conceive of Socrates as a man; moreover, one must think of the three statements involved in the argument (in-

together with it (as we have also stated), then, if what proves the existence of God were self-evident, God's existence would also be self-evident, it being apprehended together with the self-evident proof of it. But as we have shown, it is not self-evident. Therefore neither can it be proved by the self-evident. But neither can it be proved by the non-evident. For that non-evident fact which is demonstrative of God's existence requires proof. And if it should be said to be proved by means of something self-evident, it will no longer be non-evident but self-evident. Therefore the non-evident fact proving his existence is not proved by means of the self-evident. Nor is it proved by the non-evident. For whoever asserts this will be driven to infinity under our constant demands for proof of the non-evident fact brought out as proof of the one exhibited before it. Therefore the existence of God cannot be demonstrated from anything else. But if it is neither spontaneously self-evident nor proved from anything else, the existence of God will be inapprehensible.

One thing more. He who says that God exists either affirms or denies his forethought for the things in the world,[3] and if he affirms it, he affirms it either for all things or for some things. But if he had forethought for all things, there would be neither any bad thing nor any evil in the world. But they say that all things are full of evil. Therefore, God will not be said to have forethought for all things. But if he has forethought for some things, why for some things and not for others? For either he has both the will and the power to think of all things beforehand, or he has the will but not the power, or the power but not the will, or neither the will nor the power. But if he had both the will and the power, he would have forethought for all things; but *ex hypothesi* he does not forethink all things; therefore he does not have both the will and the power to take thought for all things. And if he has the will but not the power, he is weaker than that which is the cause of his inability to extend his forethought to all things. But it is against our conception of God that he should be weaker than anything. But if

---

cluding the conclusion that Socrates is mortal) together, and with the same clarity. If one fails to do this, one is not proving the conclusion.

3. The Stoics believed that God was providential reason.

he has the power of forethought for all things, but not the will, he will be considered malicious. And if he has neither the will nor the power, he is both malicious and weak. But to say this about God is impiety. Therefore God has no forethought for the things in the world.[4]

But if he takes no thought for anything, and no work or product of his exists, a person will not be able to say where we get the idea that God exists, seeing that he neither appears of himself nor is apprehended by means of any of his products. For these reasons, then, it cannot be apprehended whether God exists. And our conclusion from all this is that those who positively assert the existence of God probably are necessarily guilty of impiety.[5] For if they say that he takes thought of all things, they will be saying that God is responsible for what is evil, while if they say he takes forethought for some things, or even for nothing, they will necessarily be saying that God is either malicious or weak, which is manifest impiety.

---

4. The casual reader will think this claim queer in the light of the opening remarks of this section: previously he had said that the Sceptics affirm that the gods "are possessed of foreknowledge." And here he seems to be contradicting this claim. Of course, there is no contradiction at all here: in the first paragraph of this chapter Sextus was affirming something "undogmatically," and in this paragraph Sextus is juxtaposing one dogmatic claim against another (conflicting) dogmatic claim, just to let them cancel each other out. In the first paragraph, Sextus was affirming something without reasons, undogmatically, as part of the individual Sceptic's customary, habitual religion. The first paragraph was strictly in terms of experience and habits of upbringing, in terms of Recollective Signs. In this paragraph he is stating claims about Indicative Signs.

5. The reason this is supposed by Sextus to be a telling charge against the dogmatists is that Sextus is assuming that the reader, by virtue of his upbringing, etc., wishes to eschew impiety; certainly the Sceptics wished to eschew it because it could produce only trouble, charges and countercharges; piety is part of the Practical Criterion, which in turn is part of the Sceptic's program for attaining and keeping unperturbedness or ataraxy.

from Against the Physicists, *BOOK ONE*

On Gods

THE doctrine of gods seems to be quite the most indispensable one to the dogmatic philosophers. Hence they assert that "Philosophy is the pursuit of wisdom, and wisdom is the knowledge of divine and human things."[6] It follows that if we show that their inquiry concerning gods is subject to question, we shall virtually have proved that neither is wisdom the knowledge of divine and human things nor philosophy the pursuit of wisdom.

Now, some have said[7] that those who were the first leaders of mankind, and who first considered what is profitable for life, invented in their great sagacity both the notion of the gods and the belief in the mythical stories of Hades. For life long ago was brutish and uncivilized—as Orpheus says, there was a time

> when men gained from one another their
> Cannibal livelihood, and the stronger slew the weaker man—

6. This is a Stoic definition of wisdom—*sapientia est rerum humanarum divinarumque scientia*. The highest wisdom for Plato and Aristotle was the knowledge of divine things, forms and essences in their purity and relationships amongst themselves and with divinity; the Stoics included some of Aristotle's "practical wisdom," the knowledge of human things, in their definition of this crucial term. Still, for all, wisdom was not primarily an art of living, but was knowledge of unperceived causal forces. It is the claim to this sort of knowledge that Sextus is considering here, with reference especially to the ultimate cause, God, or the gods.

7. It is of great importance to see that Sextus is not naïve enough to propose the following aetiology as a true one—it, like the others, goes beyond the evident facts. He is proposing the following only as something to be put in the scales with opposing dogmatical views. The Sceptics did *not* deny that there are gods, nor did they propose an arbitrary, inconclusive account of the origin of the notion of godhead; they did *not* say that the notion of God is absolutely empty of reality, and a relative product of the needs, etc., of men. This is all dogmatism, to be put in antithesis with other dogmatisms. The nineteenth-century accounts of psycho-sociological origin of religion (especially Ludwig Feuerbach's *The Essence of Christianity*, and works similar to it) are as arbitrary, as dogmatical, to a Sceptic as the Platonic, Aristotelian, or Stoical accounts reaching opposite conclusions.

and for this reason they wished to put a stop to wrongdoers. First they laid down laws providing for the punishment of those who were openly doing wrong, and after this they invented gods also as overseers of all the sinful and right actions of men, so that none would dare to do wrong even in secret, but would believe that the gods

> Clad in mist go over all the earth,
> Observing examples of violence and good order
>   among men.[8]

And Euhemerus,[9] nicknamed "the Atheist," says:

> When the life of mankind was unordered, some by reason of their strength and intelligence had prevailed over the others to such an extent that all had to live according to their commands. These men, being eager to win greater admiration and dignity, invented for themselves a kind of nimbus of surpassing and divine authority, and hence were acknowledged as gods by the people.

And Prodicus of Ceos says:

> Sun, moon, rivers, springs, and in general all things beneficial to our livelihood were regarded by the ancients as gods because of the advantages derived from them, just as the Nile is so regarded by the Egyptians.

And this, he says, is why bread was worshipped as Demeter, wine as Dionysus, water as Poseidon, fire as Hephaestus, and so on with each thing that is useful. And Democritus says that there are certain images which approach men, and that some of these are beneficent and others maleficent (hence also he used to pray that he might get "propitious images"). These images, he says, are great and enormous, and though hard to destroy, are not indestructible. They foretell the future to men, since they can be observed

---

8. Cf. Hesiod, *Works and Days* 255, and Homer, *Odyssey* XVII 487. (—Tr.)

9. Euhemerus was a Sicilian who lived in Macedonia about 316 B.C. He held that the gods of Greek mythology were amplified and deified actual men and women. "Euhemerism" now means "a method of interpretation which treats myths and religious history in general as partially based upon actual history, upon real incidents."

and since they emit sounds. It was from the impressions they had
received of these very images that the ancients formed the notion
of the existence of God, there being besides these nothing else possessed of the indestructible nature of God. Aristotle said that the
conception of gods arose among men from two sources, from
events concerning the soul and from celestial phenomena. It arose
from events concerning the soul because of the inspired states of
soul occurring in sleep and because of prophecies. During sleep,
he says, when the soul is alone, it recovers its own peculiar nature
and prophesies and foretells the future. It is in this state also
during its separation from bodies at death. Certainly, too, he accepts the poet Homer as having observed this fact; for Homer represents Patroclus when he is being killed as prophesying the slay-
ing of Hector, and Hector as prophesying the death of Achilles.[1]
Now, it was because of these things, he says, that men conceived
of the existence of something divine, resembling in its aloneness
the soul, and of all things the most knowing. But of course it was
because of celestial phenomena also. For having beheld the revolu-
tion of the sun by day and the well-ordered motion of the other
stars by night, they supposed that some god must be the one
responsible for such motion and order.

Such was Aristotle's view. But there are others who say that
the mind, keen and agile in the apprehension of its own nature,
found also in itself a reflection of the universe, and formed the
notion of some surpassing power of mind, analogous to itself but of
divine nature. And there are some who have conjectured that we
have arrived at the conception of gods from the marvellous occurrences in the world. Democritus also appears to be of this opinion.
"For," says he, "when the men of ancient times saw the phenomena
in the heavens, such as thunderings and flashes of lightning,
thunderbolts and collisions of stars, and eclipses of sun and moon,
they were frightened, and imagined that gods must be the cause
of these things." Epicurus, on the other hand, believes than man's
conception of God is drawn from the presentations seen in sleep.
"For," he says, "when great images of human form came to them
in sleep, they supposed that there must exist in reality some such

---

1. Homer, *Iliad* XVI 851ff., and XXII 358 ff. (—Tr.)

gods of human form." And some have recourse to the unalterable and well-ordered motion of the heavenly bodies, and say that it was from this that our notions of the gods first originated. For just as, if a man were seated on Trojan Mount Ida observing the host of the Greeks approaching over the plains with much discipline and order,

> The knights first with their horses and chariots,
> Behind them the foot-soldiers,[2]

such a man would certainly have arrived at the notion that there exists someone who draws up such a battle array and commands the soldiers marshalled under him, such as Nestor or some other hero who knew how to

> Draw up horses and shield-bearing men,[3]

and just as a man familiar with ships is aware, as soon as he sees from a distance a ship being driven by a fair breeze and with all its sails well trimmed, that there is someone who steers its course and brings it into its appointed harbours—in the same way those who first looked up to heaven and beheld the sun running its courses from east to west, and the well-ordered dances, as it were, of the stars, inquired after the creator of this most beautiful arrangement.[4] They calculated that it had not come about by acci-

---

2. Homer, *Iliad* IV 297 f. (—Tr.)
3. Homer, *Iliad* II 554. (—Tr.)
4. This whole argument is sometimes called the "argument from design." Kant sought to undermine all such arguments as those presented in this chapter in his *Critique of Pure Reason*, in the second division (Book II, Ch. III) of his Transcendental Dialectic. The argument from design is what Kant calls a "physico-theological proof," and is "the oldest, the clearest, and the most accordant with the common reason of mankind." Moreover, he says, it is the most useful, helping us as it does to see order, causal sequences, beauty, in the universe (Chapter III, Sec. VI, pp. 519–520). Moreover, while it is heuristically and aesthetically satisfactory, it cannot be contradicted by experience itself, since even catastrophes illustrate a deep causal orderliness in the universe. Still, on pp. 522–524 of the *Critique*, Kant seeks to undermine or tone down the "dogmatic language of the overweening sophist" who proposes this argument as conclusive. Among other things, he points out that the argument from design, order in the universe, does not prove, but rather assumes, that things in the world cannot of themselves without help from God be orderly and harmonious—what if things themselves, the processes of

dent but by the agency of some mightier, imperishable nature, which was God. And some of the later Stoics say that the first men, who were born of Earth, were in intelligence much superior to the present race, as one may see from a comparison of ourselves with older men and with those heroes who, possesed as they were of an extra organ of sense in their keenness of intellect, could apprehend the nature of Divinity and conceive of certain of its powers.

Such, then, are the statements of the dogmatic philosophers on the conception of the gods. But we do not suppose that they require refutation. For the variety of assertions displayed is confirmation of the fact that they are not acquainted with the whole truth, since many ways of conceiving God can exist when that which is true in them is not being perceived.[5] And yet, even if we proceed to the particular suggestions, there will be found no certainty in any of their statements. For example, those who believe it was certain lawgivers and sagacious men who created in other men the notion of gods do not appear to attack the issue at all. The question was, after all, what was the original cause which brought men to a belief in gods? But these men miss the point when they say that certain lawgivers created in men the notion of gods. They do not see that

---

nature themselves, were intrinsically orderly? Notice how similar this argument is to that of Carneades, cited in the Introduction (p. 21). And, Kant goes on, if you question this assumption, you need to prove a cause of the intrinsically orderly stuff of the universe; this in turn leads you to talking vaguely about the "very great," "astounding," etc., nature of a being of whom we have only "relative representations," ideas derived from our own experience, ideas that get very vague when magnified to the size of a God and a universe. This proof then, like any other for Kant, moves "into the realm of mere possibilities" and is based on a hope that we may "upon the wings of ideas . . . draw near to the object— the object that has refused itself to all . . . *empirical* enquiries" (p. 524).

Despite Kant's obvious emphasis on refutation, on proved *denial*, and the Sceptic's emphasis on a suspension of judgement, the upshots of their two treatments of the argument from design are quite similar.

5. This is a dogmatic claim, a slip from Scepticism as Sextus has described Scepticism. Instead of suspending judgement simply, he is inferring from these antitheses the falsity (or at least the partial falsity or truth) of the claims that fall into these antitheses. If doubt is the suspension of judgement, no such inferences are appropriate. That is, true suspension of judgement always leaves it open or possible that a given claim be proved true *or* false, if an acceptable criterion should appear.

the original difficulty still awaits them whenever somebody asks, "But how did the lawgivers arrive at the conception of gods, if gods were not handed down to them by earlier tradition?" Further, all men have a conception of them; not, however, in the same way. On the contrary, the Persians actually deify fire, the Egyptians water, and other peoples some other such thing. It is improbable, too, to suppose that all men were assembled together by the lawgivers and then heard something about gods. The tribes of men were unmixed and at any rate unknown to each other, and as for sea voyages, history teaches us that the *Argo* was the first ship of any that sailed the seas. "Yes," perhaps someone will say, "but before all this the lawgivers and leaders of each tribe invented this idea, and that is why different peoples assumed the existence of different gods." But this is foolish. For the preconception men have about God is, again, one common to all. According to it he is some kind of a blessed living being, imperishable and perfect in happiness and non-receptive of all evil. And it is perfectly absurd that all men should hit upon the same characteristics by chance rather than being moved to apprehend them naturally. It was not, therefore, by conviction or because of any kind of legislation that the men of ancient times accepted the existence of gods.[6]

And there is an equal failure to understand the issue on the part of those who assert that the men who were mankind's first rulers and administrators of public affairs clothed themselves with greater power and honour for the submission of the multitude, and in time, when they had died, were regarded as gods. For suppose they did elevate themselves to the rank of gods. How did they themselves get a conception of gods under which to subsume themselves? This point, certainly, requires proof, but it is passed over. And not only that; what they maintain is improbable. For things made current by leaders—and especially if they are falsehoods—last only as long as the lifetime of the leaders, and are done away with when they are dead. Indeed, one might tell of many who were

---

6. Notice that Sextus is not himself making a claim about the cause of our belief in the existence of gods; he is making a counter-claim and defending it just so that we can suspend judgement on the whole problem. He is not dogmatizing here; he is developing conflicting arguments that have equal force.

made gods during their lifetime but were despised after their death, unless they had assumed some divine appellation, as did Heracles, the son of Zeus and Alcmena. For it is said that his name was originally Alcaeus, but that he usurped the appellation of Heracles, who was regarded as a god by the men of that time. Hence also the tradition about a peculiar statue of Heracles once found at Thebes, that it bore the inscription, "Alcaeus, son of Amphitryon, as a thank-offering to Heracles." And they say that the sons of Tyndareus assumed the glory of the Dioscuri, who, again, were thought to be gods, for the wise men of that time called the two hemispheres—that above the earth and that below —by the name "Dioscuri." This is also why the Poet says of them, hinting darkly at this fact:

> They are now living, now dead, on alternate days
> Each, and are honoured like gods.[7]

And they set felt caps upon them, and stars upon these, to symbolize the construction of the hemispheres. Those, then, who thus usurped the honours due to the gods somehow did better than they intended, but those who merely proclaimed themselves gods were, instead, despised.

Again, those who say that the ancients supposed that all things beneficial to life were gods—such as sun and moon, rivers and lakes, and the like—are not only championing an improbable opinion but also pronouncing the ancients guilty of the utmost stupidity. For it is not likely that they were so foolish as to suppose that things they could see perishing before their very eyes were gods, or to bear witness to the divine power of such things as could be eaten or destroyed by themselves. Some views, perhaps, are reasonable, such as believing in the divinity of the Earth—not that substance which is cut into furrows or dug up, but the pervading power in it, and its fruit-bearing, and truly most divine, nature. As for lakes and rivers and various other things of a nature to be useful to us—to believe that these are gods is a madness second to none. For on this assumption one ought also to believe that men, and especially philosophers, are gods (for they contribute to the advan-

---

7. Homer, *Odyssey* XI 303 f. (—Tr.)

tages of our life), and most of the irrational animals (for they help to perform work for us), and our household effects and everything else of even humbler character. But this is, certainly, extremely ludicrous. Therefore we must say that the view expounded is not sound.

But there is no reliance on the view of Democritus either, as he tries to explain the less doubtful by the more doubtful. For nature gives us many clues of various kinds for the solution of the problem how men acquired the conception of God; but the idea that there are existent in the surrounding air overgrown images of an appearance like that of humans, and in general other fictions of the sort that Democritus likes to invent for himself, is altogether inadmissible.[8]

One may also make the same observations in reply to Epicurus. His belief was that gods were conceived from the presentations of images of human shape received in sleep. Well, why did there arise from these a conception of gods rather than a conception of overgrown men? And in reply to all the views set forth one may say in general that men do not form a conception of God on the basis merely of a manlike living being's size, but in conjunction with the idea of his being blessed and imperishable, and of his displaying the most power in the universe. But how, or from what source, these characteristics were conceived by those who first drew from them their conception of God, is not explained by those who allege as causes the presentations occurring in sleep and the orderliness of the heavenly bodies.

But their reply to this is that while the idea of God's existence arose from the images that appear in sleep or from the observed phenomena of the universe, the notion that God is eternal and imperishable and perfect in happiness came in by analogy as an inference from mankind. For just as by magnifying ordinary man in our imagination we acquired the idea of a Cyclops, who was not like

---

8. Again it must be noticed that Sextus is making these remarks not to express his own beliefs on these unprovable matters, but to put opposing claims into antithesis, and thus secure a suspension of judgement about these matters.

> A man who eats bread, but like a wooded peak
> Of high mountains, when it appears apart from others,[9]

just so, when we had conceived of a man happy and blessed and complete with all the good things, by augmenting these characteristics we conceived of the one who was highest in these very qualities as God. And again, having imagined some long-lived man, the ancients increased his lifetime to infinity, joining to the present both the past and the future; then, having arrived at the conception of eternity, they went on from there to say that God is eternal. Those who argue thus are indeed defending a plausible view, but they are falling slowly into the mode of circular reasoning,[1] which puts them in a most difficult position. For in order to conceive a happy man in the first place, and then God by analogy from him, we must conceive what happiness is, as it is by his participation in it that the happy man is conceived. But according to them happiness is "a certain daemonic and divine nature," and he who has a well-disposed daemon is called "happy."[2] Consequently, in order to determine human happiness we must previously have a notion of "God" and "daemon," and in order to conceive God we must have previously a conception of the happy man. And so each, while it waits for its conception to come from the other, becomes for us inconceivable.

This, then, is our reply to those who inquire how men of an earlier age acquired a conception of God. Let us next look into the question whether gods exist.

Do Gods Exist?

SINCE not everything that is conceived actually partakes in existence—on the contrary, a thing can be conceived and still not

---

9. Homer, *Odyssey* IX 191 f. (—Tr.)

1. See Agrippa's modes, above, p. 73, especially the one on circular reasoning. For the most part Sextus has hitherto been using the ten modes of Aenesidemus.

2. "Happiness" in Greek is expressed by the term *eudaimonia*, which word is made up of two major parts—*eu* signifying "well-disposed" or "good," and *daimonia*, which is based on the Greek word for divinity, *daimon*. And so "happy" in Greek literally means "having a well-disposed divinity."

exist, like a hippocentaur and like Scylla—it will also be necessary, after our inquiry about the conception of the gods, to consider the question of their existence. It will probably be found that the Sceptic, as compared with those whose philosophies differ, is on the safer ground for having followed his ancestral customs and the laws. For he declares that gods do exist, and he performs everything that conduces to their worship and veneration, while at the same time he is by no means hasty in the matter of philosophic inquiry concerning them.³

Of those, then, who have examined the question of the existence of God, we have some who assert his existence, some who assert his non-existence, and some who say that he is "no more" existent than non-existent. That he exists is the contention of most of the dogmatists and is the general preconception of ordinary men. That he does not exist is the contention of those who are nicknamed "atheists," such as Euhemerus,

> A boastful old man who scribbles wicked books,⁴

and Diagoras of Melos, and Prodicus of Ceos, and Theodorus, and multitudinous others. Of these, Euhemerus said that those who were believed to be gods were actually certain men of power who for this reason had been deified by the others, and then were thought to be gods. Prodicus said that whatever benefits life was understood to be God—things such as sun, moon, rivers, lakes, meadows, crops, and everything of that kind. And Diagoras of Melos, a dithyrambic poet, was at first, as they say, pre-eminently god-fearing. He began his poem, at any rate, in this manner: "By the favour of a god and by fortune all things are accomplished." But after he had been wronged by a man who had committed perjury and suffered no punishment for it, he changed his tune and asserted that God does not exist. And Critias, one of the tyrants at Athens,⁵ seems to be from the ranks of the atheists when he says

---

3. Again the Practical Criterion appears, and the Sceptic absolves himself from the charge of being an atheist.

4. This verse quotation is from the *Iambi* of Callimachus, Greek poet of the third century B.C. (—Tr.)

5. Critias was one of the hated "Thirty" who ruled Athens for a time in 404 B.C., at the close of the Peloponnesian War. He was also a

that the lawgivers of ancient times invented God as a kind of over-
seer of the right and wrong actions of men. Their purpose was to
prevent anyone from wronging his neighbour secretly, as he would
incur the risk of vengeance at the hands of the gods. What he said
goes like this:

> There was a time when man's life was lawless
> And brutish and subservient to force;
> When there was no prize, either, for good men,
> Nor yet punishment given to the bad.
> And then, I think, men instituted laws
> As punishers, that Right could be the lord
> Of all alike, and keep Violence enslaved;
> And whoever did any wrong was punished.
> Then, since the laws would hinder them
> From doing deeds of violence openly, while yet
> They did them secretly—then, it seems to me,
> Some shrewd man, wise in judgement, first
> Invented for mortals the fear of gods,
> To serve as terror for the bad, even though
> Their actions, words, or thoughts be secret.
> And then he brought in the Divinity,
> Saying there was a God, thriving in deathless life,
> Hearing and seeing with his mind, thinking much,
> Both mindful of this world and a bearer of divine
> Nature, who could hear all that mortals speak,
> And have the power to see their every act.
> And even if you plan some evil deed in silence,
> This will not escape the gods; for that,
> There's too much wisdom in them. With words
> Like these he introduced this most alluring doctrine,
> Concealing with his lying speech the truth.
> He named, as being where the gods abide,
> That place which would have terrified them most;
> Whence, as he knew, mortals derive their fears,
> And advantage also for their wretched life:
> The vault revolving above, where he perceived
> That lightnings were, and terrible claps
> Of thunder, and the starry frame of heaven,
> An embroidery of Time, the cunning builder,
> And whence a glowing mass, a meteor, makes it way,
> And the melting rain journeys down to earth.

---

kinsman of Plato. The following extensive fragment is from his satyr-play
Sisyphus. (—Tr.)

With suchlike fears did he encircle men,
And in his speech, by playing upon these fears,
He established the Deity well, and in a fitting place,
And by laws extinguished lawlessness.

And after he goes on a little more, he adds this:

And thus, I think, did some man first persuade
Mortals to believe in a race of gods.

Theodorus, "the Atheist," is also in agreement with these men, and according to some, Protagoras of Abdera. The former, in his treatise *On Gods*, demolished with various arguments the theological beliefs of the Greeks, while Protagoras in one passage wrote expressly:"In regard to gods I can say neither whether they exist nor of what sort they are, for many are the things that prevent me." The Athenians condemned him to death for this, but he escaped, and then perished, lost at sea. Timon of Phlius[6] also mentions this story in this passage of the second book of his *Lampoons*:

Prince of all sophists then, and of all thereafter,
Lacking neither clearness of speech, nor insight, nor
    volubility,
Protagoras. They wished to make ashes of his writings,
Because he wrote that he neither knew nor was able
To perceive of what sort or who the gods might be,
Paying all heed to fairness. But this was of no
Avail. Instead, he took to flight, unwilling thus
To sink to Hades, drinking the cold Socratic drink.

And Epicurus, according to some, leaves God undisputed when addressing himself to the public, but not where the real nature of things is the issue. And the Sceptics have said that because of the equal weight of the opposing arguments gods are existent "no more" than they are non-existent. This we shall see when we have briefly run over the arguments advanced on each side of the question.

Now, those who claim that gods exist try to prove their thesis by four modes. These are, first, the agreement of all mankind; second, the ordered arrangement of the universe; third, the absurdity of the consequences of denying divinity; and their fourth and last mode

---

6. See Introduction, pp. 15-17.

is that of the refutation of the opposing arguments. Arguing from the conception common to all men, they claim that practically all men, both Greeks and barbarians, believe in the existence of divinity and for this reason are agreed in offering sacrifices and prayers and in raising temples to gods. And they differ in their methods of doing these things, as though they possessed a common faith regarding the existence of some divinity, but did not all have the same preconception regarding its nature. But at any rate, if this preconception were false, they would not all be in agreement as they are. Therefore gods exist. And besides, false opinions and occasional utterances are not kept up indefinitely, but die off with those for whose sake they were maintained. For example, men pay honour to kings with sacrifices and with all the other religious rites with which they worship gods. But they observe these rites only during the lifetime of the kings themselves, and when they are dead they omit them as being rather unlawful and impious. But the conception of the gods both existed from eternity and continues to eternity, attested as it in all likelihood is by events themselves. Moreover, even if we ought to pass over the conjecture of the vulgar and believe, instead, those men who are wise and of the highest order of genius, we can readily see that poetry produces no great or illustrious work in which God is not the one vested with the authority and power over the events taking place, just as he was by the poet Homer in the war he recorded between the Greeks and the barbarians. And we can also readily perceive that the majority of the physicists are in accord with poetry, for Pythagoras and Empedocles and the Ionians and Socrates and Plato and Aristotle and the Stoics, and perhaps also the philosophers of the Garden[7] (as Epicurus testifies *expressis verbis*), leave God undisputed. Therefore, just as, if our inquiry were concerned with some visible object, it would be reasonable for us to rely on those with the sharpest vision, and if it were concerned with some audible object, to rely on those with the sharpest hearing, just so, when we are examining an object observed by reason, we ought not to rely on any but those of acute intellect and reason, such as were the philosophers.

But to this the opposite party have their standard rejoinder.

---

7. I.e., the Epicureans. (—Tr.)

They argue that all men also have a common conception in regard to what the legends say about Hades, and that they have the poets in agreement with them, and even more so in this regard than in the case of the gods. Nevertheless, they say, we would not assert that the stories told of Hades are factually true. If we did, it would be because we fail to understand in the first place that it is an attribute not only of the fiction about Hades but in general of every legend to contain inconsistencies and to be impossible, as this one was:

> And I saw Tityus, son of glorious Earth
> Lying on the ground, and he covered nine roods.
> A pair of vultures, sitting on either side, tore his liver,
> Deep inside. And his hands could not ward them off,
> For he had dishonoured Leto, renowned consort of Zeus.[8]

For if Tityus was lifeless and had no consciousness, how was he amenable to punishment? And if he had life, how was he dead? And again, when it is said:

> Yes, and I beheld Tantalus suffering great pain
> Standing in a lake that was laving his chin,
> Eager to quench his thirst, but unable to reach his drink.
> For each time the old man bent forward, eager to drink,
> His drink was lost as the water receded, and at his feet
> Black earth would appear, parched by a god.[9]

For if he never tasted any liquid or food, how did he survive, instead of perishing from a lack of the necessaries of life? And if he was immortal, how could he be in such a state? An immortal nature is inconsistent with pains and torments, since everything that feels pain is mortal.

Of course,[10] the myth did thus contain within itself its own refutation, but the notion of gods is not of this kind, nor was there a suggestion of inconsistency in it; on the contrary, it appeared to be in accord with the facts. Nor is it possible, for that matter, to suppose that souls move downwards; for since they are composed of fine particles, and are of a fiery no less than an airy nature, they

---

8. Homer, *Odyssey* XI 576 ff. (—Tr.)
9. Homer, *Odyssey* XI 582 ff. (—Tr.)
10. This is the reply of the Stoics. (—Tr.)

are borne upwards to the higher regions instead.[1] They also continue in their own existence, and are not (as Epicurus said) "dissipated like smoke when released from their bodies." Nor was it the body that controlled them previously, but it was they that were the causes of the body's coherence, as they also were, much earlier, of their own. For when they have left the dwelling of the sun, they inhabit the region below the moon. There, because of the purity of the air, they take more time for remaining, having like the other stars suitable nourishment in the steam exhaled from the earth, and having nothing in those regions which would dissolve them. If, then, souls live on, they are the same as daemons, and if daemons exist, we must also say that gods exist, and that to their existence the preconception regarding what the stories say about Hades is by no means prejudicial.

Such, then, is the argument from the belief in God common to and agreed on by all. But let us also examine the argument from the orderly arrangement of the surrounding universe. Now, the substance of existing things, they say, is of itself motionless and formless, and must be given motion and form by some cause. On this account, just as when we have seen a very beautiful work of bronze we are anxious to learn who the craftsman is, inasmuch as the material by itself is motionless, so also when we behold the matter of the universe in motion and possessing form and orderly arrangement, we might with good reason look into the cause of its motion and of the many kinds of form it possesses. And it is probable that this is nothing other than some power which pervades it, just as our soul pervades us. This power, then, is either self-moved or it is moved by another power. And if it is moved by a different power, it will be impossible for that different power to be moved unless it is moved by still another power, which is absurd. There exists, therefore, some power which is of itself self-moved. This would, then, be divine and eternal. For it will have been in motion either from eternity or from some definite point of time. But it will not have been

---

1. Again, Sextus is not to be read as defending this claim—he is simply putting in opposing, equally plausible claims to counterbalance the ones he is trying to cast doubt upon. He has no doctrine of soul, let alone one so close to the Stoics' notion of a soul made up of *pneuma*, or a fiery substance.

in motion from some definite time, for there will exist no cause why
it should be in motion from some definite time. Therefore the power
which moves matter and brings on ordered forms of generation and
change in it must be eternal, and from this it would follow that it
is God.—Moreover, that which is productive of what is rational and
wise is in any case itself both rational and wise. But the power
spoken of above is at any rate of such a nature as to construct man.
Therefore it must be rational and wise, and this is a characteristic of
divine nature. Gods, therefore, exist.

Also, bodies are divided into those which are unified, those which
are composed of things joined together, and those which are composed of separate things. Now, unified bodies are those dominated
by a single "cohesion,"[2] as are plants and animals. Bodies composed
of things joined together are those composed of elements which are
nearly alike and which tend to make up some one thing which is the
total of them, such as chains and cupboards and ships. Bodies composed of separate things are those composed of things which are dis-
joined and separate and exist by themselves, such as armies and
flocks and choruses. Since, now, the universe too is a body, it is
either a unified body, or one composed of things joined together, or
one composed of separate things. But it is composed neither of
things joined together nor of separate things, as we show from the
"sympathies"[3] connected with it. For it is in accordance with the
waxings and wanings of the moon that many of our land and sea
animals perish and increase, and that ebb-tides and flood-tides occur
in certain parts of the sea. And likewise it is in accordance with
certain risings and settings of the stars that changes of the surrounding atmosphere as well as all kinds of changes in the weather take
place, sometimes for the better, sometimes with pestilential results.
From these facts it is evident that the universe is a unified body.
For where bodies are composed of things joined together, or of
things which are separate, the parts do not "sympathize" with each
other, since, for example, if all the soldiers in an army have been
killed, one who may have survived appears to have no ill effects

---

2. The Stoics believed in a principle or force that held inorganic
bodies together, and they called this force *hexis*, "attraction," or "holding."
3. The explanation of this term immediately follows.

communicated to him. But in the case of unified bodies there exists a certain "sympathy," since when a finger is cut the whole body is affected sympathetically. And so the universe too is a unified body.

But since bodies are divided into those which are held together by mere "cohesion," those held together by "nature," and those held together by "soul" (such as stones and sticks by cohesion, plants by nature, and animals by soul)—then certainly the universe too is controlled by one of these. And it will not be held together by mere cohesion, for the things dominated by cohesion (such as sticks and stones) do not admit of any change or mutation to speak of, but merely undergo a condition produced by their own expansion or compression. The universe, on the other hand, admits of considerable changes, the atmosphere sometimes becoming icy and sometimes hot, and sometimes dry, sometimes damp, and sometimes undergoing alterations in some other way in accordance with the motions of the celestial bodies. The universe, then, is not held together by mere cohesion. But if not held together by this, then certainly by nature. For even the things controlled by soul were, long before that, held together by nature. Necessarily, therefore, it must be held together by the best nature, since it embraces the natures of all things. But that nature which embraces the natures of all things must have enclosed within it those natures which are rational. But that nature which embraces the rational natures is in any case rational also. For it is not possible for the whole to be inferior to the part. But if that nature which governs the universe is the best, it will be intelligent and good and immortal. And if it is such, it is God. Gods therefore exist.

And inasmuch as there exist on land and in the sea, in spite of the density of their parts, a variety of animals which share in the faculties of soul and of the senses, it is all the more probable that there exist some animals with soul and intelligence in the air, which in comparison with land and water possesses a high degree of purity and clearness. And in agreement with this is the saying that the Dioscuri are good daemons, "saviours of well-benched ships," and this one:

> For on the bounteous earth are thrice ten thousand
> Of Zeus's immortal watchers of mortal men.[4]

---

4. Hesiod, *Works and Days* 252 f. (—Tr.)

But if it is probable that animals exist in the air, it is at any rate reasonable to suppose that animal life should exist in the ether also, which, since men derived their faculty of intellect from it, is also the source of man's share in that faculty. And granted that ethereal animals exist, and are thought to be far superior to terrestrial animals because they are imperishable and ungenerated, it will be granted that gods also exist, since they do not differ from these.

And Cleanthes[5] used to argue thus:

If one nature is better than another nature, there must exist some best nature; if one soul is better than another soul, there must exist some best soul; and if, again, one animal is better than another, there must exist some best animal; for such things do not lend themselves to an extension *ad infinitum*. And so even as neither nature nor soul is capable of becoming better and better to infinity, so the animal is not capable of this, either. But one animal is, nevertheless, superior to another. A horse, for example, is stronger than a tortoise, a bull stronger than a horse, and a lion stronger than a bull. And of all, no doubt, of the terrestrial animals man is pre-eminent and superior in disposition both of body and of soul. Therefore there must exist an animal which is the most excellent and the best. And yet man can hardly be the very best of animals. For one thing, he lives in evil all his life, and if not that, for the greater part of it (for if he ever attains goodness, he attains it late, and at the sunset of life). Also, he is a thing which is subject to death, is feeble, and is in need of any number of aids, such as food and coverings and all the other things necessary for the care of the body, which stands over us like some hateful tyrant, demands its daily tribute, and threatens us with disease and death if we should fail to provide for washing it, anointing it, clothing it, and feeding it. Consequently man is not a perfect animal, but incomplete and far removed from perfect. That animal which is perfect and best will be better than man and will be completely supplied with all the virtues and not receptive of any evil. And this animal will not differ from God. Therefore God exists.[6]

---

5. See Introduction, p. 18.

6. This argument was to be used most effectively by St Thomas in his *Summa Theologica* (Part I, Question 2, Article 3), and was called by him the argument "from the gradation to be found in things." St Thomas wrote:

Now the maximum in any genus is the cause of all in that genus, as fire, which is the maximum of heat, is the cause of all hot things. . . . Therefore there must also be something which is to

Well, such is the argument of Cleanthes. But Xenophon, the Socratic, has also propounded an argument for the existence of gods. He attributes the proof to Socrates, whose words in the course of his examination of Aristodemus I quote:

> Tell me, Aristodemus, are there any persons whom you hold in admiration on account of their skill? Why, yes, he said. Who are they then? Well, I admire Homer for his poetry, and Polycletus for his statuary, and Zeuxis because of his painting. You approve these then, do you not, because of the fact that the works they turned out were products of extraordinary craftsmanship? Why, yes, he said. If, therefore, the statue of Polycletus should take on the added excellence of animation, would you not approve of the artist far more? I certainly should. Now, when you see a statue you say it has been wrought by some artist; but when you see a man with an agile soul and a well-arranged body, and when you then see the position of his parts and the use made of them, and that in the first place he was made to stand upright, and was given eyes to see visible things, and hearing to hear audible things—do you not believe that he is the handiwork of some extraordinary mind? And what would be the use of smell, if nostrils had not been added, and likewise what would be the use of flavours, if a tongue to judge them had not been placed in him? And (he says), when you know that you have in your body a small part of the great quantity of earth that exists, and a little of the great quantity of water existing, and the same with fire and air, well then, if mind is the only thing nowhere existent, where in the world do you think you were lucky enough to get hold of yours?[7]

Such, then, is the argument of Xenophon, the inductive force of which is as follows: "Of the great quantity of earth existing in the universe you possess a small part, and of the great quantity of water existing in the universe you possess a small part. Therefore of the great quantity of mind existing in the universe you also possess a small part. The universe is therefore intelligent, and consequently is God." But some seek to obviate the argument by remaking its

---

all beings the cause of their being, goodness, and every other perfection; and this we call God.
The argument in this form occurred in Aristotle's *Metaphysics* (this was Aquinas' source), and was to be used a great deal in Italian Platonic philosophy (especially in the writing of Marsilio Ficino).
7. Cf. Xenophon, *Memorabilia* I 4, 2 ff. (—Tr.)

premisses, thus: "Of the great quantity of earth existing in the universe you possess a small part. And of the great quantity of water existing in the universe you also possess a small part, and of air and fire as well. You also possess, therefore, some small part of the great quantity of gall existing in the universe, as well as phlegm and blood." It will follow that the universe is both gall-producing and productive of blood—an absurd conclusion. But the defenders of the argument claim that the parallel argument is dissimilar to that of Xenophon. For he bases his inquiry on simple and primary bodies such as earth and water and air and fire, but those who employ the parallel argument have made a side-leap to compounds. For gall, blood, and all other fluids in the body are not primary and simple but compounded of primary and elemental bodies.

The same argument can also be propounded in this form: "If there were not something earthy in the universe, there would not be anything earthy in you either, and if there were not something wet in the universe, there would not be anything wet in you either, and so likewise with air and fire. Hence, also, if there were not some mind in the universe, there would not be any mind in you either. But there is some mind in you; therefore there is mind in the universe also, and as a consequence the universe is intelligent. But if it is intelligent, it is God." The argument which takes the following form serves the same function: "Now, if you were to see a well-wrought statue, could you be in doubt as to whether it was the work of a skilled mind? Or would you not be so far removed from any suspicions on this account that you would even go on to admire its excellence of workmanship and its artistic quality? Now, in this case you observe the statue, which is external to you, and ascribe it to an artificer, asserting that there must exist some craftsman who made it. Is it consistent, then, when you consider the mind inside you, which in its so great diversity excels any statue or any painting, to suppose that, if generated, it is the creation of chance? Is it not rather the creation of some craftsman possessed of surpassing power and intelligence? He could reside nowhere else but in the universe, as he governs and generates and increases the things in it. But this craftsman is a god. Therefore gods exist."[8]

---

8. This argument is related to the argument from design (see above, p. 182, fn. 4).

And Zeno of Citium, taking his cue from Xenophon, argues thus:

> That which sends forth a seed of a rational thing is itself also
> rational; but the universe sends forth a seed of a rational thing;
> therefore the universe is rational. And in this conclusion its ex-
> istence is included *a fortiori.*

The plausibility of his line of argument is obvious. For the beginning of motion in all that is "nature" or "soul" seems to come from
the "ruling part" of the soul, and all the powers sent out to the
parts of the whole are sent out from the ruling part as from a well-
spring, so that every power existing in a part exists also in the whole,
because it is distributed from its ruling part. Hence the power that
the part has must have existed much earlier in the whole. For this
reason, if the universe sends forth a seed of a rational animal, it does
not do this by throwing off superfluities, as man does; rather, in so
far as it contains seeds of rational animals, it contains the whole of
them—and this not as we might say of a vine, that it "contains"
grape-stones, that is to say individually, but because generative
principles of rational animals are contained in it. What he is saying,
then, is this: "The universe contains generative principles of rational animals. Therefore the universe is rational."

And again Zeno says:

> The rational is better than the non-rational. But nothing is better
> than the universe. Therefore the universe is rational. And it is
> the same with the intelligent and that which partakes of anima-
> tion. For the intelligent is better than the non-intelligent, and the
> animate better than the non-animate. But nothing is better than
> the universe. Therefore the universe is intelligent and animate.

Virtually the same argument is found in a passage[9] of Plato,
where he writes as follows (I quote):

> Let us, then, state the reason why the creator created this whole
> world of becoming. He was good, and in him who is good there
> cannot be any jealousy about anything. Being himself free of
> jealousy, he wished all things to be as much like himself as pos-
> sible. And one would do best to accept the view of wise men
> that it is this, above all, which is the supreme originating cause
> of becoming and of the universe.

---

9. *Timaeus* 29 D ff. (Jowett's translation, pp. 13–14).

Then he goes on a little farther to add:

> It was this reflection, no doubt, that led him, when he was fash-
> ioning the universe, to put reason in soul, and soul in the body,
> so that the work he produced might be by nature the fairest and
> best. Thus, then, if we are to credit the likely account, we must
> say that this universe is in truth a living being with soul and in-
> telligence that came to be by the providence of God.

He was expounding virtually the same argument as Zeno, for the
latter also declares that the universe is most fair, as it is a work produced according to nature and, according to the likely account, a
living being with a soul, intelligent and rational.

But Alexinus matched Zeno's argument with one of his own in
this form:

> The poetic is better than the non-poetic and the grammatical
> better than the non-grammatical, and so with the other arts: that
> which is considered to be in accordance with their rules is better
> than that which is not. But there is not a single thing better than
> the universe. Therefore the universe is poetic and grammatical.

The Stoics meet this parallel argument with the observation that
Zeno has taken what is absolutely better, that is, the rational over
the non-rational, the intelligent over the non-intelligent, and the
animate over the non-animate, while Alexinus has not. For the po-
etic is not in an absolute sense better than the non-poetic, nor the
grammatical better than the non-grammatical. There is, consequently, a great difference to be observed in their arguments. For—
consider—Archilochus, who is poetical, is not better than Socrates,
who is non-poetical; and Aristarchus, who is grammatical, is not
better than Plato, who is non-grammatical.

Furthermore, the Stoics and those who agree with them also
try to demonstrate the existence of the gods from the motion of the
universe. For that the universe is in motion, everyone will admit, as
there are many things which lead to this conviction. It is moved,
then, either by nature or by deliberate choice or by a vortex[10] and

---

10. The vortex, or *dine*, of Democritus was an aspect of the mechan-
ical necessity that holds in his material universe; the material of the
world is atoms and the void in which the atoms move; now, these atoms
move about in complexes, or vortices, and the lighter parts of these swirl-

of necessity. But it is not reasonable to suppose it is moved by a vortex and of necessity. For the vortex is either disorderly or well ordered. And if it is disorderly, it will not be able to move anything in an orderly manner. But if it moves anything with order and harmony, it will be divine and marvellous. For it would never be moving the whole in an orderly and preserving way if it were not intelligent and divine. And if it were this, it would no longer be a vortex, for a vortex is disorderly and short-lived. Consequently the universe will not be moved, as Democritus said, of necessity and by a vortex. It will not be moved by a non-perceptive nature, either, inasmuch as the intelligent nature is superior to this. And such natures are seen to be contained in the universe. It too, then, must necessarily possess an intelligent nature by which it is moved in an orderly way, and this, naturally, is God.

Again, mechanisms with automatic movement are more marvellous than those without. We are struck with admiration, for example, when we behold the sphere of Archimedes, in which sun and moon and the rest of the stars are in motion. Not that we are astonished at the wooden parts, or at their movement—no, it is the craftsman and the causes of the motion that we admire. Hence, in the degree that the percipients are more marvellous than the things perceived, in that degree the causes of the motion of the former are the more marvellous. For since a horse is more marvellous than a plant, the cause of the horse's motion is also more marvellous than the cause of the plant's. Also, since the elephant is more marvellous than a horse, so also the cause of the elephant's motion, which enables him to carry so large a weight, is more marvellous than that of the horse's motion. Also, more marvellous than all these—to apply the highest analogy—is the moving cause of the sun, and of moon and stars; and above these, as being their cause, is the nature of the universe. For the cause of the part does not extend to the whole, nor is it the cause of the whole. Rather, the cause of the whole is extended down into the parts, for which reason it is also

---

ing complexes are forced outward, while the heavier parts cluster in the middle; the ultimate nature of everything in the universe, mind included, is determined by the density or proximity of these atoms with each other in an atom-complex, or vortex. See Windelband, *A History of Philosophy*, pp. 109–116.

more marvellous than the cause of the part. Consequently, since
the nature of the universe is the cause of the orderly arrangement
of the whole universe, it will be the cause of the parts also. And if
this is so, it is the most excellent. And if it is the most excellent, it
is both rational and intelligent and, what is more, it will be eternal.
But such a nature is the same as God. There exists, therefore, something which is God.

Moreover, in every body which consists of many parts and which
is controlled by "nature,"[1] there exists some part which is the dominant one, just as in the case of ourselves this part is variously claimed
to exist in the heart or in the brain or in some other part of the body,
and in the case of plants—somewhat differently—is said in some to
be in the roots, in others in the foliage, and in others in the heart-
wood. Consequently, since the universe too is multipartite and is
controlled by nature, there will exist in it some part which is the
dominant one and which first begins its motions. And this can be
nothing, they say, but the nature of existing things, which is God.
God therefore exists.

But perhaps some will say: "From this argument it results that
the earth is the most authoritative and most dominant element in
the universe, and that the air is even more authoritative and dominant. For without these it is not possible for the universe to exist.
Consequently we shall say that both the earth and the air are God."
But this is foolish, and like saying that the wall is the most dominant
and authoritative thing in a house, "for without it the house cannot
exist." For just as in this case, while the house cannot indeed exist
without a wall, the wall is certainly not pre-eminent over and better
than the master of the house, so it is in the case of the universe. It
is impossible for the structure of the whole to exist without earth
and air, yet these are not pre-eminent over the nature controlling
the universe, and this is not different from God. Therefore God
exists.

This, then, is the type of argument they have on this head. Let
us consider next the mode concerned with the absurdities consequent upon abolishing the Divinity. If gods do not exist, piety does

---

1. By "nature," or *physis*, is meant "the total structure," which has
many parts but is dominated by its total structural pattern.

not exist, as it exists only in relation to gods.[2] For piety is "the science of service to the gods," and there can be no service to things which do not exist; hence there will also be no science concerning this service. And just as there cannot be a science concerned with service to hippocentaurs, since they are non-existent, so also, if the gods are non-existent, there will be no science concerned with service to them. Consequently, if gods do not exist, piety is non-existent. But piety does exist, so we must say that gods exist. And again, if gods do not exist, holiness is non-existent, since it is "a kind of justice toward gods." But according to the common notions and preconceptions of all men, holiness exists. On this account there must be something holy. And therefore the Divinity exists.—Assuming however, that gods do not exist, wisdom is abolished, since it is "the science of things divine and human." And just as there exists no science of things human and hippocentaurean because of the fact that humans exist but hippocentaurs do not exist, by the same token there will also be no science of things divine and human,[3] because while men exist, gods do not. But it is in any case absurd to say that wisdom does not exist; therefore it is also absurd to claim that the gods are non-existent.

And furthermore, since there has also been brought up the matter of justice in the intercourse of men with one another and with the gods, if gods do not exist, justice will not exist either, which is absurd. Now, Pythagoras and Empedocles and the whole crowd of the Italian philosophers declare that we have a certain community of interest not only with one another and with the gods but also with the irrational animals. For there is one spirit which pervades all the universe like a soul, and which also makes us one with those animals. Hence, if we kill them and eat their flesh we shall be doing wrong and committing a sacrilege, because we are destroying our kin. And it was for this reason that these philosophers recommended abstinence from animal food, and declared those men were impious who

Stain the altar of the Blessed with the warm blood of victims.

---

2. This last clause is corrupt in the MSS., and no satisfactory emendation has been offered. The context would seem to require something like what is here given. (—Tr.)

3. This is the Stoic's definition of wisdom, but was rather widely held at the time of this writing.

And Empedocles says somewhere:

Will you not cease from the evil sound of murder? Do you not see
That you are devouring one another in the carelessness of your
    minds?

And:

A father, lifting his son now changed in form,
Slaughters him with a prayer, the fool! The sacrificers wonder
At his cries for mercy. But he, again deaf to reproaches,
Prepares an evil banquet in his halls after the slaughter.
Likewise, a son takes his father and children their mother,
And, robbing them of life, devour their own flesh and blood.

This, then, was the advice of Pythagoras, but he was mistaken.[4] For
it does not at once follow that, if some spirit exists which pervades
both us and the irrational animals, there must exist some kind of
justice between us and them. Consider this, that there is also a
spirit running through stones and through plants so as to unite us
to them, yet there is no such thing as justice between us and plants
and stones. We certainly commit no injustice when we cut and saw
bodies of this kind. Why then do the Stoics assert that men have a
certain relationship of justice and intercourse with one another and
with the gods? Not on the grounds that there exists a spirit that
runs through all things—since that would be retaining a relationship of justice between us and the irrational animals—but because
we possess a reason which extends both to one another and to gods.
In this the irrational animals have no share and thus will have no
claim to a relationship of justice with us. Consequently, if the conception of justice hinges on any community feeling between men
and between men and gods, then if gods do not exist, justice will
necessarily be non-existent also. But justice is existent. We must
affirm, then, that gods exist.

Further, if gods do not exist, prophecy does not exist either, as
it is "the science of observing and interpreting the signs given by
gods to men," and inspiration and astrology do not exist either, nor

---

4. Remember that here and in the whole context, Sextus is not
necessarily stating his own beliefs; rather, he is pitting one dogmatic
argument against its opposite, and trying to show how, equally plausible,
they cancel each other out.

divination, nor prediction by dreams. But it is absurd to abolish such a multitude of things which are already believed in by all men. Therefore gods exist.

Zeno used to propound this argument also: "One may reasonably honour the gods. But if they are non-existent, one may not reasonably honour them. Therefore gods exist." But to this argument some construct a parallel argument: "One may reasonably honour wise men. But if they are non-existent, one may not reasonably honour them. Therefore wise men exist." This was not pleasing to the Stoics, as their "wise man" has remained undiscovered up to now. But Diogenes, the Babylonian, says in reply to this parallel argument that the second premiss of Zeno's argument really means this: "But those whose nature does not imply existence one may not reasonably honour." For when it is accepted in this meaning, it is plain that gods are of such a nature as to exist.[5] And if this is so, then they actually do exist. For once granted they ever were existent, they are also now existent, just as, if atoms existed, they exist now also, for it is implied in the conception of such bodies that they are imperishable and uncreated. Hence the conclusion deduced by the argument will also be consistent. But it does not follow that wise men actually exist just because they are of such a nature as to exist. Others, however, say that Zeno's first premiss, that "one may reasonably honour the gods," is ambiguous, for while it means in the first place "One may reasonably honour[6] the gods," it also means "One may respect" them. It is the first, they say, which is taken as premiss, and this, in the case of wise men, is false.

These arguments, then, are fairly typical of the arguments brought forward by the Stoics and by representatives of the other schools to prove the existence of gods. It will be our next task to point out that on the other hand those arguments which prove the non-existence of gods are themselves not inferior to these as far as the equal validity of their persuasiveness is concerned. And so, now, if gods exist, they are living beings. And using the same argument with which the Stoics tried to prove that the universe is a living

5. This argument is a first cousin or ancestor to St Anselm of Bec's "ontological argument," according to which the very nature of God implies that it is impossible for him not to exist.
6. I.e., actively, by means of worship. (—Tr.)

being, one might go on to prove that God too is a living being. For a living being is better than what is not a living being. But nothing is better than God. God, therefore, is a living being, since, incidentally, we have in support of this argument also the common conception of mankind, seeing that the ordinary man, the poets, and the majority of the best philosophers testify to the fact that God is a living being—so as to confirm the logic of our conclusion. For if gods exist, they are living beings. But if they are living beings, they have sensation, for every living being is conceived qua living being by its participation in sensation. But if they have sensation, they also taste bitter and sweet. For they do not perceive objects of sense through some other sense without perceiving them through the sense of taste as well. Hence, too, simply to prune away from God this or any other of his senses is an altogether unconvincing procedure. For if man has a greater number of senses than God, man will be superior to him. What we really ought to do, instead of robbing him of the five senses—as Carneades said—is rather to ascribe to him, together with these five which are present in all, a number of additional ones, so that he will be able to apprehend a greater number of objects.[7] We must declare, then, that God possesses a sense of taste, and that by means of this sense he perceives things that can be tasted. But if he perceives by means of a sense of taste, he perceives sweet and bitter. And if he perceives sweet and bitter, he will be well pleased with certain things and displeased at others. And if he is displeased at certain things he will also be receptive of vexation and of change for the worse. But if this is so, he is perishable. Consequently, if gods exist, they are perishable. Therefore gods do not exist.

If, however, God exists, he is a living being. If he is a living being, he also possesses sensation. For it is precisely the fact of possessing sensation that differentiates a living being from what is not a living being. But if he possesses sensation, he hears and sees and smells and touches. And if this is so, there are certain things in the realm of each sense which attract or repel him, for example in the realm of sight, things which are symmetrical rather than otherwise,

---

7. See above, pp. 57-59, where this possibility is used in explaining the ten modes or tropes of Aenesidemus.

and in the realm of hearing, sounds which are harmonious rather than those which are not, and so on with the other senses. But if this is so, there must be certain things which are vexatious to God; and if there are certain things which are vexatious to God, God is subject to change for the worse, hence also to destruction. Therefore God is perishable. But this is in violation of what was the common conception of him. Therefore the Divinity does not exist.

The argument is still more effective if based on a single sense, sight, for instance. For if the Divinity exists, it is a living being. And if it is a living being, it sees, for

He is all eye, all mind, all ear.[8]

And if he sees, he also sees both white and black things. But since white is what makes vision "divided" while black is what makes vision "confused,"[9] God has his vision made divided and confused. And if he is receptive of division and confusion, he is also receptive of destruction.[1] Therefore if the Divinity exists, it is perishable. But it is not perishable; therefore it does not exist.

Again, sensation is a kind of alteration. For it is impossible for a thing which apprehends by means of a sense to escape alteration and remain, instead, in the condition it was in before the apprehension. And so if God has sensation, he also undergoes alteration. But if he undergoes alteration, he is receptive of alteration and change. And if he is receptive of change, he will at all events be receptive of change for the worse. And if this is so, he is also perishable. Therefore it is also absurd to claim that he exists.

An additional argument is this. If a Divinity exists, it is either limited or unlimited. And it cannot be unlimited, as in that case it would be both motionless and inanimate. For if the unlimited moves, it goes from place to place. But if it goes from place to place,

---

8. A verse of Xenophanes. (—Tr.)

9. This passage alludes to the doctrine of the *Timaeus* Sec. 67, according to which white objects divide the stream that flows from the eyes, while black objects compress and confuse this stream.

1. The words translated as "divided" and "confused" would in such a context normally mean "piercing" (or "discerning") and "blurred." The argument, however, is a verbal one, and hinges on the use of the abstract nouns "division" and "confusion," which suggest destructibility. (—Tr.)

it is in place; and if it is in place, it is limited. Therefore, if there is anything unlimited, it is motionless; or, if it moves, it is not unlimited. In the same manner, it is inanimate also. For if it is held together by soul, this involves at all events a movement from the central parts to the ends and from the ends to the central parts. But in the unlimited there is no centre or end. Consequently, the unlimited is not animate either. And hence if the Divinity is unlimited, it neither moves nor is animate. But the Divinity does move, and is thought to participate in animation. The Divinity is not, therefore, unlimited.—Nor, again, is it limited. For since the limited is a part of the unlimited, and the whole is better than the part, it is evident that the unlimited will be better than the Divinity and will have control of the divine nature. But it is absurd to say that anything is better than God and has control of the nature of God. Therefore the Divinity is not limited either. But if it is neither unlimited nor limited, and no third possibility besides these can be conceived, the Divinity will be nothing.

Again, if the Divinity is anything, either it is a body or it is incorporeal. But neither is it incorporeal, since the incorporeal is inanimate and without senses and capable of no activity, nor is it a body, since every body is both subject to change and perishable, while the Divinity is imperishable. Therefore the Divinity does not exist.

If, however, the Divinity exists, it is in any case a living being. If it is a living being, it is at all events all-virtuous and happy (and happiness cannot subsist apart from virtue). But if it is all-virtuous, it also possesses all the virtues. But it cannot possess all the virtues without possessing both self-control and endurance. And it cannot possess these virtues unless there exist certain things which for God are hard to abstain from and hard to endure. For self-control is "a disposition not to overstep the usual bounds of right reason, or a virtue which enables us to rise above those things which seem hard to abstain from." For a man is exercising self-control, they say, not when he abstains from a moribund old woman, but when he has it in his power to enjoy a Laïs or a Phryne or some such woman and then abstains from her. And endurance is "the knowledge of things endurable and not endurable, or a virtue which enables us to rise above those things which seem hard to endure."

For it is the man who holds out under the knife and the cautery who shows endurance, not the man who is drinking honeyed wine. There will, then, exist certain things which for God are hard to endure and hard to abstain from; otherwise he will not possess these virtues, I mean self-control and endurance. And if he does not possess these virtues, since there is no middle ground between virtue and vice, he will possess the vices which are opposed to these virtues, such as moral weakness and incontinence. For just as a person who does not possess health has a disease, so he who does not possess self-control and endurance has the opposite vices, which is an absurd thing to say in the case of God. And if there exist certain things which for God are hard to abstain from and hard to endure, there also exist certain things which can change him for the worse and cause him vexation. But if this is so, God is receptive of vexation and of change for the worse, and hence also of destruction. Consequently, if God exists, he is perishable. But the second is not so; therefore neither is the first.

Further, in addition to the preceding arguments, if the Deity is all-virtuous, he also possesses courage. And if he possesses courage, he possesses "knowledge of things fearful and not fearful and intermediate." And if this is so, there must exist something which to God is fearful. For manifestly, the courageous man is not courageous because he has a knowledge of what sort of things are fearful to his neighbor, but because he knows what is fearful to himself, and this is not exactly the same as what is fearful to his neighbour. Consequently, since God is courageous, there exists something which to him is fearful. If there exists something fearful to God, there exists something which causes God vexation. And if this is so, he is capable of vexation, and thus also of destruction. Hence, if the Divinity exists, it is perishable. But it is not perishable, therefore it does not exist.

Again, if the Divinity is all-virtuous, it possesses also greatness of soul. And if it possess greatness of soul, it possesses "knowledge which causes it to rise above events." If this is so, it must occur that the Divinity sometimes rises above contingencies. And if this is so, there exist certain contingencies which are vexatious to it, and thus it will be perishable. But this is not so, therefore the original proposition is not so, either.

Another argument. Since God possesses all the virtues, he possesses also wisdom. If he possesses wisdom, he possesses also "knowledge of what is good and bad and indifferent." And if he possesses knowledge of these things, he knows what sort of things good things and bad things and indifferent things are. Now, since pain is one of the indifferent things,[2] he knows both pain and what its real nature is. And if this is so, he must have experienced it, for if he had not experienced it, he would not have acquired a notion of it. On the contrary, just as a man without experience of white and black colour owing to congenital blindness cannot possess a notion of colour, so likewise God cannot possess a notion of pain either, without having experienced it. For when we, who have had frequent experience of pain, are unable to gain a clear conception of the specific quality of the pain suffered by gouty persons, or to conjecture how it is from their descriptions, or even to hear consistent accounts of it from the sufferers themselves, because they all explain it differently and some say they feel it is like a twist, others like a fracture, and others like a stabbing—this being so, surely if God has no experience of pain at all, he cannot possess a notion of pain. "Heavens!" they say, "it is not pain he has experienced, but pleasure; and it is from the latter that he has the conception of the former." But this is foolish. In the first place, it is impossible to form a notion of pleasure without having experienced pain. For it is the nature of pleasure to exist proportionately to the removal of everything that gives pain. In the second place, even if this point is conceded, it again follows that God is perishable. For if God is receptive of such relaxation,[3] he will also be receptive of change for the worse, and is thus perishable. But this is not so; consequently the original proposition is not so either.

And if the Divinity is all-virtuous and possesses wisdom, it also possesses good counsel, inasmuch as "Good counsel is wisdom in matters requiring deliberation." And if it possesses good counsel, it deliberates. And if it deliberates, there must be something that is non-evident to it. For if there is nothing non-evident to it, it does

---

2. According to the Stoics. (—Tr.)
3. I.e., of such pleasure. The word *diachysis* means "merriment," "cheerfulness," as well as "diffusion," "relaxation," "dissolution." This argument is at least partly a verbal one. (—Tr.)

not deliberate, and also possesses no good counsel, since deliberation pertains to something non-evident, being "a search for the
right course of action in the present circumstances." But it is
absurd for God not to deliberate or possess good counsel. He does
possess it, therefore, and there is something non-evident to him.
And if there is something non-evident to God, it could hardly be
anything else, primarily, but something like this—namely, whether
there exist in the infinite any things capable of causing his destruction. But if this is non-evident to him, he will at all events be afraid,
on account of his anxiety concerning these things which tend to his
destruction and which cause him to be in a state of alarm and
commotion. And if he gets to be in this kind of a commotion, he
will be receptive also of change for the worse, and hence he will
be perishable. From this it follows that he does not exist at all.

And besides, if nothing is non-evident to God, but he from his
nature is *ipso facto* capable of apprehending all things, he does
not possess art. Rather, just as we would not say of the frog or the
dolphin, animals which swim naturally, that they possess the art
of swimming, in the same way we would not say of God, whose
nature it is to apprehend all things, that he possesses art, since art
appertains to things which are non-evident[4] and not immediately
apprehended. But if God possesses no art, he will not possess the
art of living either, and if this is so, neither will he possess virtue.
But if God does not possess virtue, he is non-existent. And again,
God being rational, if he does not possess virtue, he possesses at
all events its opposite, vice. But he does not possess vice, its opposite. Therefore God possesses art, and there exists something which
is non-evident to God. From this it follows that he is perishable,
as we concluded previously. But he is not perishable, therefore he
does not exist.

Also, if (as we have shown) he does not possess wisdom, he
does not possess temperance either. For "temperance is a state
which preserves the decisions of wisdom in the matter of preferences and aversions." And besides, if there is nothing that will set
in motion God's desires, and nothing that will attract God, how

---

4. See above, p. 100, for the distinction between kinds of evidence;
Sextus is not here referring to the eternally hidden, but only to the
temporarily out-of-sight.

shall we, as long as our conception of temperance corresponds more or less to this definition of it, say that he is temperate? For just as we would not say that a pillar possesses temperance, in the same way we cannot rightfully say that God is temperate. And if these virtues are stripped from him, justice is also, and the remaining virtues as well. But if God possesses no virtue, he is nonexistent. And the antecedent is true; therefore the consequent[5] is true.[6]

Again, if the Divinity exists, either its possesses virtue or it does not. And if it does not, the Divinity is worthless and unhappy, which is absurd. But if it does possess it, there will exist something which is better than God, for just as the virtue of a horse is better than the horse itself and the virtue of a man is better than its possessor, in the same way the virtue of God will also be better than God himself. But if it is better than God, it is plain that, as he is found wanting, he will be in a bad state, and will be perishable. But if there is no intermediate alternative between the opposites, and God is seen to fall under neither of the opposites, we must say that God does not exist.

Further, if he exists, he is either endowed with speech or dumb. But to say that God is dumb is perfectly absurd and is in conflict with the common notions of him. But if he is endowed with speech, he employs utterance and possesses organs of speech, such as lungs and windpipe and tongue and mouth. But this is absurd, and comes close to the story-telling of Epicurus. Therefore we must say that God does not exist. For of course if he employs speech, he converses. And if he converses, he assuredly converses in some language or other. But if this is so, why does he use the Greek tongue

---

5. The "antecedent" (clause) and the "consequent" (clause) are technical terms of Stoic logic, and designate the two clauses of the major premiss of the typical Stoic hypothetical syllogism: "If it is day, it is light." (—Tr.)

6. A slight change of logical form occurs here. Previously Sextus has been using the form *modus tollens* (If A, then B; it is not the case that B; therefore it is not the case that A: if it is raining, then it is cloudy; it is not cloudy; therefore it is not raining). Now he uses *modus ponens*: If A, then B; A; therefore B: if it is raining, then it is cloudy; it is raining; therefore it is cloudy. Both types of argumentation are valid: given the truth of the first "If . . . then . . ." assertion, the conclusion or last remark must be true.

rather than the non-Greek? And if the Greek, why the Ionian
dialect rather than Aeolic or any of the others? He certainly does
not use them all; therefore he uses none. For if he uses Greek, how
will he use the non-Greek, unless somebody has taught him? And
if he uses the non-Greek, how will he converse with us, unless he
has interpreters similar to the men we have who are capable of
interpreting? We must declare, then, that the Divinity does not
employ speech, and is consequently non-existent.

Again, if the Divinity exists, it is either corporeal or incorporeal.
But it will not be incorporeal, for the reasons stated in the foregoing. And if it is corporeal, it is either a compound formed from
the simple elements or it is a simple and elementary body. And if
it is a compound, it is perishable, for everything that is a product
of a combination of things must necessarily be dissolved and perish.[7]
And if it is a simple body, it is either fire or air or water or earth.
However, no matter which of these it is, it is inanimate and irrational, which is absurd. If, therefore, God is neither a compound
nor a simple body, and there is no further alternative, one must
declare that God is nothing.

Such, then, is the character of these arguments. And some have
also been propounded in the form of a sorites[8] by Carneades. These
his pupil Clitomachus has placed on record as being the most excellent and effective. They are like this. If Zeus is a god, Poseidon
is also a god:

For we are three brothers, by Kronos, and Rhea bore us,
Zeus and myself, and Hades the third, ruler of those below.
All was divided three ways, and each got his share of
    honour.[9]

So if Zeus is a god, Poseidon will also be a god, since he is his
brother. And if Poseidon is a god, the Acheloüs also will be a god.
And if the Acheloüs, then the Nile also. If the Nile, then every
river as well. If every river, the streams also will be gods. If the

---

7. This claim, that the composite is necessarily transient, had even
then a long history, but it is by no means self-evidently clear or valid.

8. A sorites is a chain of arguments, the conclusion of one forming
the premiss of the next – in effect, a chain argument which links the first
premiss to the last conclusion, if it is validly done.

9. Homer, *Iliad* XV 187 ff. (—Tr.)

streams, then the torrents also. But the streams are not gods; therefore Zeus is not a god, either. But if gods existed, Zeus too would be a god; therefore there are no gods.

Further, if the sun is a god, day also will be a god. For "day" is nothing other than sun above the earth. And if day is a god, the month will be a god too, for it is a whole compounded of days. And if the month is a god, the year too will be a god, for the year is a whole compounded of months. But this is not so; therefore the original proposition is not so, either. Apart from this, they say, it is absurd to say that day is a god, but that morning and midday and afternoon are not.—If, again, Artemis is a goddess, Enodia too will be a goddess, for the latter is supposed to be a goddess equally with the former. And if Enodia is a goddess, so are Prothyridia and Epimylios and Epiklibanios.[1] But this is not so; therefore the original proposition is not so, either.—If, again, we say that Aphrodite is a goddess, Eros too will be a god, as he is a son of Aphrodite. But if Eros is a god, Eleos too will be a god, for both are affections of the soul, and Eleos is an object of worship just as Eros is. The Athenians, for example, have several altars to Eleos.[2] And if Eleos is a god, Phobos is too:

> I am the unsightliest god to look at,
>   for my name is Fear,
> And of all the gods I share least in beauty.[3]

And if Phobos is a god, then the rest of the affections of the soul are too. But these are not gods; therefore Aphrodite is not a goddess either. But if gods existed, Aphrodite too would be a goddess; therefore there are no gods.—Again, if Demeter is a goddess, Ge too is a goddess; for Demeter, they say, is nothing else than "Ge-meter."[4] If Ge is a goddess, the mountains too and the peaks and every stone will be a god. But this is not so; therefore the original proposition is not so either.—Carneades also propounds other such

---

1. Enodia, Prothyridia, Epimylios, and Epiklibanios are epithets of Artemis meaning "of the wayside," "of the vestibule," "of the mill," and "of the oven." (—Tr.)

2. *Eros* (Amor), "Love"; *Eleos*, "Pity." *Phobos* (next sentence) is "Fear." (—Tr.)

3. This is a fragment from a comedy, author unknown. (—Tr.)

4. *Ge* is "Earth," *meter* is "mother." (—Tr.)

sorites-arguments for the non-existence of gods, but the general character of these is sufficiently revealed in those set forth above.

Well now, such are the arguments attempted on both sides, for the existence of gods and for the non-existence of gods. Their logical consequence is the Sceptics' suspension of judgement, especially since in addition to them there is also the diversity of views on the part of ordinary people about gods. For different people have differing and discordant notions about them, with the result that it is possible neither to believe all of them, as they are conflicting, nor to believe some of them, on account of their being of equal force. Further confirmation of this is furnished by the myth-making of the theologians and poets, which is full of all kinds of impiety. Hence Xenophanes too, in his criticism of Homer and Hesiod, says:

> Homer and Hesiod have ascribed to the gods everything
> That is, with men, disgraceful and blameworthy:
> Stealing, adultery, and deceiving one another.

Bibliography

A. *Ancient Sources*

A COMPLETE English translation (with accompanying Greek text) of the surviving works of Sextus Empiricus is

[1] *Sextus Empiricus.* 4 vols. Translated by R. G. Bury. London, 1933–44, Loeb Classical Library.

The best Greek text of Sextus is the Teubner edition:

[2] Mutschmann, H., and Mau, J., eds. *Sexti Empirici Opera.* 3 vols. Leipzig, 1954, 1962. Vol. 4 of this edition is an invaluable Greek word index by K. Janáček.

Much of our evidence concerning Pyrrho and Timon comes from their *Lives* in

[3] Diogenes Laertius. *Lives of Eminent Philosophers*, vol. 2. Translated by R. D. Hicks. London, 1925.

The ancient evidence concerning Pyrrho is collected in

[4] Caizzi, F. D. *Pirrone Testimonianze.* Naples, 1981.

A major source for academic scepticism is Cicero's *Academica*, available in

[5] Cicero. *De Natura Deorum and Academica.* Translated by H. Rackham. London, 1933, Loeb Classical Library.

[6] Reid, J. S., ed. *M. Tulli Ciceronis Academica.* London, 1885. Reprint, Hildesheim, 1966. This important edition of the Latin text has an introduction and copious notes.

Three essays by Galen that discuss empiricism and methodism, two traditions of ancient medicine closely related to scepticism, and their relation to Dogmatism are translated in

[7] Galen. *Three Treatises on the Nature of Science.* Translated by M. Frede and M. Walzer. Indianapolis, 1985. This work includes a useful introduction by Frede.

The ancient evidence on the sceptical modes is newly translated and extensively discussed in

[8] Annas, J. and Barnes, J. *The Modes of Scepticism.* Cambridge, 1985.

St. Augustine attacks academic scepticism in

[9] St. Augustine. *Contra Academicos.* Translated by J. J. O'Meara. London, 1951, Ancient Christian Writers No. 12.

217

B. *Secondary Literature on Ancient Scepticism*
The beginning student may wish to start with the articles, "Hellenistic Thought" and "Skepticism," and on the various sceptical philosophers in
[10] Edwards, P., ed. *The Encyclopedia of Philosophy*. 8 vols. New York, 1967. The article on Sextus Empiricus was written by Philip Hallie.

The best introductory survey of philosophy in the Hellenistic period, including scepticism, is
[11] Long, A. A. *Hellenistic Philosophy*. London, 1974.
For a recent, briefer survey, see
[12] Sedley, D. "The Protagonists." In [20], pp. 1–19.

The best and most influential general treatment of ancient scepticism is still
[13] Brochard, V. *Les Sceptiques grecs*. Paris, 1923, 2d edition.
General studies in English include
[14] Stough, C. L. *Greek Scepticism*. Berkeley and Los Angeles, 1969.
[15] Bevan, E. *Stoics and Sceptics*. New York, 1959.
[16] Zeller, E. *Stoics, Sceptics, and Epicureans*. Translated by S. F. Alleyne. London, 1870. This is part of Zeller's magisterial history of Greek philosophy, now somewhat out of date.

The most important general studies in foreign languages are
[17] dal Pra, M. *Lo scetticismo greco*. Rome-Bari, 1975, 2d edition.
[18] Robin, L. *Pyrrhon et le scepticisme grec*. Paris, 1944.
[19] Goedeckemeyer, A. *Die Geschichte des griechischen Skeptizismus*. Leipzig, 1905.

The following collections include papers on ancient scepticism.
[20] Schofield, M., Burnyeat, M., and Barnes, J., eds. *Doubt and Dogmatism*. Oxford, 1980.
[21] Barnes, J., Brunschwig, J., Burnyeat, M., and Schofield, M., eds. *Science and Speculation*. Cambridge and Paris, 1982.
[22] Burnyeat, M., ed. *The Skeptical Tradition*. Berkeley and Los Angeles, 1983. Almost half the papers in this important volume are devoted to ancient scepticism.

[23] Giannantoni, G., ed. *Lo Scetticismo antico*. Naples, 1982.
A comprehensive bibliography of scholarship on ancient scepticism is contained in [23]. For shorter bibliographies, see [8] and [20].

For Pyrrho and Timon, see
[24] Flintoff, E. "Pyrrho and India." In *Phronesis* 25, 1980, pp. 88–108.
[25] Long, A. A. "Timon of Phlius: Pyrrhonist and Satirist." In *Proceedings of the Cambridge Philological Society*, n.s. 24, 1978, pp. 68–91.

On academic scepticism, see
[26] Striker, G. "Über den Unterschied zwischen den Pyrrhoneern und den Akademikern." In *Phronesis* 26, 1981, pp. 153–69.
[27] Glucker, J. *Antiochus and the Late Academy*. Göttingen, 1978. Hypomnemata 56.
[28] Sedley, D. "The End of the Academy." In *Phronesis* 26 1, 1981, pp. 67–75.
[29] Couissin, P. "The Stoicism of the New Academy." In [22], pp. 31–64.

On Sextus Empiricus, see
[30] Chisholm, R. "Sextus Empiricus and Modern Empiricism." In *Philosophy of Science* 8, 1941, pp. 371–84.
[31] House, D. K. "The Life of Sextus Empiricus." In *Classical Quarterly* 30, 1980, pp. 227–38.
[32] Long, A. A. "Sextus Empiricus on the Criterion of Truth." In *Bulletin of the Institute of Classical Studies* 25, 1978, pp. 35–49.
[33] Janáček, K. *Sextus Empiricus' Empirical Methods*. Prague, 1972.

On the Sceptics' methods of argument, see
[34] Striker, G. "Sceptical Strategies." In [20], pp. 54–83.
[35] ———. "The Ten Tropes of Aenesidemus." In [22], pp. 95–116. See also Annas and Barnes [8]; this book provides both a historical interpretation and a philosophical evaluation of the tropes. Written for the beginning student, it also contains much material of interest to the scholar.

Some of the best recent work on ancient scepticism has revolved around the question whether or in what sense the ancient sceptic held beliefs. See

[36] Frede, M. "Des Skeptikers Meinungen." In *Neue Hefte für Philosophie* 15/16, 1979, pp. 102–29.

[37] Burnyeat, M. "Can the Skeptic Live His Skepticism?" In [20], pp. 20–53; and [22], pp. 117–48

[38] Barnes, J. "The Beliefs of a Pyrrhonist." In *Proceedings of the Cambridge Philological Society* 29, 1982, pp. 1–29; also in *Elenchos* 4, 1983, pp. 5–43.

[39] Burnyeat, M. "The Sceptic in His Place and Time." In *Philosophy and History*. Cambridge, 1984, pp. 225–54.

[40] Frede, M. "The Sceptic's Two Kinds of Assent and the Question of the Possibility of Knowledge." In *Philosophy and History*. Cambridge, 1984, pp. 225–78.

Myles Burnyeat has written many other articles on ancient scepticism, including

[41] Burnyeat, M. "Protagoras and Self-Refutation in Later Greek Philosophy." In *The Philosophical Review* 85, 1976, pp. 44–69.

[42] ———. "Idealism and Greek Philosophy: What Descartes Saw and Berkeley Missed." *The Philosophical Review* 91, 1982, pp. 3–40.

C. *Modern Scepticism*

Richard Popkin's survey of early modern scepticism is a classic of intellectual history:

[43] Popkin, R. *The History of Scepticism from Erasmus to Spinoza*. Berkeley and Los Angeles, 1979, 3d edition. See also his collection of essays:

[44] ———. *The High Road to Pyrrhonism*. San Diego, 1980.

Among many works relevant to scepticism in this period, the three most important are

[45] de Montaigne, M. *The Complete Essays of Montaigne*. Translated by Donald Frame. Stanford, 1958. The long essay, "Apology for Raymond Sebond," draws heavily on Sexus.

[46] Descartes, R. *Meditations on First Philosophy*. Indianapolis, 1979.

[47] Hume, D. *A Treatise of Human Nature*. Edited by L. A. Selby-Bigge. Oxford, 1888. Of particular interest are Book 1, Part 2, "Of knowledge and probability," and Part 4, "Of the sceptical and other systems of philosophy."

For more on early modern scepticism, see the articles in [22]. The notes to these articles can serve as a guide to further reading, as can the—voluminous—notes and bibliography to [43]. One important book too recent to be cited in these sources is

[48] Fogelin, R. *Hume's Scepticism in the Treatise of Human Nature*. London and Boston, 1985.

D. *Scepticism in Contemporary Philosophy*

Although scepticism has been a central concern of contemporary philosophy, contemporary discussions of scepticism have been focussed on the problem of scepticism concerning the external world, a problem that the ancients did not confront as such (although some of their arguments are relevant to it). Some classic works of twentieth-century philosophy that discuss scepticism are

[49] Santayana, G. *Scepticism and Animal Faith*. New York, 1923.
[50] Ayer, A. J. *The Problem of Knowledge*. Hammondsworth, Middlesex, England, 1956.
[51] Austin, J. K. *Sense and Sensibilia*. Edited by G. J. Warnock. Oxford, 1962.
[52] Moore, G. E. "Proof of an External World." In *Philosophical Papers*. London, 1959, pp. 114–25. Other papers in the collection—on common sense, scepticism, and certainty—develop the point of view of this one.

One of the greatest philosophers of the twentieth century, Ludwig Wittgenstein, worried a great deal about scepticism. This concern shows itself through all his later work but most of all in his posthumously published

[53] Anscombe, G.E.M., and von Wright, G., eds. *On Certainty*. Translated by Anscombe and D. Paul. Oxford, 1969. This book includes comments on Moore's "Proof of an External World," in [52].

Two recent books that defend scepticism are

[54] Unger, P. *Ignorance: A Case for Scepticism*. Oxford, 1975.

[55] Naess, A. *Scepticism*. London and New York, 1968. Naess explicitly aims to defend Pyrrhonian, not "modern," scepticism, and his book contains an extended philosophical discussion of what it is like to *live out* ancient scepticism.

A rich and thought-provoking, but difficult, book that discusses scepticism in relation to many aspects of life and literature is

[56] Cavell, S. *The Claim of Reason: Wittgenstein, Skepticism, Morality, and Tragedy*. Oxford and Cambridge, Mass., 1979.

The significance of "modern" scepticism is assessed in

[57] Stroud, B. *The Significance of Philosophical Scepticism*. Oxford, 1984. This very clearly written book is accessible to beginners, yet valuable to specialists as well.

E. *Editions Cited in This Text*

The following editions are cited in the footnotes of this book.

Aquinas, St. Thomas. *Basic Writings*. Edited by A. C. Pegis. New York, 1945.

Hume, D. *Hume's Treatise*. Edited by L. A. Selby-Bigge. Oxford, 1951.

Kant, I. *Immanuel Kant's Critique of Pure Reason*. Edited by N. K. Smith. London, 1933.

Plato. *The Dialogues of Plato*. Translated by B. Jowett. New York, 1937.

Russell, B. *Sceptical Essays*. New York, 1961.

Wittgenstein, L. *Philosophical Investigations*. Oxford, 1953.

Index of Names

General Index

Ability, 33
Absolutely non-evident objects, 100
Absolute judge, 62
Absolute nature, 66
Absolute truth, 109n, 175n
Absolutes, 62n, 67
Absurdity, 170
Academic philosophy, 31, 91–97
Academics, 10, 16–24, 31n, 94, 95n, 157, 159, 162
Academic Sceptic, see Academics
Academy, 10, 17, 95
Academy, Middle, 91, 96
Academy, New, 91, 94–96
Academy, Old, 91
Accidents, 124
Acoustic affection, 149
Action, 49, 94n, 160
Actions, everyday, 16, 40
Adela, 13
Ad infinitum argument, 64, 114, 145, 146, 167
Admixtures, 44, 64–65
Adultery, 69
Adverbial philosophy, 80n
Aetiological tropes, 25
Aetiologists, 77–78
Aetiology, 179n
Affection, acoustic, 149
Affirmation, 33, 34n, 81
Age, 59–61, 90, 141
Agent by whom, 131
Agoge, 11, 12, 14, 15, 17
Agreement of all mankind, 191–193
Akatalepsia, 14
All things non-apprehensible, 84
All things undetermined, 83
Alleys, blind, 39n
Alteration, 154
Alteration and God, 207
Anaesthesia, 6, 9

Analytic philosophies, 158n
Anapodeictic, 51n
Anatomy of doubt, 4, 5
Ancients, 185
Animals, differences in, 45–54; featherless, 134; irrational, 49–51, 53, 186, 203, 204; rational, 108n, 132, 133, 199; variation in, 44
Animate God, 208
Antinomy, first, 112
Antithesis, 32, 33, 183n, 186
Apathy, 11
Aperient, 128n
Aperient drugs, see Aperient function of doubting
Aperient function of doubting, 7, 9, 39n
Aphasia, 6, 7, 14
Aporetic, 32
Apparatus, dialectical, 16
Apparent proof, 49
Apparent things, 68
Appearance, 32, 33, 39–41, 43, 50, 57, 78, 81n, 98, 152
Appearances, clear, 160; denial of, 38
Apple, 38, 57, 58
Apprehending presentations, 152, 159–167, 169
Apprehending sense-impression, 97
Apprehension, 106, 153
Arbitrariness, 39n
Arche, 7, 35n
Argument, chain, 213n; circular, 62, 72–76, 104, 146, 166; ontological, 205; opposed, 33, 85; Sophistical, 110; tested, 146; untested, 146; veiled, 162; weak, 128
Argument from design, 182n
Argus, 51

227